NELSON
SYSTEMS
ENGINEERING

VCE Units 1–4

third edition

Pat O'Neill

Aaron Powter

NELSON
A Cengage Company

Australia • Brazil • Japan • Korea • Mexico • Singapore • Spain • United Kingdom • United States

Nelson Systems Engineering VCE Units 1–4
3rd Edition
Pat O'Neill
Aaron Powter

Publishing editors: Kirstie Irwin, Debbi Barnes
Project editor: Jocelyn Hargrave
Editor: Joy Window
Proofreader: Nadine Anderson-Conklin
Indexer: Ann Philpott
Cover designer: Miranda Costa
Text designer: Miranda Costa
Cover image: Shutterstock.com/gualtiero boffi
Permissions researcher: Corrina Tauschke
Production controller: Erin Dowling
Reprint: Magda Koralewska
Typeset by Cenveo Publisher Services

Any URLs contained in this publication were checked for currency during the production process. Note, however, that the publisher cannot vouch for the ongoing currency of URLs.

For product information and technology assistance,
in Australia call **1300 790 853**;
in New Zealand call **0800 449 725**

For permission to use material from this text or product, please email
aust.permissions@cengage.com

National Library of Australia Cataloguing-in-Publication Data
Nelson Systems Engineering : VCE Units 1 - 4 / Pat O'Neill,
Aaron Powter.

3rd ed.
9780170227452 (pbk.)
Includes index.
For secondary school students in years 11 and 12.

Systems engineering--Textbooks.
Victorian Certificate of Education examination--Study guides.
Technology--Study and teaching (Secondary)--Victoria.

Powter, Aaron.

620.0011

Cengage Learning Australia
Level 7, 80 Dorcas Street
South Melbourne, Victoria Australia 3205

Cengage Learning New Zealand
Unit 4B Rosedale Office Park
331 Rosedale Road, Albany, North Shore 0632, NZ

For learning solutions, visit **cengage.com.au**

Printed in China by 1010 Printing International Ltd
12 13 14 15 16 27 26 25 24 23

Contents

Acknowledgements

The authors would like to acknowledge the following people for their contributions and support in writing this book:

- Dr Chris Anderson, Rex Candy, Dr David Vercoe, Nicolas Hogios and Darren Privitera for their time and expertise in writing the case studies

- Peter McNeill and Brian Ramsay for material and advice

- VCE Systems Engineering students Amir Alic (Taylors Lakes Secondary College) and Robin Kent (Northern College of the Arts and Technology) for their sample design and planning folio material.

Author profiles

Pat O'Neill is technology coordinator and teacher at Taylors Lakes Secondary College and teaches VCE Systems Engineering and VCE Product Design and Technology. Pat wrote the previous editions for VCE Systems Engineering and Systems and Technology studies. He has been involved in technology education for a number of years as a VCE reviewer, assessor and lecturer, and as president of the subject association. Pat has received awards from TEAV and ACET for his contribution to technology education.

Aaron Powter is a technology teacher at the Northern College of the Arts and Technology. Aaron predominately teaches in both VCE Systems Engineering and VET Engineering programs. He has been involved in Secondary Education for the past ten years and has worked for both Education Queensland and DEECD in Victoria. Aaron is a VCAA assessor for Systems Engineering and a sessional lecturer. He is a qualified engineer with an extensive background in mechanics and engineering integrated systems. Aaron holds a passion for radio-control aircraft, robotics and mechatronics.

ISBN 9780170227452

Introduction

Nelson Systems Engineering has been written and updated to address the revised VCE Systems Engineering study design. Its chapters examine the principles, concepts and practices set out throughout the study. Common themes throughout the study are those of understanding, problem-solving and arriving at appropriate solutions. These skills and characteristics are important to use all in our daily lives.

Chapter 9 'The systems engineering process' assists you with these areas of learning as it takes you through the design and planning process in detail and uses sample folio material to illustrate how to develop a good folio for project work. Chapter 10 'Production: equipment, safety and materials' supports Chapter 9 and your production processing and safety tasks as you progress through the course.

A sound knowledge of systems is important to your understanding of systems design, configuration and manufacturing. Chapter 1 'Understanding systems' introduces you to methods of identifying and describing different types of complex systems. Other chapters have been written and revised to assist your learning and understanding of systems, including Chapter 4 'Mechanical systems', Chapter 5 'Electrotechnology' and Chapter 8 'Testing engineering systems'.

Given the current and future directions in technological developments in the areas of microelectronic, robotics, remote and control technologies, Chapter 6 'Integrated and digital manufacturing' and Chapter 7 'Integrated control systems' have been written to introduce you to important knowledge and concepts within these themes and to encourage you to develop projects using these technologies. As technologists we should be aware of social and technological developments and how they influence and shape our lives and our environments. Chapter 2 'Technology systems in society' and Chapter 3 'Energy systems' both examine past, current and some predicted developments and outcomes that are, or soon will be, familiar to us all.

A number of chapters and themes are supported by relevant expert case studies to address specific themes or important concepts in systems engineering: energy, control technology, industrial design, energy and environment, testing and manufacturing. These have been written by experienced professionals who have expert knowledge in a wide range of technologies in their fields. You will find that the book provides you with learning activities as you work through and at the conclusion of each chapter. These assist you with your understanding and learning of the relevant material, specific topics and sections in each chapter. The appendixes 'Revision tasks' and 'A–Z: Systems terminology' are important in your learning as they help you to reflect and revise your technical knowledge and language in the field of systems engineering.

As the beginning to this introduction points out, technology plays a significant and essential part in all our lives. We use it in different areas of society for the home, energy production, manufacturing, chemical processing, transportation, agriculture, communications, health services, sport, leisure industries, recycling and many more. Most of these interact and depend on one another to function effectively. When they do this we call them systems. The term 'system' means that something has been constructed in an organised way for a particular purpose.

We go through our daily routine with ever-increasing contact and reliance on new and developing technological systems, many of which we simply take for granted. If we stop to think how we use technology each day and how much we depend on it, we may even surprise ourselves. For instance, we use alarm clocks to wake us; shower using hot and cold water; prepare breakfast using kettles, cookers and microwave ovens; and then go to school or work using some means of transport, such as cars or trains. Throughout the day we come into contact with and use many other technological systems and devices, including televisions, computers, buses, speed cameras, elevators and mobile phones. For these systems to function effectively, a considerable amount of energy is required. Our electricity supply system, for example, uses energy sources such as gas, oil, solar, wind and coal for its production, and is an essential feature of most working technical systems.

For practical reasons, we often integrate or connect a number of different systems. For instance, the manufacturing industry needs the chemical and transport systems as support. At another level, a motor vehicle would not function if the steering or electrical systems failed. When we speak of planning, arranging and integrating technologies, we really mean that we are 'constructing' or 'engineering' technical systems.

The necessary planning and organisation of systems is performed by technologists (experts in technology), such as engineers, scientists, inventors and innovators, who are committed to turning theory and ideas into action. As different technological systems rely on one another to function, it is important that the design, configuration and production of these are correct and well thought out. This task is what we refer to as 'systems engineering'. In practice, systems engineering needs to combine social, scientific, mathematical, environmental and technical knowledge to arrive at effective practical solutions to tasks or problems.

Our increasing use of technology has created rapid change in society and how we do things, especially in the past 10 to 20 years. We need only look at industrial applications to see how things have progressed since the introduction of steam-powered machines during the 18th century, to the development of mechanical and electrical systems in the 19th century, followed by the electronic, microelectronic, automated and controlled methods of production throughout the 20th century to the present.

As a result of these changes we need to learn and develop new skills. With increased automation and the use of robots in many industries, less manufacturing labour is needed. This, however, has brought an increasing demand for new and emerging skills in areas such as microelectronics, programming, robotics, communications, energy management, electrotechnology, systems analysis and servicing. In doing so, technology has made life easier for some by taking on the mundane, routine and dangerous jobs.

We have become familiar with many more user-friendly and personal technologies, and the benefits have reached us all. Vehicle cruise and climate control, smart phones, smart homes, mobile broadband, GPS and automated banking are just a few. We continue to be exposed to more recent experimental and technological developments, such as supercapacitors, LCD screens and displays, mini fuel cells, electric and hybrid vehicles, solar-powered homes, multiscreen television, voice recognition and video calls. The increasing rate of technological innovation (systems and applications) and change has been phenomenal.

We should not ignore the fact that technology can also be harmful, through misuse, pollution, wastage and overexploitation of the Earth's natural resources to satisfy our ever-increasing demands. To overcome these problems we should continue, as a matter of necessity, to research and develop more efficient ideas, lean design, green technology and resource-preserving solutions to our living requirements.

The study of Systems Engineering is about encouraging you as a student to become a practical problem-solver and to increase your awareness and understanding of practical applications of technology in society and a systems approach to this. In doing so, you will gain knowledge and skills in working with electronic and mechanical systems and the integration and control of these. You will become more involved with the technological processes, such as the systems engineering process in designing, planning, manufacturing, testing, maintaining and evaluating systems. We hope you will use this knowledge and experience in your everyday life to help you make decisions, analyse situations, consider options, think logically and solve real-life problems.

ISBN 9780170227452

Legislation and safety

In systems production work, students are involved in a range of practical activities. In doing so, they may work with materials, components, chemicals, powered mechanical equipment and electrical power supply. Working with potentially hazardous materials, substances and equipment requires that all health and safety issues should be considered and then practically implemented. In Victoria, the relevant legislation for electrical safety is the *Electrical Safety Act 1998* and its associated regulations.

Only people holding an appropriate and current electrical licence are permitted to perform electrical work on systems that require voltage greater than 50 volts AC or 120 volts ripple-free DC. Students are not permitted to carry out any electrical work on systems above 50 volts AC or 120 volts ripple-free DC. Any systems that meet the above specifications must comply with the *Australian/New Zealand Wiring Rules* (AS/NZS 3000:2007). General requirements for electrical equipment can be found in AS/NZS 3100:2009 and AS/NZS 3760:2010 for in-service safety inspection and testing of electrical equipment. Energy Safe Victoria (**www.esv.vic.gov.au**) is the safety regulator responsible for electrical and gas safety in Victoria.

The systems engineering process

The systems engineering process illustrated below represents the stages followed in managing and developing a systems engineering project. This is examined and explained in detail in Chapter 9.

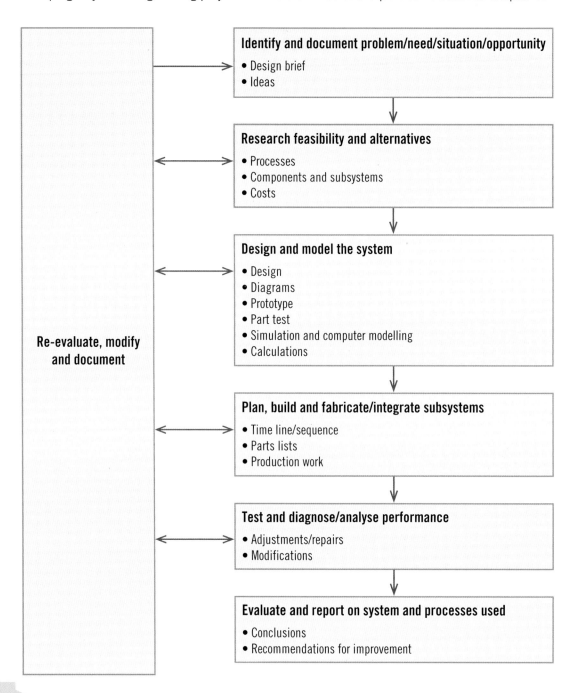

Re-evaluate, modify and document

Identify and document problem/need/situation/opportunity
- Design brief
- Ideas

Research feasibility and alternatives
- Processes
- Components and subsystems
- Costs

Design and model the system
- Design
- Diagrams
- Prototype
- Part test
- Simulation and computer modelling
- Calculations

Plan, build and fabricate/integrate subsystems
- Time line/sequence
- Parts lists
- Production work

Test and diagnose/analyse performance
- Adjustments/repairs
- Modifications

Evaluate and report on system and processes used
- Conclusions
- Recommendations for improvement

The systems engineering process

ISBN 9780170227452

Unit outcomes guide

A quick reference guide to where to find the most relevant sections and topics for each VCE Systems Engineering Outcome in Unit 1

Unit 1 Outcome	Chapter topics and case study titles
1	**Chapter 1: Understanding systems** – identifying systems, systems and subsystems, open and closed loop systems, using diagrams, describing complex systems
	Chapter 4: Mechanical systems – motion and force, mechanisms and applications, mechanical principles, calculations, friction, understanding and describing mechanical systems
	Chapter 6: Digital manufacturing – computer-aided design, computer-aided manufacture, industrial machines and equipment
	Chapter 7: Control systems – microcontrollers, PLC basics, remote and radio control
	Case study 6: Vehicle style and design
	Chapter 9: The systems engineering process – about design, why design?, designing systems, design and production process
2	**Chapter 8: Testing engineering systems** – why test systems, causes and effects of faults, test equipment, fault finding
	Case study 5: Testing flight data systems
	Chapter 9: The systems engineering process – design and production process, testing and evaluating
	Chapter 10: Production: equipment, safety and materials – equipment, safety procedures, risk assessment, materials for systems production

A quick reference guide to where to find the most relevant sections and topics for each VCE Systems Engineering Outcome in Unit 2

Unit 2 Outcome	Chapter topics and case study titles
1	**Chapter 1: Understanding systems** – identifying systems, systems and subsystems, open and closed loop systems, using diagrams, describing complex systems
	Chapter 4: Mechanical systems – motion and force, mechanisms and applications, mechanical principles, calculations, friction, understanding and describing mechanical systems
	Chapter 5: Electrotechnology – electrical principles, basic circuit theory, component function and operation, open and closed loop circuits, integrated circuits, power supplies, designing and making systems, project ideas
	Chapter 6: Digital manufacturing – computer-aided design, computer-aided manufacture, industrial machines and equipment
	Chapter 7: Control systems – microcontrollers, PLC basics, remote and radio control
	Chapter 9: The Systems Engineering Process – designing systems, design and production process, planning
	Case study 6: Vehicle style and design
2	**Chapter 8: Testing engineering systems** – why test systems, causes and effects of faults, test equipment, fault finding
	Chapter 9: The systems engineering process – production process, planning, testing and evaluating
	Chapter 10: Production: equipment, safety and materials – equipment, safety procedures, risk assessment, materials for systems production
	Case study 5: Testing flight data systems

ISBN 9780170227452

A quick reference guide to where to find the most relevant sections and topics for each VCE Systems Engineering Outcome in Unit 3

Unit 3 Outcome	Chapter topics and case study titles
1	**Chapter 1: Understanding systems** – identifying systems, systems and subsystems, open and closed loop systems, using diagrams, describing complex systems, systems operating sequence
	Chapter 4: Mechanical systems – motion and force, mechanisms and applications, calculations, friction, understanding and describing mechanical systems, pneumatics, autotechnology
	Chapter 5: Electrotechnology – electrical principles, basic circuit theory, component function and operation, open and closed loop circuits, integrated circuits, power supplies, designing and making systems, project ideas
	Chapter 6: Digital manufacturing – computer-aided design, integrated systems, remote control technology, industrial machines and equipment
	Chapter 7: Control systems – microcontrollers, PLC basics, remote and radio control
	Chapter 9: The systems engineering process – designing systems, design and production process, production planning and project management, test procedures, planning tests
	Chapter 10: Production: equipment, safety and materials – equipment, safety procedures, risk assessment, materials for systems production
	Case study 4: Remote control systems
	Case study 6: Vehicle style and design
2	**Chapter 1: Understanding systems** – identifying systems, systems and subsystems, open and closed loop systems, using diagrams, describing complex systems
	Chapter 2: Technology systems in society – systems in society, appropriateness of technological systems, technology and the environment, new and emerging technologies
	Chapter 3: Energy systems – different types, energy sources, renewable and non-renewable, energy conversion in systems, effects of energy use, environmental considerations
	Case study 3: Solar house

A quick reference guide to where to find the most relevant sections and topics for each VCE Systems Engineering Outcome in Unit 4

Unit 4 Outcome	Chapter topics and case study titles
1	**Chapter 8: Testing engineering systems** – causes and effects of faults, test equipment, test procedures, measurement, getting accurate results, fault finding, maintenance procedures
	Chapter 9: The systems engineering process – production process, planning, testing and evaluating
	Chapter 10: Production: equipment, safety and materials – equipment, safety procedures, risk assessment, materials for systems production
	Case study 5: Testing flight data systems
2	**Chapter 1: Understanding systems** – identifying systems, systems and subsystems, open and closed loop systems, using diagrams, describing complex systems
	Chapter 2: Technology systems in society – systems in society, appropriateness of technological systems, technology and the environment, new and emerging technologies
	Case study 1: Water treatment and recycling system
	Case study 2: Manufacturing and technology
End-of-year examination	**Section: Revision tasks**

ISBN 9780170227452

1

UNDERSTANDING SYSTEMS

In this chapter you will learn about the nature of the things that we regard as everyday systems and how we understand and describe them efficiently and effectively. Systems are characterised by their configuration and the tasks they perform. Some are automatic; others need to be operated manually. The material in the chapter explains how we identify, define and categorise different kinds of systems and the techniques for describing systems accurately and clearly.

Identifying systems

As the introduction to this book points out, the term 'system' means that something has been constructed in an organised way for a particular purpose. This could be a collection of existing systems integrated (as subsystems) to form a new and more complex system, or a simple system made up of basic components and parts.

Systems are usually described by their function or the task they are required to do. Transport systems, education systems, security systems, communication systems, health systems and air conditioning systems are just a few examples.

A system has three main stages in its operation: input, process and output.

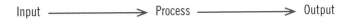

Input ⟶ Process ⟶ Output

LEARNING ACTIVITY 1.1

1 Copy the above statement and diagram into your notebook, and then list three devices that you consider to be systems and three you do not.

2 Give reasons for your choices.

Input, process and output (IPO)

- **Inputs** include energy, information and materials. These are needed for the system to function. For example, an input to an electric kettle is electricity.

- **Process** operations convert the input to the required output. Something is happening; basic to complex activities are involved. An electric kettle heating element converts electrical energy into heat energy.

- **Outputs** are produced by the process stage. These should be planned or 'desired outputs' of the system. An electric kettle produces heat and boiled water.

Systems also have 'undesired outputs' due to inefficiencies such as friction, heat losses, noise and exhaust. They usually waste energy, are slower, need higher maintenance and have a shorter life as a result.

Systems are more effective if they have some means of **control** to monitor their operational functions and to make adjustments so the desired outputs are maintained. Information on the condition of the process and output is monitored and fed back to the controller. This can be either human intervention (often unreliable) or more effective automatic control. An automatic kettle has a thermostat on/off sensor to control the input.

To establish whether or not what seems to be a system actually is one and to explain its characteristics, we use what is called a 'systems approach' to describe it. Here we can compare the system to agreed 'definitions' or guidelines (as set out below); then we break the system down into a basic form, often using diagrams to show its major features without having too much complexity or the need for technical detail. We can also design and construct systems in a similar way. All systems should conform to a four-part definition. This is shown in the diagram on page 3.

Shutterstock.com/Rick Lord

ISBN 9780170227452

Defining and describing systems

For a system to be recognised as such, it should conform to a four-part definition of what a system actually is:

1 A system should have a name or title that usually describes its purpose.

2 Systems have inputs, processes, outputs and some means of control.

3 Systems within more complex systems are known as **subsystems**.

4 Major parts or subsystems of a system should be connected in some organised way. If any of these were to fail or change, the system would change or malfunction.

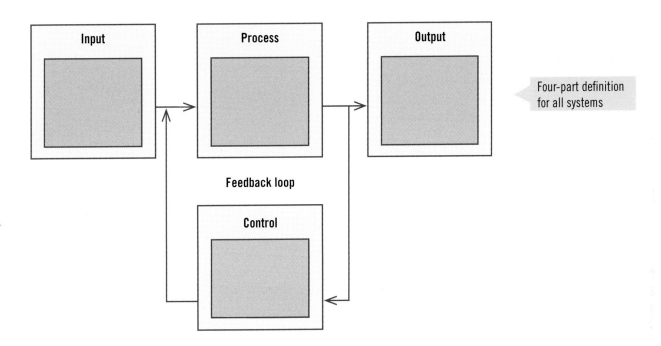

Four-part definition for all systems

LEARNING ACTIVITY 1.2

Discuss your interpretation of each part of the definition with a group of students in class. Use a working system in your classroom as a focus for your discussion.

Subsystems

Subsystems have their own inputs, processes and outputs. They are major functional parts of an operational system and are referred to as 'systems within systems'. Subsystems should be connected to contribute to the overall function of the system. Integrated or complex systems contain a number of subsystems. Motor vehicles, for instance, are complex systems that have quite a number of subsystems.

Vehicle subsystems include electrical, mechanical, cooling, steering, transmission, braking and locking. All of these contribute to the operation of the vehicle and the failure of one or a number of them would significantly affect the system. Independently, or removed from the system, they serve very little or no purpose.

Some examples

Bathroom shower system

If you examine a shower as a 'warm water supply system' you can see that it has 'inputs' of hot and cold water. The 'process' is the adjustment of the taps to mix the water supply. The 'output' is water at a desirable temperature. Human control is attempted, but this is not very effective as water is wasted in the process. Heating, water supply and mixer subsystems exist. If the hot water input supply failed, the output water spray would be cold.

Alamy/InsideOutPix

LEARNING ACTIVITY 1.3

1 List the stages involved in using the shower and describe what the user must do to set the water spray at a comfortable temperature.

2 Find out how this can be done automatically.

Home heating system

At a more complex level we know that a 'gas-ducted home heating system' has 'inputs' of electricity, air and gas. The 'process' is the gas being ignited to heat the air that is then fed through ducts to the outlets in various rooms. The 'output' is warm air at a determined temperature. The thermostat is used to 'control' the system by switching it on and off. Subsystems within the heating system are energy supply, temperature control, heaters and fans. The system is organised so as to allow the energy supply to enter the heater where warm air is produced. Fans then distribute this warm air. If the electricity supply failed or the ducts became disconnected, there would be no output of warm air at the vents.

ISBN 9780170227452

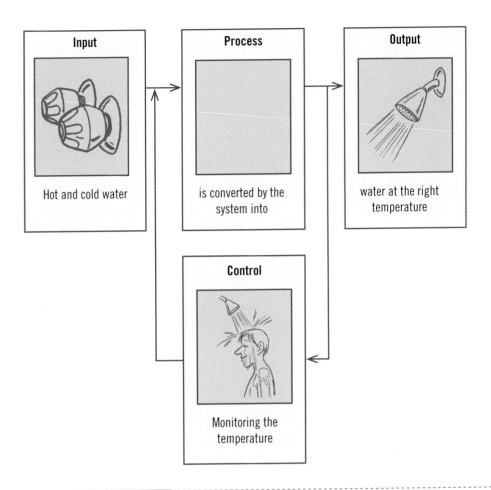

Input	Process	Output
Hot and cold water	is converted by the system into	water at the right temperature

Control

Monitoring the temperature

LEARNING ACTIVITY 1.4

1 Draw a simple diagram to explain how a home heating system operates.
2 Which do you think is most efficient, the shower or the heating system? Explain why.

Using diagrams to describe systems

Both of the previous systems are reasonably easy to describe verbally or in written form when we break them down into separate stages and subsystems. When systems become complex, a simple way of describing them is to use diagrams. We can do this in basic form by using flow diagrams with words as headings and linking them in sequence with lines to show relationships and arrows to show flow and direction. Flow block diagrams containing information can be used to represent stages and subsystems. Arrows and lines can be used to show connections and flows between stages.

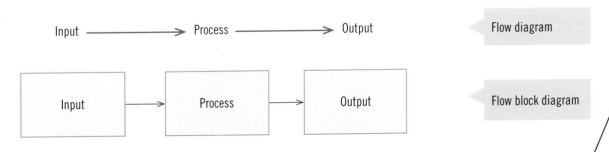

Input ⟶ Process ⟶ Output — Flow diagram

Input	Process	Output	— Flow block diagram

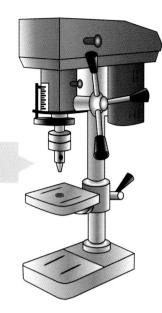

Drilling machine: open loop system

Open loop systems

The shower and heating systems operate differently to each other. The shower needs human intervention to manually operate, switch and adjust the system in providing the required output. The user becomes the monitor/controller of a technical system and is often unreliable and inefficient in this role. Systems such as this are known as **open loop systems**. Other examples of open loop systems are drilling machines, desk lamps, concrete mixers, car jacks, hair dryers and key-operated lock devices.

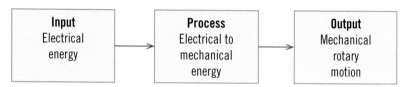

Input	Process	Output
Electrical energy	Electrical to mechanical energy	Mechanical rotary motion

Closed loop systems

Systems that work independently (such as home heating systems) are **closed loop systems**. Closed loop systems, being automatic, have sensors that monitor and enable them to modify and control the system in some way so that a desired output is constantly achieved. For example, a home heating system has a thermostat to monitor the output or room temperature. In this system

Robot arm: closed loop system

Corbis/John Zich/zrImages

information is fed back to the controller, which switches the system on and off at the required temperature. This process is termed a feedback loop. Examples of closed loop systems are air conditioning units, engine cooling systems, home security systems, vehicle climate control, thermostatically controlled ovens and robots.

A robot arm, as a system, can be controlled and maintained by a computer programmer interfaced to it. Put simply, electrical energy is supplied as the input to the system. Current goes to the motors and stepper motors which activate and create movement as an output. The computer is programmed to control the input and process, using sensors to assist with monitoring the process and output movement. The sensors feed information to the controller; this decides if action or modification of the input or process is required to maintain the desired output.

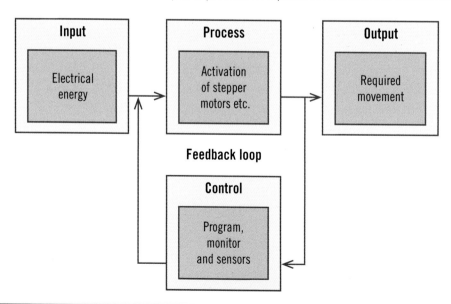

Input	Process	Output
Electrical energy	Activation of stepper motors etc.	Required movement

Feedback loop

Control

Program, monitor and sensors

ISBN 9780170227452

LEARNING ACTIVITY 1.5

1 From the table below, determine which devices are systems and which are not.

2 Of the devices you have identified as systems, indicate in the right-hand column which are open and which are closed. Identify any that are not systems. Three have been done for you.

3 Select one from each category (open, closed, not a system) and state why you think they are so.

Which are systems?	Category: Open loop, closed loop or not a system
Saxophone	
Motor bike	
School	
Pencil	Not a system
Dishwasher	
Mobile phone	
Drilling machine	
Table lamp	
ATM	
Alarm clock	
Bench vice	
Garden watering hose	
Vehicle cooling system	Closed loop
Computer desk	
Hair dryer	Open loop
Traffic lights	
iPod	
Bicycle	
Gym rowing machine	
Spanner	
Wind turbine	
Electric guitar	

Describing complex and integrated systems

The closed loop diagram of the robot arm gave just enough detail of its configuration and function without being confusing. This is essential when describing systems, especially to someone who is unfamiliar with the technology. Where more detail is required, such as numerical values, subsystem operations and sequences, we can add blocks to the diagram and increase the amount of information within each block. A written description should always be given.

We frequently use this method of describing systems when planning and designing projects for production tasks. Further examples of this concept are given throughout this book in relevant sections.

Typical flow block diagrams for complex systems

The first is a flow block diagram for a drilling machine – an open loop system with subsystems as part of the process, shown outside the process block.

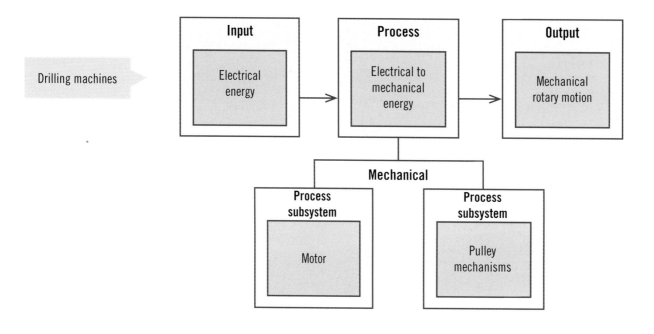

Next is an open loop system with two subsystems as part of the process, shown inside the process block.

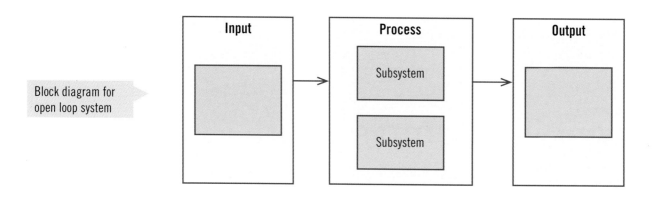

ISBN 9780170227452

Here is a closed loop system with two subsystems as part of the process, shown inside the process block.

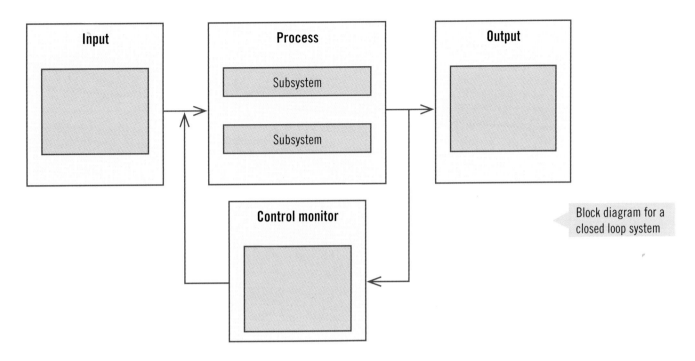

Block diagram for a closed loop system

Next is an automatic heating system – a closed loop system (monitors the process and sends information back to the controller). Two subsystems as part of the process are shown outside the process block.

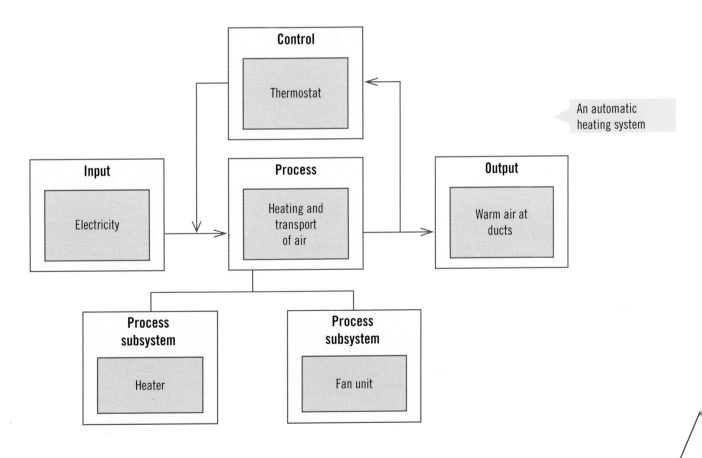

An automatic heating system

Last is a complex flow block diagram for a closed loop system (desirable and undesirable outputs).

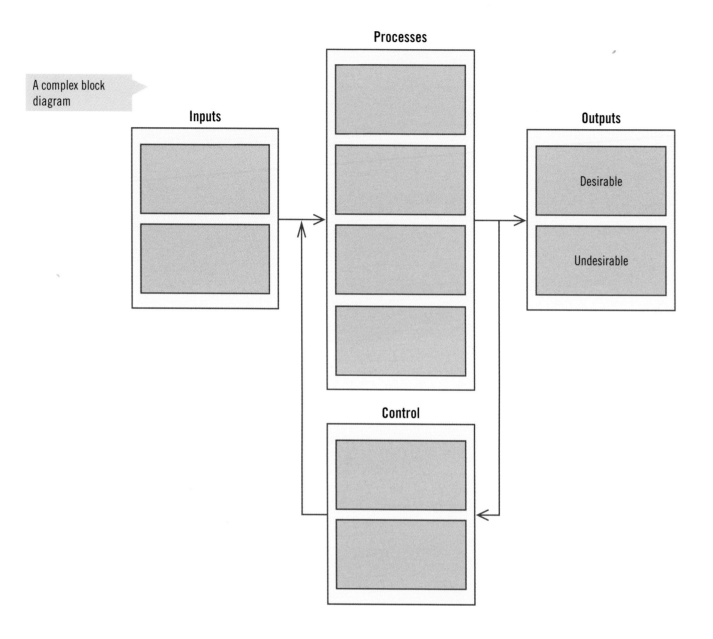

A complex block diagram

Processes

Inputs

Outputs

Desirable

Undesirable

Control

ISBN 9780170227452

1 Complete and label a flow block diagram for an open loop system used in your classroom.
2 Complete and label a flow block diagram for a closed loop system used at home.
3 Complete the missing details in the table below.
4 Discuss your answers with your teacher and class group. *Note*: Some of the systems listed are open loop, so their only means of control is manual.

System	Input	Process	Control?	Output
Electric motor	Electricity	Conversion of electricity to mechanical energy		Mechanical rotary motion
Mobile phone				
Electric oven	Electricity		Switches, timer, thermostat	
Wheel brace				
Bicycle pump	Human kinetic energy, air			
Car brakes				

Explaining a system's operating sequence

We also use diagrams to explain how and in what sequence systems actually operate. By introducing blocks (symbolic blocks that represent functions, operations or tasks such as on/off and decision), we can get a clearer representation of a system's dynamics.

The diagram on page 12 is an example of systems planning, operating, monitoring and decision-making. The diagram represents the operation of a closed loop system as the process and output are both monitored and controlled. The decision stage represents the monitor/controller, which switches the heater on and off automatically.

Human beings function in the way shown in the sequence diagram each time we make decisions and perform everyday activities and tasks.

Room heater system

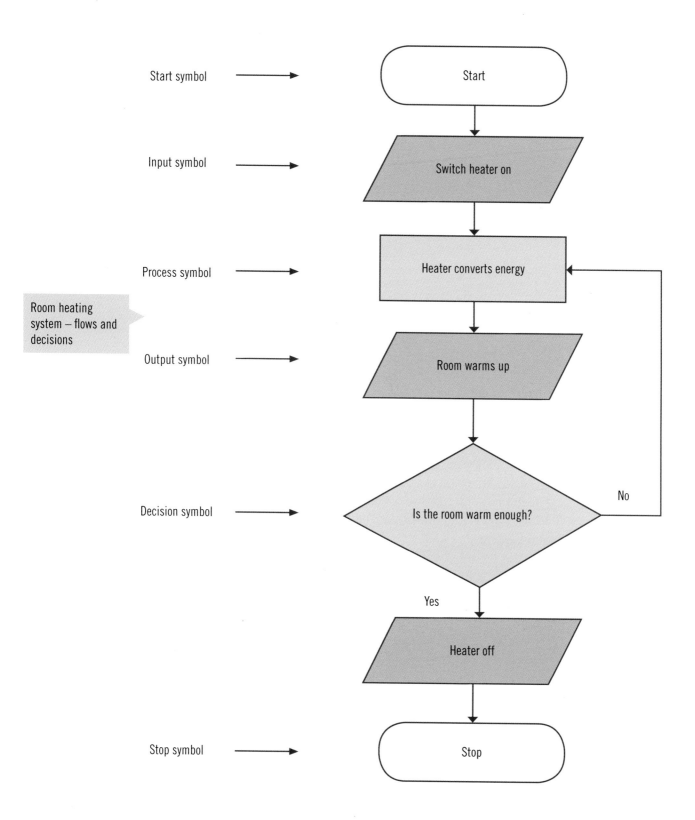

Start symbol ⟶ **Start**

Input symbol ⟶ **Switch heater on**

Process symbol ⟶ **Heater converts energy**

Room heating system – flows and decisions

Output symbol ⟶ **Room warms up**

Decision symbol ⟶ **Is the room warm enough?** — No

Yes

Heater off

Stop symbol ⟶ **Stop**

ISBN 9780170227452

LEARNING ACTIVITY 1.7

1 Copy the different diagram symbols below into your notebook and define each one.

2 Think of a decision that you made and enacted today. Draw a diagram of your own to represent the process you went through, the decision you made, and the action you took.

3 Complete the diagram below to represent an automatic garage door operation.

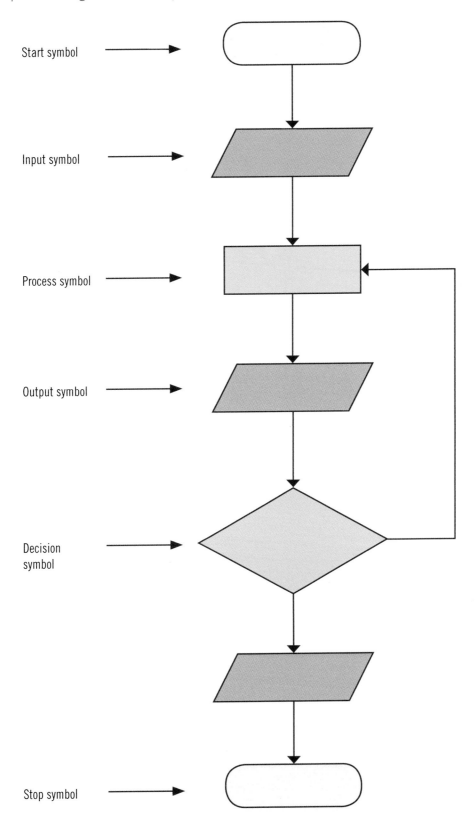

Different kinds of systems

Technological systems have many applications and come in different forms. In systems engineering we look at and work with electrical, electronic and mechanical systems. We also attempt to arrange these into integrated (electromechanical) systems, as most modern systems function in this way. Elevators, motor vehicles, mobile phones and computers are examples in which the above kinds of systems are integrated as necessary features.

Electrical systems

Electrical systems take electricity as a raw form of energy. Electricity is supplied to electronic and mechanical systems and devices such as power tools, machines, motors and lights. In electrical systems the supply is not modified, but it is when it reaches the various devices it is connected to. Typical electrical systems are power grids supplying businesses, railway networks and road lighting. House circuits and motor vehicle electrics are other examples, with cars using batteries as their power sources.

Electronic systems

Electronic systems use and modify electricity to operate and control electronic devices and mechanical systems. Electronic systems have enabled us to develop and increasingly use control systems that are automatic and require little or no human intervention. Electronic **circuits** use a range of electronic components including resistors, transistors, diodes, capacitors and more complex devices such as integrated circuits and supercapacitors. We find electronic systems everywhere, with computers, microwave ovens, digital cameras, GPS devices and security systems being just a few of the systems that operate in this way.

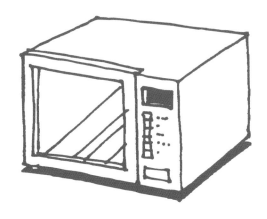

ISBN 9780170227452

Mechanical systems

Mechanical systems are arrangements of components organised to change motion from one form to another. They control the speed, direction and force of the moving parts to achieve a desired output. Mechanical systems also include pneumatic and hydraulic devices. They are made up of components such as gears, racks and pinions, levers, valves and cylinders. Car jacks, air pumps and bicycles are examples of these. Motor vehicles consist of many mechanical systems or subsystems, such as steering, braking and transmission.

Integrated systems

When systems are constructed by combining mechanical, electrical and electronic systems we identify them as integrated or electromechanical systems. Most modern systems are integrated and controlled. Many are completely free of human intervention! Washing machines, robots, motor vehicles, elevators, dishwashers, aircraft, automatic doors and remote controlled systems are examples of integrated systems.

Weblinks

www.technologystudent.com

Google Images search: flow block diagrams

END-OF-CHAPTER ACTIVITIES

1 What does the term 'system' mean?

2 Explain each of the following.
   a Input
   b Process
   c Output

3 Define and give three examples of subsystems.

4 Explain what is meant by 'control' in a closed loop system.

5 a Name three open loop systems.
   b Name three closed loop systems.

6 Complete a systems diagram for an open loop system that you are familiar with.

7 Complete a systems diagram for a closed loop system that you are familiar with.

8 Produce a poster or a PowerPoint presentation to show and explain the difference between open loop and closed loop systems. Describe the purpose of the feedback loop.

9 a Name five mechanical systems.
   b Name five electronic systems.

10 a List five integrated systems.
   b Choose two of these systems and say why you think they are so.

11 What are the reasons for having sensors in systems?

12 Clearly explain, with examples, what is meant by undesirable outputs.

13 Describe advantages, disadvantages and interesting features of control systems using a PMI (plus, minus, interesting) chart.

ISBN 9780170227452

CASE STUDY 1

Water treatment and recycling system

This case study is by Dr David Vercoe (chemist), who specialises in flocculation chemistry and is employed as the regional manager (south-eastern Australia) for Ovivo, a global waste water engineering company. The company aims to create value in water through innovation, creativity and expertise in industrial, municipal and waste water treatment. Dr Vercoe's role at Ovivo is to ensure that the chemistry of the waste water systems built and serviced in his region is correct and to ensure that all the equipment is running at its highest efficiency. This case study deals with the need to treat industrial waste water prior to disposal and recycling for good environmental and financial reasons.

A number of the issues raised in Chapter 2, 'Technology systems in society', such as new and innovative technologies, environmental concerns and recycling, are explored and implemented through the scenario described by the writer. Note also how the writer follows the techniques used in Chapter 1, 'Understanding systems', to describe a system by using schematic, IPO, flow diagrams and images to communicate what is done and how the technology and situation achieve positive outcomes.

Issues

Why does industry have to treat its waste water? Why can't it simply go down the drain and be forgotten about? It is now well known and understood that the environment is fragile and needs to be looked after. Industry cannot throw its hard waste into the gutter out the front of its factory.

It can no longer dispose of liquid waste down the sewer; the waste first has to be treated to remove impurities.

A secondary issue which is driving industry in treating its wastewater is the cost of water. Australia is overall a dry continent and, with the country coming out of one of its biggest droughts, water is a finite resource and therefore relatively expensive to industry.

To put water usage of some industry plants into perspective, the average household bathtub holds approximately 80 L whereas a processing plant can use over 10 to 20 thousand times that in a day – a huge cost. Treating and recycling the water using its own processes will provide the plant with a huge saving, which can then be passed down to the consumer.

There are many ways in which waste water can be treated. The type of treatment plant will always be defined by the industry type, the level of water purification required, the footprint (area) available to a treatment plant, and the cost. Simple treatment may include screening, where the solid material is screened out, or clarification, where the solid material is either allowed to settle to the bottom of a pond and pumped out or treated with a polymer and then skimmed off the surface.

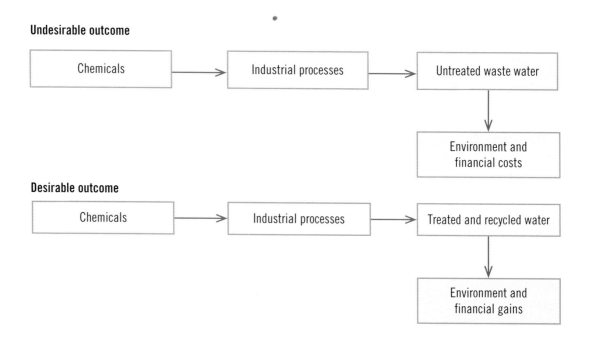

Scenario

A malting company in regional Australia has recently upgraded its water treatment plant to allow for the reuse of its wastewater. Before the upgrade the wastewater was treated in anaerobic ponds where large aerators were used to promote biological destruction of the nutrients; the aerators were then turned off to allow the solids to settle to the bottom of the pond and the waste water was then sent to the sewer. The issues with this plant were odour and the rapid rising of the solids level in the anaerobic ponds so that the solids had to be continually sucked out (involving extra cost); the cost of the increasing volume of water being used and sent to the sewer was becoming too expensive.

ISBN 9780170227452

The customer wanted to recycle as much water as possible to help reduce costs, but the recycled water had to be of a certain quality as it was going to be reused in food (malt). The following schematic diagram was suggested and implemented to assist the customer with the wastewater treatment requirements.

The process

Screening

Wastewater from the existing factory sump is pumped to a static screen to remove coarse solids. Screened effluent is then fed to an externally fed rotary screen to remove fine solids to protect membrane sheets from perforation and clogging.

Solids removed from the screen are discharged to the screenings bin for disposal.

Effluent equalisation

Screened effluent enters the equalisation tank by gravity drainage from the adjacent rotary screen. The equalisation tank also serves as a balance tank, damping volumetric feed fluctuations to allow the process downstream to operate at set hydraulic profiles.

Aeration

The existing aeration pond is kept and the aerators are upgraded to allow for maximum oxygen uptake by the waste water stream.

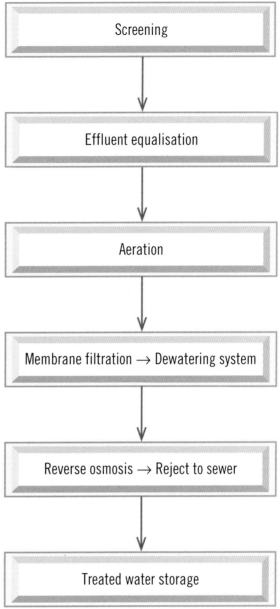

Online process monitors measuring dissolved oxygen concentration, temperature and pH are added to ensure the conditions are optimum for bacterial life.

Membrane filtration/dewatering

The mixed liquid (or waste stream) is then passed through a membrane filtration. In this process the stream is passed through a series of membranes under pressure, screening down to approximately 0.08 microns (μm). This system is a batch system which helps prevent the membrane pores from clogging. It removes only solid material, and relies on the performance of the 'bugs' in the aeration pond to consume all the inorganic material before it reaches the membrane. As it is a batch process and a filter, the solids content of the membrane filter will slowly increase over time. To combat this, liquid with high levels of solids is systematically 'dewatered' by being pumped to the centrifuge where a polymer flocculant is added; after the waste is spun at high speeds, a high-solid waste is separated from the water. This water is then sent back to the aeration pond to rejoin the process.

Reverse osmosis

The conditioned membrane bioreactor (MBR) permeate will be pumped at high pressure through a reverse osmosis unit, removing many of the viruses and dissolved salts in the water. Reverse osmosis results in a high quality permeate for reuse as well as a reject stream of concentrated salts (brine), which can be sent to the sewer. Antiscalants, sodium metabisulphite and hydrochloric acid are added to remove scalants and foulants that form on the membrane surfaces and reduce the oxidation potential of trace residual chlorine.

The water quality results can be seen in the photograph below.

From left to right, the water samples are as follows: reverse osmosis-treated water sample, reverse osmosis reject to sewer sample, MBR permeate sample, aeration pond sample and feed sample

Results

The recovery rate of 'clean' water out of the reverse osmosis unit is approximately 75%, so the customer has been able to save money by reducing their discharge volume, and also through discharging a cleaner waste stream down the sewer. The other saving is through not having to purchase the same amount of water through the water authority.

It is estimated that the plant will pay for itself in eight months.

2

TECHNOLOGY SYSTEMS IN SOCIETY

In this chapter you will learn about technology systems, how we use them and what impact they have upon social, natural and working environments. The rate of technological change is faster than ever before with many technological innovations being introduced daily. In fact, technology change is happening so fast that some futurists think that the rise will soon be unmeasurable. This chapter looks at a range of technologies that we frequently interact with. Several new and emerging technologies are examined and their roles and functions analysed.

Technology systems for sport and leisure

Systems play a great part in our leisure times. They are part of our hobbies or sporting activities, such as radio control models (cars, aircraft and boats), watercraft, gym equipment, fishing rods, scooters, bicycles and tricycles, skateboards and rollerblades. The electronic scoreboards at sport venues and the electronic beam that helps us detect when the ball goes out of court in tennis are systems. Athletes are fitted with wireless monitors to check and analyse their heart rates and monitor their cadence, such as bicycle crank revolutions per minute.

Sports equipment such as an electric treadmill keeps the average person fit and helps athletes prepare for sporting events. These treadmills are integrated systems that use electric, electronic and mechanical systems to control their incline and velocity, and operate different exercise programs. The use of microelectronics is greatly on the increase.

Sports monitor

Alamy/Hugh Threlfall

Blood pressure monitor

Most of these systems are not essential to our lives; however, some are important in terms of our general wellbeing. More recent developments include the global positioning system (GPS) and digital wrist monitors to check time, speed, distance and heart rate.

Audio and video systems, televisions, mobile phones

Music player

We use systems that entertain, such as DVD players, radios, televisions and interactive computer games, to name just a few. Millions of these entertainment systems are sold every year throughout the world. They help us enjoy our leisure time, but there remain some concerns about their use, such as children watching too much television.

Mobile phones are small, portable and full of features. They have become mobile interactive communication devices, not just phones. They are multifunctional devices that enable you to send emails, use GPS, type text, take photographs and videos, play downloaded and uploaded music, and give you access to the Internet and thousands of commercial apps. People and services can be accessed more easily at any time and in most places. This has given people freedom to make phone calls while sitting on a tram or waiting to go into a meeting, though mobile phone use is restricted in some places. In many workplaces employees have company mobile phones; theoretically they can be accessible at any time. While there are advantages in having and using a mobile phone, there are also some disadvantages: some of us don't want to be contactable all the time. There are also some (unfounded) concerns about the health risks of using a mobile phone on a regular basis. Recent research has shown that the risk of crashing a car goes up four times while using a mobile phone while driving.

DVD player

Shutterstock.com/H. Brauer

Standby function

Most audiovisual systems (such as televisions, stereos and computers) are powered by mains electricity via rectified power extreme low voltage (EVL) or by batteries. Many have a 'standby' function when switched off using a remote control. Some have permanent electronic displays. Even when the system is switched off via a remote control, it still uses

ISBN 9780170227452

some electrical energy while on standby. Government bodies have estimated that between 5 and 10% of Australia's electricity is used by products left on standby. Hence, local governments have endorsed energy-saving devices that turn off mains power at the power point when the device has been inactive for a predetermined time. It has been estimated that some households can save up to $140 per annum on their energy bills. This amounts, Australia-wide, to the output of four power stations and the release of millions of tonnes of greenhouse gases. Disposal of batteries used in portable devices creates soil pollution problems because of their chemical contents.

LEARNING ACTIVITY 2.1

1 Name two systems used in the home for entertainment. Explain two benefits and two negative aspects of each system.

2 List four systems used for leisure or sports activities. Select one and discuss it in terms of the following.

- How the system operates in terms of input, process and output
- Whether the system is totally new, or a replacement or a modification of a similar system
- The positive and negative effects of the system on the user

3 What is the main advantage and main disadvantage of the 'standby' function?

4 Work in small groups to research jet skis. Information to be gathered could include:

- When were jet skis developed?
- How do they work?
- What are some of the safety issues around their use?
- What other impact might they have on the environment?
- What restrictions have been placed on their use?
- Who can use them?

Groups are to compile their findings and prepare a class presentation that includes a graphic display and an oral presentation. The presentation should include a clear outline of the benefits and costs of jet skis. The graphic display could for instance include one or more of the following: posters, PowerPoint presentations, videos, photographs, brochures and articles.

5 The introduction to this chapter talks about futurists hypothesising about technological change and how rates of advance may soon be immeasurable. Research 'Technological singularity' and 'The spike by D. Broderick', and write a detailed paragraph that compares and contrasts both theories.

Technology in transport

Transport is an interesting area to look at in terms of technological change and its effect on society and the environment. People have seen transport as a necessity for many thousands of years, using animals, water and the wind to move about locally and internationally.

Transport across the seas: ships and aircraft

The nature of transport, particularly in the Western world, has changed dramatically, partly due to the desire to move people and goods more quickly and over longer distances, especially across the stretches of water that separate the continents. Sailing ships and then steam-powered vessels were used for travelling across water until the 20th century. The design of these ships was progressively improved so that they increased in size, shape and power to allow transatlantic and then world crossings, providing passengers relative comfort and moving ever larger quantities of goods. Cargo ships are now so large that the sea bed has to be deepened in some places to allow them through and passenger ships are now mostly used for holiday cruises. Passenger and car ferries are used for short channel or similar crossings, and water taxis are gaining popularity. Ships are still, however, a fairly slow form of transport (compared with air travel) and people today prefer to travel long distances as fast as possible.

iStockphoto/© Simon Bradfield

Air travel that can carry many people fast over long distances has had a great impact on our lives. In countries such as Australia, an island with relatively few close neighbours, this has been particularly significant. While ships are still used for transporting cargo and for leisure cruising, planes have become the main form of transport used to move people and goods over long distances. Aircraft have also led to a large increase in the amount of domestic travel undertaken by Australians – for both work and leisure. We can now travel from one side of Australia to the other in about four hours using a jet turbine engine.

iStockphoto/© Ermin Gutenberger

ISBN 9780170227452

Personal and public transport

Australia is a very large country and the distances between major cities historically created transport problems. Two hundred years ago people and goods were moved by horses, wheeled vehicles, boats and ships. Steam engines and railways soon replaced the horse, and large numbers of people and large amounts of goods could be moved quickly over very long distances. By the middle of the 20th century the internal combustion engine was used to power an increasing number of cars, trucks and buses.

Most Australian families have come to rely on at least one car for their everyday transport. It is seen by many to be not only convenient, but also essential. Cars are one of the greatest users of energy. They are generally inefficient in their use of energy and they cause a great deal of pollution (air and noise) and contribute to the greenhouse effect, as well as creating increasing traffic congestion.

Public transport is an alternative used by many people. For some this is the most convenient way to get to work; others may not be able to afford to run a car, and there are some people who are concerned about the effects that cars have on the environment. As we are becoming more health conscious, many people opt for walking or riding a bicycle to work or school as a way of exercising while travelling. For some, these options are simply far more convenient and faster than driving a car, especially in capital cities. A bicycle is far easier to park than a car.

A tram for public transport

While cars (often relatively new cars) are common in most parts of Australia, there are proportionally far fewer cars in most developing countries. This is mainly due to the cost of purchasing and running a car, limited access to spare parts, and poor road networks. Walking is a common mode of transport in many countries and, in some, animals are still used to transport both people and goods. Bicycles are popular in countries such as China. The type of transport used in a country will generally be determined by the wealth and technical expertise of that country. This will affect not only the individuals who live there, but also the way in which goods are transported within as well as into and out of the country. This in turn will affect the availability of goods and services.

LEARNING ACTIVITY 2.2

1   List four systems that are used for transportation over water. State at least one advantage of each one.

2   List six systems used for transportation over land. State at least one advantage of each one, and list the type (or types) of fuel or source of energy of each.

3   Write down a list of 10 questions you would ask a person of about 90 years about the development of transport over his or her lifetime.

4   Select a particular model of a car. List three model variations of the same car available to the car buyer, and explain in each case why someone would buy that particular model.

5   Work in small groups to research air travel today. What effect has it had on our lives in terms of the following?

   • Travel

   • Work

   • The environment

Each group member should investigate one of the areas above. The information is to be pooled and the group should develop a visual presentation of their findings. The presentation needs to identify and discuss at least two effects that air travel has had on each of the three areas listed (possibly one advantage and one disadvantage).

6 Using the Internet, define the term 'golden age of aviation'.

7 What did Boeing design and build in the 1960s that changed the way people travelled around the world? Explain what effect this had on other modes of transport.

Technology systems in the home

Our homes are full of different types of technologies. We use technologies to prepare food, to heat and cool homes, to provide light, to protect us and to entertain us. The impact of technological development on our home lives has been significant. In the following pages we will look at some of the systems that are used in the home.

Systems used for heating and cooling

Electricity and gas are the most common forms of energy that are used to heat and cool our homes. Many different types of heating and cooling systems can be seen in the home, including ducted heating, wall-mounted heaters, fan heaters, solar heaters and reverse-cycle air conditioners.

The efficiency of a heating system in terms of both its heating efficiency and energy efficiency can vary dramatically depending on the device. For instance, in many homes with ducted heating, energy can be wasted as all areas of the room are heated even when they are unoccupied. New improvements allow us to select which rooms are to be heated or cooled, reducing the amount of energy that is wasted.

Fan heaters are useful because they are portable and can heat a small space quickly, but they use a relatively large amount of power and are therefore expensive to run.

Thermostats are common on most heating devices. Before thermostats, heat control was achieved manually by turning the heater off when the room became too hot and on again when it cooled down. Thermostats have allowed us to set a particular temperature to control the heater to turn itself on and off automatically.

Oil and water are also used in heating systems. The oil or water is usually heated within the system and the heat from this is radiated to heat the room. In the past, wood and coal were commonly used as fuel for both cooking and heating. In some rural areas with access to timber, the use of wood fires is still quite common, but open fires are no longer allowed in most cities because of air pollution.

A fan heater

Shutterstock.com/objectsforall

Some people like the look of an open fireplace, and gas fires that look like wood fires are now available.

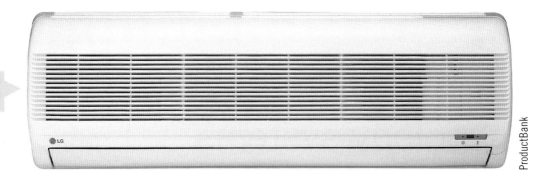

Reverse-cycle air conditioner

ProductBank

Electric fans and air conditioners are examples of systems used for cooling. Air conditioning is often used, especially in office buildings and shopping centres. It is only in more recent times that cooling systems have become common in homes. There are increasing numbers of air conditioners available as the demand for them has increased. Reverse-cycle air conditioners, which allow the systems to be used for either heating or cooling, are now quite popular. This is an example of the move towards products and systems that have more than one function.

When people are making choices about heating they need to consider a number of things, including:

- their needs in terms of heating

- the type of home they are heating

- cost (to install and to run)

- energy efficiency (which relates to the cost of running the heating).

LEARNING ACTIVITY 2.3

1   List the various types of heating appliances that can be used in the home. In each case state its source of energy.

2   Select one type of heating appliance in the home. Explain its operation in terms of input, process and output.

3   Is the system chosen for Question **2** an open loop or a closed loop? Explain your answer.

4   Name three different types of cooling appliances. Explain briefly the advantages and disadvantages of each type.

5   Name two household appliances that have more than one function. Explain briefly the functions of each appliance you have selected.

6   Research alternative energy sources that can be used for cooling, heating and cooking. List these in your workbook and provide a brief explanation of their operation and use.

Systems used in food preparation: kitchen appliances

A large number of the systems that we have at home are used to prepare food. Larger items such as refrigerators, ovens and cooktops are found in most homes. Appliances such as kettles, can openers, food processors, rice steamers, blenders, electric pans, electric knives, sandwich makers, microwave ovens and bread makers are very popular devices with many of us.

The type, size and efficiency of these devices have improved as a result of developments in technology. Toasters are a good example of this. Toasters are now available in many different colours and some will take many slices of bread of different thicknesses. There are controls that vary the length of time the heating element is turned on so that you can choose how much the bread is toasted. Toasters are now much easier to clean and some (like many other appliances) have even been designed to be the centrepiece of the kitchen!

In Australia most families also have a barbecue. Outdoor cooking is considered to be part of Australian life. There have been many developments in an effort to improve and diversify the range of barbecues available. Barbecues are available in many sizes, shapes and colours. Many barbecue systems now include an oven and rotisserie. There are electric barbecues as well as bottled or mains gas barbecues and some that use combustible materials or heat beads.

A toaster

Gas barbecue

Shutterstock.com/Xebeche

iStockphoto/© ep stock

Systems used for cleaning: vacuum cleaners, washing machines, dishwashers

Cleaning is an interesting area to consider in terms of technological change as many products or systems have been developed to make our lives easier. Most of our homes have a washing machine of some sort, and many will have a clothes dryer and a dishwasher. Let's consider the development of the washing machine.

Initially washing was done either in rivers or using water carted from rivers, lakes or wells to a particular location where people washed clothing and other items. There are many countries in the world where this still happens. The provision of running water in homes meant that water no longer had to be carried great distances and washing could be done in the home. For many this dramatically reduced the amount of time that was required for washing.

In the 1860s people used wooden boxes for agitation to 'tumble wash' their clothes. By 1914 these were driven by electric motors (which could be quite dangerous). Developments since that time mean that we can now have a washing machine that automatically fills up with water, agitates and rinses our clothes. We are able to control the machine in a number of ways, including the size of the load, the amount of hot and cold water that is used, the length of the cycle, the spin speed and the time it will start washing. This control also means that we can be more efficient in our use of energy. For instance, we can use hot water only when we think it is needed, saving the energy required to heat the water. We can control the amount of water we use to suit the size of the load, with further water and energy savings. Front-loading machines are gaining popularity as they use less water than top-loading machines. These improvements in washing machines mean that we can now put on a load of washing and go to another task while the clothes are being washed, or simply relax!

A vacuum cleaner is another cleaning device that is present in most homes. The design of vacuum cleaners has changed over the years. We now see a vast array of models ranging from small portable machines to heavy-duty vacuum cleaners. The original designs for vacuum cleaners all incorporated a bag to collect the dust. Now there are bag-free vacuum cleaners on the market. Initially the design focus was purely on function with little thought given to the aesthetics or look of the machine. Now you will find vacuum cleaners in a variety of colours and shapes, as we have moved to developing household products that are more pleasing to the eye.

Front-loading washing machine

Shutterstock.com/Sashkin

Vacuum cleaner – an example of form and function

iStockphoto/© craftvision

LEARNING ACTIVITY 2.4

1 List 10 appliances used in the modern kitchen.

2 Access YouTube on the Internet. Watch 'The secret life of machines' – the vacuum and washing machine episodes.

3 Outline how the activity of cleaning clothes has developed over the years.

4 Outline the changes in the design of vacuum cleaners.

5 What is the main advantage of a front-loading washing machine over a top-loading one?

6 Gather information on an appliance used in the home. Collect brochures and user manuals, or view appliances in shops and search the Internet.

   a Name the appliance you selected and identify three models by manufacturer or by some other means.

ISBN 9780170227452

b Compare the models in terms of price, design and ease of use.

c Which model appeals to you the most? Why?

d Which models do you think would most appeal to the 'average' household? Why?

e Outline one feature that you would like to include in the appliance and that is not already there. Explain your choice of feature.

Systems used for safety and protection: smoke alarms, RCDs and security alarms

Systems such as smoke alarms and **residual current devices** (RCDs) have decreased the risk of injuries and even death in cases of house fires and electric shocks respectively. Smoke alarms can identify and monitor air density and the presence of radioactive particles absorbed by smoke. A sensor detects that change and sets off an alarm. The RCD detects any electric current that is likely to give an electric shock. It does this by constantly monitoring the currents in both the active and neutral wires. If the currents are unequal (earth leakage occurs due to a fault or accident), the device shuts off. The electricity supply is cut off in a split second to prevent electric shock or electrocution.

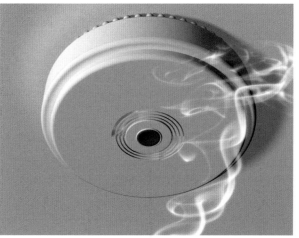

Smoke alarm

Shutterstock.com/Paul Fleet

Many homes and businesses are now fitted with security systems and alarms, some linked to professional security monitors and relevant authorities. These alarms rely mainly on sensors that detect movement.

Energy use and efficiency in the home

When designing systems for the home we need to consider energy efficiency. There has been a greater focus in recent years on improving systems so that they will be more energy efficient. This has come about partly because of concerns about the amount of energy we are using and the long-term effect on the environment. People have also recognised that the more efficient their systems are, the lower the running costs (for instance, for electricity and gas). Many appliances now have a star rating. A more efficient refrigerator is allocated more stars than a less efficient one.

Modifications have been made to many household products to improve their energy efficiency, including:

- baths replaced by showers

- shower roses that spray less water

- small, medium and large load options on washing machines, and the use of front-loading machines

- lights with automatic switches

- fan heat-extraction units

- heaters with in-built fans and thermostat control

- compact fluorescent light bulbs.

Kilowatt hours and megajoules

The amount of electrical energy used in the home is measured in kilowatt hours (kWh) and the total kilowatt hours used would be shown in the electricity bill. One kilowatt hour of electrical energy costs about 25 cents. The cost is less for consumption in 'off peak' periods. A heater rated at 2 kilowatts and operating fully for 3 hours will consume 6 kilowatt hours of electrical energy. We simply multiply the kilowatts by the hours.

The amount of natural gas energy is measured in megajoules (MJ). One megajoule costs about 1.5 cents. The energy used by gas appliances is directly related to the volume of gas used. This is detailed in the gas bill.

LEARNING ACTIVITY 2.5

1 List five design changes that have improved the efficiency of systems used in the home. Explain in what way the change or device has increased the efficiency.

2 Ask your parent or guardian for a copy of your home electricity bill. Examine it closely and note your household consumption across the months. Has it been up, down or constant? Explain your findings.

3 A 2 kilowatt heater is used continuously for 6 hours. Calculate the energy cost in dollars if one kilowatt hour costs 20 cents.

4 An electric meter reads 64 580 and three months later it reads 65 372. The difference gives the number of kilowatt hours used by the household. The standard service charge by the electricity provider is $30.00, which is added to the energy cost. Calculate the total amount for the electricity bill.

5 What assumption have you made in your working out in Question 3?

Technology in the workplace

Computer systems: mainframes, desktops and laptops

The word 'computer' comes from the word 'compute'. According to the *Macquarie Dictionary* 'compute' means to calculate. The first computers can be linked to attempts to find ways to make calculating easier. Computers have evolved over a long period of time and there have been many developments that have affected their design and the way in which they operate. Some of the first computers that resemble (even if only in broad terms!) the computers we use today needed paper tape with holes punched in it to feed information into them. The tape was used to 'tell' the computer what to do. Early computers had relatively little memory when compared to computers we use today, so they needed some of the information fed into them at the time of use.

ISBN 9780170227452

In recent times there have been significant advances in computer technology, including the development of laptops and tablets, and an array of associated electronic devices, such as the modem, USBs, laser printers, scanners and digital cameras. Each of these changes has allowed us to use computers in different situations and in a range of ways. They have also led to a significant increase in employment opportunities in the broad area of computing.

Technological development will continue as we have new and changing needs. One of the challenges for us as designers of new systems is to identify where the real needs are and to ensure that the new systems are appropriate for the situations they are designed for. Laptop computers with a clockwork mechanism for power or which can be hand-'wound' (using a dymo mechanism) have been developed for use in countries where mains electricity and batteries are not easily available.

Computers have had a huge impact on work practices in an office. Most people in the office have a personal computer on which they work and store a great deal of business information. In the past many people would have had administrative assistants to help with, for instance, writing letters and filing information. There are now far fewer of these people employed and the expectation is that people will be in charge of their own administration as they have their own computer on their desk.

A desktop computer

Shutterstock.com/mmaxer

A laptop computer

Using computers, we can now have meetings between people in different states or countries using Skype or webinars or other systems. This can reduce the number of meetings that people need to attend, and can dramatically reduce the amount of travel needed for business purposes. Laptop computers have allowed people to take their computers with them when they attend a meeting or travel interstate or overseas. They can continue to work while travelling – for instance, on an aeroplane.

There are negative impacts of using computers in the office, such as:

- health problems related to posture and watching a monitor screen for long periods of time

- overuse of email communication for trivial messages (many workplaces now have restrictions on how people use email)

- employees using email chains to communicate with one another where face-to-face meetings would be more productive.

1 List the benefits and the negative impacts of computers:

   a in the workplace

   b at home and in schools.

2 Make a list of five technological systems used in the workplace and outline briefly the output of each system.

3 Outline three systems that are no longer used in the workplace and have been replaced by new systems performing the same functions. Name the new systems.

4 Sketch a purely mechanical system you would come across in a small workshop. Indicate the input and the output of the system. Outline the mechanical principle that underpins the operation of the system.

Technology and the work environment

The changes to technology in the workplace have had a huge impact on the nature of work. Technological systems are used in all types of work for a range of purposes. In the manufacturing industry we use machines to manufacture products, and to transport them to their point of sale. Offices use a range of systems, such as telephones and computers, in an effort to improve the efficiency of the workplace. The infrastructure in any workplace – power, lighting, heating, cooking facilities and so on – is supported by technological systems. In the retail industry, systems such as electronic cash registers and barcode readers are essential. Consider all of the systems that are used in the hospitality industry. The local mechanic uses a range of systems to service your family car. All workplaces use technological systems in some

An automated teller machine

Shutterstock.com/Rafael Ramirez Lee

way, and these will have an impact on the way in which the workplace functions. For instance, machines have now replaced people in many industrial situations:

- Robots are used to do repetitious, dirty or dangerous tasks.
- Most business is done online using computers.
- Automated teller machines and Internet banking have reduced the need for tellers in banks.

There have been significant changes to the office environment and these have had a great impact on the way in which the office operates. Communication is vital to most workplaces, but especially in an office. The methods of communication and the ease with which we can now communicate with people in other parts of the city, state, country or world have changed a great deal. The development of the telex in the 1960s allowed businesses to communicate in text form with people in different places. The facsimile (fax) machine was developed, allowing us to send different types of information (images and handwriting) quickly and easily. Now we have modems that allow us to send information via a computer. Scanners, digital cameras and mobile phones mean that we can send a greater range of images and graphics as well. Emailing, web cam, Skype and video conferencing allow us to have online discussions, thereby enabling businesspeople to negotiate and respond quickly to information without actually having to meet in person.

Vast amounts of energy are used in the manufacturing industry – most of it in the manufacture and transport of materials and products. There is also a proportion of energy used for heating, lighting, hot water, food preparation facilities or in a canteen, for instance. Without technological systems industry would not exist. There have been many changes and improvements made to the systems to try to have both a more efficient and a more comfortable workplace.

Developments in industry, particularly in terms of improving the efficiency of machinery, have had a great impact on the nature of industry. What is the impact of this on society?

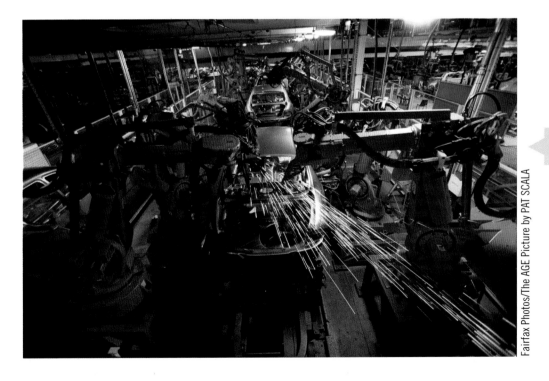

Robot arms used in car manufacturing

Fairfax Photos/The AGE Picture by PAT SCALA

Some people would argue that these tasks were boring or dangerous and that it is better for a machine to do it. Others say that the use of robots means more unemployment because the workers who are displaced experience problems in finding alternative work.

There is no doubt that using robots and machinery for some tasks has meant that many industries have reduced the incidence of accidents in the workplace. The downside is the increase in unemployment. There will be many new jobs created by the introduction of new machinery, robots and computers. For instance, there has been an increase in the need for service engineers, technicians and computer specialists. The problem for society is that the workers displaced by technology will not have the skills needed for the new jobs.

Lean manufacturing

Not only have industry and business become more efficient with the introduction of new technologies, but major changes in how work is planned and completed have also increased output and efficiency. Industry has developed a 'leaner' approach to its business and production plans. The term 'lean manufacturing' has been applied to the processes where structured planning, minimalist design, streamlined production, reduced machining, full recycling and minimal waste, an efficient production line and mass production are all important features.

In the future, new technological developments in industry will continue to change the nature of the work. This means that as designers and technologists we need to be able to adapt to these changing needs.

The 'Manufacturing and technology' case study discusses lean manufacture in greater depth, together with some of the concepts discussed previously in this section.

LEARNING ACTIVITY 2.7

1 Name and explain briefly the functions of two systems used in an office environment and two systems used in a manufacturing industry.

2 Choose one of the systems from Question 1 and outline its effect on the work environment and work practices.

3 Describe two ways in which energy efficiency could be improved in a system in the home, and two ways it could be improved in a system in the workplace.

4 List and explain three advantages and three disadvantages of using robots in industry.

Technology and the environment

When we analyse and design systems we need to consider both the effect of the system on the environment and the appropriateness of the system for the situation for which it is intended.

When we use systems there will be some sort of effect on the environment. We need to assess this impact as part of designing systems. When we talk about systems and the environment there are a number of things to consider:

- the energy sources and forms that will power the system

- the polluting effect on the natural environment, including the flora and fauna, and the atmosphere

- the effects of the system on people and society.

Energy sources: renewable and non-renewable sources

Systems need energy to operate. Computers, for instance, use electrical energy from a power station or batteries made of materials and chemicals. Cars use the chemical energy from petrol, LPG and even batteries. The source and form of energy used for a system will to some degree determine the impact that the system has on the natural environment.

Some energy sources, such as solar, wind and waves, are renewable, while others, like coal and gas, are not. We need to take into consideration the benefits and issues associated with using different energy sources and materials when we are making decisions about how the system will operate. What energy source is least likely to have a detrimental effect on the environment? Can it be used in this particular design?

There are many forms of waste and pollution that have an impact on the environment, and as such need to be considered in terms of the systems we use and design.

Newspix/Aaron Francis

Shutterstock.com/IKO

Air pollution: the greenhouse effect

Systems are a significant contributor to air pollution. Burning fossil fuels, such as coal and oil, produce gases that pollute the air. Two systems are the main cause of this form of pollution. The first comprises the coal- and oil-fired systems that generate electricity, and the second is the internal combustion engine. Any system that involves burning or heating materials is a potential cause of air pollution. Air pollution causes health problems and contributes towards the global warming effect.

A gardener's glass greenhouse used for growing plants traps heat. It lets heat from the sun's rays in but does not allow it to get out, hence warming the interior. What we call 'greenhouse gases' act just as glass does, allowing heat from the sun to pass through but trapping it and keeping the Earth warm. Carbon dioxide, water vapour, methane and nitrous oxides are examples of greenhouse gases. Without these gases the Earth would be much cooler and in most places uninhabitable. A build-up of these gases will, however, make the Earth too warm for many species. This is what has happened since the concentration of these gases has increased. Car engines and power stations release carbon dioxide as a by-product, and this contributes to the greenhouse effect. Global temperature is rising as is sea level, flooding low-lying areas.

The burning of coal and oil also increases the acid content in rain. The rain that falls is called acid rain and reduces plant growth and development. Many countries have been affected by acid rain. As a result, many vehicles are now fitted with emission control devices to reduce pollution, and current technological developments are being made in storing carbon dioxide gas from power stations under pressure deep underground. Neither are really satisfactory, hence the ongoing research and introduction of hybrid and electric vehicles, and worldwide trends towards growth in renewable energy technologies.

Soil and water pollution

Using old, disused products (such as computers) as landfill often causes soil pollution. A computer contains a lot of toxic material. The cathode ray tube used for the monitor can contain a kilogram or more of lead, a poisonous metal. Lead is used to shield users from harmful radiation. There is also some lead in the solder used in soldering components.

Toxic chemicals are used in the plastic as flame retardants. Many chemicals can be recovered upon recycling but this takes time, effort and money. Aluminium can be extracted from the disk drives, copper and plastic from the wires, and precious metals such as gold, silver and platinum from other parts. Some manufacturers are now building systems that are easier to dismantle and recycle. They are using clip-ins instead of screws wherever possible and the same type of plastic throughout.

Spilt or waste materials from industrial systems also pollute the soil. Oil that leaks from storage tanks and waste from processing that is dumped in tips are examples of soil pollution from systems. Smoke alarms contain a small amount of radioactive material. Chemicals and other substances used in systems often find their way into waterways and ground water.

Noise and visual pollution

People who live near freeways or aerodromes are affected by the noise created by traffic. Mechanical systems produce noise when operating, and designers have to consider ways of reducing this problem. There is concern that listening to very loud music will lead to premature deafness, especially among young people.

Visual pollution

iStockphoto/© Skyhobo

ISBN 9780170227452

There are many examples of systems that spoil the view of our environment. Electricity transmission pylons and lines, mobile phone towers, wind farms, chimneys that carry the exhaust gases from furnaces and the overhead wires on tramway systems are all examples of visual pollution.

LEARNING ACTIVITY 2.8

1 Explain the greenhouse effect and name two technological systems that contribute to the effect. Explain in what ways they contribute to the effect.

2 Dumping your old computer in the local tip causes soil pollution. Explain how. Suggest ways of reducing this kind of pollution.

3 Cars cause a great deal of pollution. Find out about at least two improvements that have been made to cars to reduce the pollution they create. Identify the problem that the improvement addressed in each case, discuss how it works and explain what impact this improvement has had or will have.

4 List five systems that have some visual impact on the environment. Select one and explain the impact. Is there an alternative system that could be used? Are there ways in which the visual impact could be reduced?

Appropriate technology

We use technology every day in many of the things that we do. Technology will often make tasks easier. Instead of hand washing dishes we may have a dishwasher. We could have a remote-controlled garage door that can be opened and closed without needing to get out of the car. Portable power tools, such as saws and drills, have replaced many hand tools.

Wants and real needs

Technology has been used to address needs in society, but many of the new developments now are about making our lives easier, comfortable, safer and more entertaining. There are many examples of real needs ('technology pull') such as those in health and medical technology and increasingly in new technologies to address environmental issues. However, there is also a great deal of development in technology that is more about wants than real needs. For instance, using a dishwasher instead of washing dishes by hand is about making our lives easier, rather than being a real need. The new ideas are still legitimate, but we need to be aware of the purposes of the systems we develop and of their effects on society.

Designing water pumps is a need.

Alamy/© Finnbarr Webster

Designing an automatic sprinkler system – a need or want?

Shutterstock.com/PozitivStudija

'Needs' vary significantly depending on the environment. In a particular country there may be a 'need' to design a water pump that can be easily operated by a range of people in a village, and which uses an energy source that is readily available all year round. In another situation there may be a 'need' for an automatic sprinkler system so that someone doesn't have to stand around watering the garden. In reality the automatic sprinkler is not needed, but it does make life easier. In designing systems it is important for us to be able to identify the situation or environment in which the system is to be used and to address the problem accordingly.

Systems control gives better output and at other times it allows us more time to do other things. For instance, ovens can now be set to automatically come on at a particular time, which has allowed people to start cooking dinner while still on their way home from work. DVD players can be programmed to record a program while we are out so we can watch it at our convenience. Telephone messages can be accessed from another location, so that we can check messages even when not at home. All of these things are aimed at making our lives easier and more efficient.

Many of the new developments have been in the area of control. For example, motor vehicles are basically the same as the previous versions or series, with maybe some style and safety variations. What has changed is how we control its operation. Vehicle computer systems control the engine, brakes, suspension, speed, environment and many other features such as video, audio and GPS to improve standards of comfort and safety when we are driving.

Motor vehicle

Shutterstock.com/Maksim Toome

To be able to judge the appropriateness of a system, consideration needs to be given to who will be using the system and where it will be used. For instance, if you were designing a toy or game for a young child, the game would need to be simple to use, be made out of non-toxic materials, and have no sharp edges and no small parts that might be broken off or swallowed.

It is extremely important to consider the environment or situation in which the system is to be used as it will affect the form of energy and the materials that will be used in the system. If we look at transport, for example, the type of transport that would be appropriate in a city could be quite different to that which is appropriate on a farm or in a rural area. We need to ensure that systems are designed to suit the environment in which they will be placed.

The technology must suit the situation and be suitable for the people who will use it. The intended users of the system need access to relevant resources and knowledge to be able

ISBN 9780170227452

to operate and repair the system. Many systems are now designed in such a way that they cannot be repaired easily, or the repair cost is higher than the replacement cost. The culture and environment within a country all need to be considered. Remember that inappropriate technology is bad design.

LEARNING ACTIVITY 2.9

1 Explain the difference between a 'need' and a 'want' in regard to technological systems.

2 Name five technological systems that you would classify as needs rather than wants. Briefly explain your reasoning.

3 Name two systems that have an element of control and explain the controls and their benefits.

4 Compare the uses and effects or implications of using a manual water pump and an electrical water pump. In what situations or environments could a manual (possibly mechanical) pump be the more effective system and when might an electrical pump be more appropriate?

5 List two advantages and two disadvantages of electronic equipment that is costly or difficult to repair.

6 Select a household product (such as a toaster, refrigerator, television or washing machine) and investigate its development. Find out when it was invented, what system it replaced, some of the changes in designs for the product over time, how it is operated, and what energy sources and forms have been used to operate it. Discuss the advantages and disadvantages of the product as it is now in terms of its energy source and forms, its operation and its effect on the environment in which it is situated.

7 Why was the development of the laptop computer significant? What are the advantages of using a laptop? What are two disadvantages of using a laptop?

8 Design a system that can be used to heat food when you are camping. First you need to identify the requirements (it needs to be light, portable, easily carried, and so on). Then you need to design and produce the system.

9 Compare a microwave oven to a conventional oven. List the similarities and differences in terms of the following.
   • How each heats food
   • The time each takes to heat the food
   • The advantages and disadvantages of each method

10 Describe two ways in which energy efficiency could be improved in a system in the home and two ways it could be improved in a system in the workplace.

11 List three ways in which you could use a system to cross a river. Identify a situation where each of these would be the most appropriate method to use.

12 Identify one technological development that is designed to reduce the negative impact of a system on people. Explain what the development is and how it reduces the impact.

Recent and emerging technologies

Technology is changing at an ever-increasing pace. It took humans a couple of million years to invent the wheel. About 5000 years later the steam engine was invented. Steam engines

Digital camera

Shutterstock.com/taelove7

and steam trains revolutionised industry and transport. Then within 100 years, diesel engines and electric motors were developed to bring about further change.

The first computers were large – the size of a room – but technological developments made computers small and portable within only 50 years. We have seen many other new technologies within that same time span.

Recent technologies such as iPods, Blu-ray and DVD players and mp3 players have replaced older ones, such as magnetic tape cassettes and video cassettes.

Even the newest systems will be replaced soon as we discover and develop new ways of storing and transmitting digital signals. This section will outline some of the technologies developed recently and others that are likely to have an impact later in the 21st century.

Audio and video

Recording, storing and playing back audio and video signals for most of the 20th century relied on analogue technology. Advances in digital technology in the last two decades have made most audio analogue systems, such as vinyl record players and magnetic cassette decks, obsolete. This also applies to other systems such as film cameras. The difference between analogue and digital signals is explained in Chapter 5, 'Electrotechnology'.

Older systems used magnetic tape and vinyl discs to store information, and electromechanical devices like tape recording heads and a stylus to record and retrieve the information in analogue form. The flow of electrons in wires and components has provided the basis for the operation of most of the electrical and electronic systems we use or have used in the past.

We are, however, using light more and more to send, store and process information. This is because devices that use light are much faster and can store more data than those relying on electric currents. An example is the use of lasers in DVD (digital video disc) players. New systems use laser beams and compact discs to do the same job in digital format. Lasers are used not only in DVD players but also in the storage systems for computer hard drives.

The word 'laser' is an acronym for **l**ight **a**mplification by the **s**timulated **e**mission of **r**adiation. A laser is a light beam made up of light purely of one colour or wavelength. The shorter wavelength is best for digital work. Any other light beam would not be as pure, being made up of a mixture of colours of varying proportions.

A laser beam is emitted from a laser diode just as coloured light is emitted from a light-emitting diode (LED). The difference between the two devices lies in the kind of semiconductors used to make the diode. Early lasers used materials that resulted in the emission of long wavelengths in the red region of the light spectrum. CD players in the 1990s were the first to use these red lasers. These lasers could be used for audio purposes but not for processing video images, as in DVD players, which require higher data storage densities. This eventually came with the arrival of shorter wavelength blue lasers. Research into new semiconductors like gallium nitride and improved manufacturing techniques led to the development of these lasers. Systems such as laser printers and projection televisions also use lasers, and benefited from the research.

DVD players have mechanical components and moving parts. They have electric motors and gearing systems. Personal music players such as the iPod, however, have no moving parts. All the music is stored in microchips in digital format. Music and words need no longer be stored on vinyl, tape or even compact disc. Radio stations are using the technology to make programs available over the Internet as podcasts or by streaming.

With digital music systems we can listen to music stored in home computers in every room in the house using a wireless remote. The system links the computer, the audio system and the remote control.

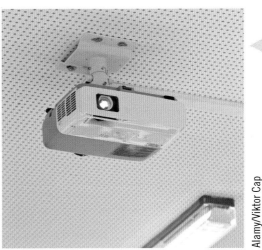

A digital audio system

Shutterstock.com/Zakharoff

Television: LCD and plasma

A television set converts TV microwave signals into sound and pictures. Liquid crystal display (LCD) screens and plasma screens are now rapidly replacing the cathode ray tube screen. They are commonly used in display screens, computer monitors, aircraft cockpit displays and instrument panels. The signals are also changing from analogue to digital to give clearer, sharper pictures and allow more features to be transmitted. In a plasma screen a gas stored in small cells called pixels provides the colours needed. There are thousands of these cells between two plates of glass. In an LCD TV, a liquid crystal solution is trapped between two sheets of special glass called polarised glass. Electric voltages applied to the gas or solution eventually lead to the emission of coloured light.

- LCD television sets can be thinner and consume less power than the plasma sets, but offer a narrower viewing angle.

- The plasma sets can be larger and offer better contrast than the LCD sets.

- The trend is to develop 'crossover products' where one single product performs a number of functions such as an audio system, DVD player and projector all combined, or a music player and a mobile phone combined.

- There is lower power consumption.

Shutterstock.com/Pakhnyushcha

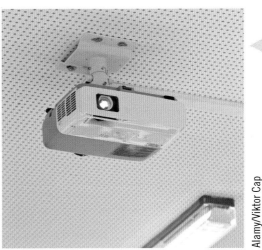

LCD television and DVD projector (crossover product)

Alamy/Viktor Cap

Light displays: light-emitting diodes

Electric light bulbs use electricity to make light, but most of the energy input is wasted as heat. An LED converts the energy directly to light. Numerical displays in the first electronic calculators used LEDs. They were not bright enough to be used elsewhere. LEDs use semiconducting materials that determine the colour and the brightness. Green and red LEDs have been around for some time, but recent developments in the production of new materials like gallium nitride have resulted in the production of blue LEDs. Any visible colour can be made from the right combination of red, green and blue light. Bright full-colour displays are now possible.

A good example is the use of LEDs for speed signs and traffic lights. The electric bulbs used before lasted for about a year and wasted energy. LEDs now are brighter, can last up to 15 years and use 90% less energy.

LEDs in new traffic lights and speed signs

Shutterstock.com/Harris Shiffman

Alamy/David Moore/Victoria

Battery technology: fuel cells

A fuel cell is basically a system that produces electricity from chemicals, just as a car battery would. The process is very similar to that in a car battery in that a chemical reaction results in one plate gaining an excess of electrons and forming a negative terminal, the **cathode**, and the other losing electrons and forming a positive terminal, the **anode**. A fuel cell, however, uses different materials and not all of them are contained inside the cell. One type of cell is fuelled by hydrogen gas and oxygen gas. These two gases are pumped from outside into the cell. They are kept apart by the plates and the electrolyte.

The amount of electrical power produced depends on many factors, such as the gas pressure, the materials used and the temperature of the cell. Fuel cells work at temperatures ranging from about 60°C to as much as 1000°C. The cells are connected in series to form a fuel–cell stack. This increases the voltage available. Fuel cells have been used as a source of power in spacecraft and trialled in some vehicles like buses.

- A fuel cell causes much less pollution than an internal combustion engine.

- Hydrogen as a fuel is plentiful and can be extracted from water or natural gas.

ISBN 9780170227452

One problem has been storing and delivering the gas to users. The gas has to be stored under pressure on the vehicle. It has been difficult to store an amount large enough to provide a good driving range before refuelling.

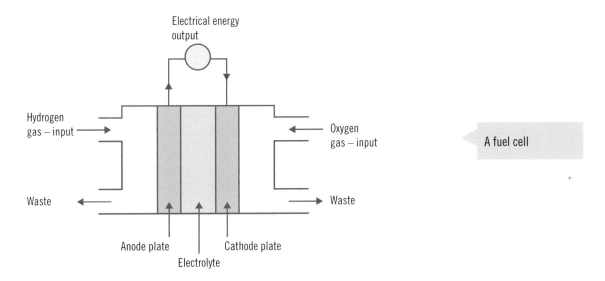

A fuel cell

Vehicle technology

Petrol, diesel and gas from fossil fuels power nearly all the cars. The emissions arising from these sources of energy as they burn create a great deal of pollution, as mentioned earlier. Vehicles driven by electric motors were developed to overcome the problem, but they have limitations. The batteries have to be constantly recharged using mains electric power after relatively short trips. Such vehicles are still used in situations where constant recharging and length of trips are not issues.

Hybrid vehicles (with two or more power sources, including petrol, diesel, hydrogen and electricity), most commonly combining both a conventional petrol engine and an electric motor, have recently been developed. Hybrid cars are now available to the average car buyer at an affordable price. A computer controls the power distribution according to the driving conditions. As you switch on the ignition and drive off, only the electric motor is used and no petrol is burnt. The petrol engine is activated when extra power is needed, such as for fast acceleration or when climbing hills. During braking the electric motor acts as a generator of electricity. The kinetic or motion energy of the car is converted to electrical energy that is used to charge the battery. This overcomes the problem of constantly having to use mains electricity for battery charging.

A hybrid car

Shutterstock.com/Boykov

Hybrids come in different forms, including:

- series hybrid – battery powered with an engine fitted to run the generator

- parallel hybrid – an electric motor and engine running separately or together to power the vehicle systems

- hybrid fuel – dual mode.

Cars are already packed with electronics and electronic gadgets. Developments in vehicle wireless technology to link the various systems are well advanced. A wireless device can interact with other systems. You can link your mobile phone, security alarm system and personal computer to your car, allowing you to transmit music and movies to your car audio and video systems. Satellite services can then transmit streamed audio and video to cars. Cars can be networked so that drivers can communicate with each other.

Car manufacturers may even be able to monitor all the systems in your car and alert you if something is faulty or is going to break down. Safety belts and airbags have contributed a great deal to a reduction in road deaths and injuries. The focus is now shifting towards comfort and accident prevention. Driverless trains and planes with autopilots are already operating, but driverless computer-controlled cars are still in the research and development stage. Furthermore there is the problem of adapting the road network to such cars. There are, however, developments in other areas that will reduce driver errors. Devices that warn the driver of a dangerous situation are now being fitted to some cars. A digital camera fitted to the door mirror detects overtaking traffic, especially around the blind spot area, and warns the driver. A similar camera fitted to the rear view mirror detects the white lines used as lane markers and warns a driver if he or she gets distracted or falls asleep, and drifts out of the lane.

Supercapacitors

A **capacitor** is a device that stores electric charge. You can read more about traditional and basic capacitors in Chapter 5, 'Electrotechnology'. These capacitors do not store large amounts of electricity and do not deliver large currents. The newer **supercapacitors** can do this, which makes them suitable as battery replacements in cordless power tools and even as electricity storage tanks in renewable energy systems. They can be used in cars to kick-start the starter motor and hence reduce the load on the battery, which will then last longer. In hybrid electric cars they can be charged by converting the energy normally wasted when braking. The stored energy in the capacitor can then be used to accelerate the car.

Power surges can damage electrical equipment. Capacitors are used to absorb these surges and protect the equipment. Supercapacitors are better than traditional ones as they not only cope with higher surges but also react faster.

- Supercapacitors use a carbon surface to store electric charge. The surface area and energy density available are thousands of times greater than in traditional capacitors that use metal surfaces.

- Supercapacitors can be charged and recharged much faster than traditional ones and they do not deteriorate over time so they last longer.

- They have a larger output power.

ISBN 9780170227452

Solar towers

Solar towers use the energy from the sun but in a very different way to solar cells. A solar tower uses the fact that the sun heats the air and that hot air rises as it is lighter than cold air. The force provided by the rising hot air can be used to turn turbine blades. The turbines operate generators and electricity is produced.

Collectors, often in the shape of wide and high upturned funnels made of concrete and steel, are used to collect the surrounding hot air. The hot air is channelled through the funnel structure, moving at speeds up to 40 kilometres per hour. A collector can be hundreds of metres high, and fixed a few metres above ground.

A solar tower

Shutterstock.com/paulrommer

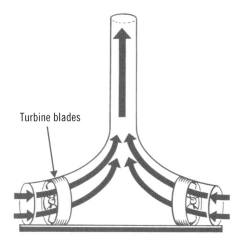

Airflow in a solar tower

Turbine blades

Combined heat and power

The efficiency of a solar tower can be improved by including a network of tubing filled with water. The water can be stored and used at night to continue the supply of hot air. Solar towers are particularly suited for remote areas as they are relatively simple in their construction and without complex technology. The hot water produced in the system can also be distributed to local networks. This technique and integration of heat distribution to customers is known as combined heat and power generation (CHP).

Solar air turbines

Other technologies aimed at reducing greenhouse gas emissions, such as solar air turbines that use heat for generation purposes, are being developed to different levels throughout the world. These are based on the Brayton and Rankine (thermodynamic) cycles of converting waste heat and pressure into useful work and electricity generation. Unlike CHP, which utilises water for heat and recycling, and other fossil fuel generation methods, solar air turbine technology utilises hot air directly for generation to complete a renewable, clean, closed loop cycle.

How solar air turbines work

- Concentrated solar energy is reflected by custom designed mirrors (heliostats) to a solar receiver located on top of a tower. The receiver houses the air turbine and air compressor.

- Air is drawn into the compressor; then compressed and sent to the solar receiver.

- The air in the solar receiver is heated to over 1000°C using concentrated solar energy.

- The hot air is directed through turbines to generate electricity.

The CSIRO in Australia has developed a large-scale demonstration site for international research and to commercially develop solar energy technologies. The site covers 4000 square metres. Although the site is being used for research it is capable of powering approximately 200 homes. The CSIRO is also researching methods of heating compressed air by using natural gas combustion to overcome unsuitable weather conditions. Also being researched is high temperature solar energy storage. For information on this, visit the CSIRO's integrated Rankine cycle project.

Solar ventilators

Weblink

www.csiro.au/en/
Outcomes/Climate/
Energy/Renewables-
and-Smart-Systems/
Integrated-Rankine-
Cycle-Project.aspx

Solar ventilators are devices that use solar panels to collect and generate power to run ventilation systems. This is a particularly useful development that has great potential in hot sunny climates to emit heat from roof cavities and living spaces. By using renewable energy as a power source, there is no need to use grid supply electricity and the need for air conditioning and its related expense is greatly reduced or eliminated.

Nanotechnology

A 10-cent coin is about 1 millimetre thick. If you could slice the coin into one million slices, then each would be 1 nanometre thick. Atoms and molecules, the building blocks of matter, are so small that we indicate their sizes in nanometres. Nanotechnology uses actual existing atoms and molecules, shuffles them around and makes new materials. The technology will also enable us to miniaturise machines, with limitless possibilities.

Microscopic machines may one day be used in medicine.

Coneyl Jay/Science Photo Library

ISBN 9780170227452

LEARNING ACTIVITY 2.10

1 **a** List five devices or systems that have been used or are currently being used to store sound.

   b Select two and discuss their advantages and disadvantages.

2 What do the letters in the word 'laser' stand for?

3 **a** Explain the difference between a laser beam and ray of light from a torch.

   b What is the difference between a red laser and a blue laser?

4 What do the letters LCD stand for?

5 What are the advantages and disadvantages of LCD televisions over plasma televisions?

6 What are the advantages of LED displays over light bulbs?

7 **a** Explain briefly how a fuel cell works.

   b Research the different materials that are used in its construction and the waste this cell produces.

8 Explain how the efficiency of a solar tower can be improved.

9 State and explain one advantage and one disadvantage of owning a hybrid car.

10 Explain the function of the computer in a hybrid car.

11 Search the Internet for information on solar air turbines. Where are they located near you?

12 **a** Explain what a solar ventilator is.

   b Draw an input, process, output (IPO) diagram for this system.

Weblinks

www.howstuffworks.com

www.technologystudent.com

www.renew.org.au

www.energyquest.com.au

www.csiro.au

www.allhybridcars.com

1 List four sources of energy we can use for heating. Discuss the advantages and disadvantages of each.

2 What factors need to be considered when choosing a heating system for a house?

3 List the measures that can be taken to reduce heat loss in a house.

4 Gas-powered refrigerators once competed with electric refrigerators. They had many advantages and yet lost out. Research and find out:
   - how they worked compared with the electric version
   - their advantages
   - why they lost out to the electric version.

5 Sketch two types of coffee-making appliances used in the kitchen. Outline for each of them the input, process and output.

6 Induction cooking is a different way of heating food and cooking to gas or electric cooking. Induction cookers can replace gas or electric ones. Research this type of cooker and write a report that compares them with the gas and electric versions.

7 Select a developing country and look at the mode of transport that is commonly used in that country. Explain possible reasons why that mode of transport is used and the implications of this for the people, the society and the environment.

8 State the units used to measure energy consumption in the home for:
   a gas energy
   b electrical energy.

9 Outline the methods that have been used over the years to record and store music.

10 State the storage medium (material) for each of the methods in Question **9** and explain how it performs the task.

11 What are the advantages of a DVD player over a videotape player?

12 A fishing rod is a simple mechanical lever system. Sketch one and indicate the load, the effort and the pivot or fulcrum, as a person lifts a fish out of the water.

13 List three models of passenger aircraft. How many engines does each use and where are they positioned?

14 List six devices found in the modern car but which were not available 20 years ago.

15 Name three sources of power for trains.

16 Explain how manufacturers of computers have made the recycling of old computers easier. What materials in these computers can be recycled?

17 List three systems that you think contribute to each of the following.
   a Visual pollution
   b Noise pollution
   c Water pollution

18 What are the causes of soil and water pollution? Suggest some measures that may reduce this type of pollution.

19 What are the design considerations when designing a toy for a four year old?

20 Are the systems listed below wants or needs? Explain your answer.
   a Petrol lawn mower
   b Hearing aid
   c Game player
   d Toilet cistern

21 Vinyl record players are hardly used these days. List four other systems you think are hardly used or have been completely replaced.

22 Research cathode ray tube, LCD and plasma television sets and draw up a table to show how they work, and their advantages and disadvantages.

23 Draw an input, process and output block diagram for a solar tower to explain how the tower works.

24 Name three other systems that make use of the sun's energy.

25 List what you think are the advantages and disadvantages of a hybrid car compared with a petrol engine car.

26 Draw a block diagram to show the operation of a hybrid car.

CASE STUDY 2

Manufacturing and technology

This case study briefly examines the role of manufacturing industries in society. New technology has created many changes in how goods are produced. Manufacturers can access an array of engineered systems to enable them to produce goods from small-scale to mass-produced items in the most efficient and cost-effective way. Industry needs to be more efficient in order to survive in a competitive world with diverse market sectors. Automation has played a major part in steering the direction of modern industry and how things are produced. Besides creating changes in production methods, technology can also affect those employed by altering their work roles and improving health and safety conditions.

This case study by author Pat O'Neill creates useful links between this chapter and the more specific case studies in this book.

Technology and society

Technology plays an important role in all of our lives. We use technology in many different ways to make our social lives and work tasks easier. Using technology is therefore an advantage if we want to maintain an organised lifestyle. Our interactions with technology include activities such as preparing meals, sport training, banking, computing, operating machines and listening to music. Without technological devices or appliances our lifestyles would be considerably different.

Technology in the home

We also rely on technology to get us to and from school and our place of work. Have you ever considered how life would be without motor vehicles or a reliable transport system? The modern workplace obviously relies on technology to do business and to produce goods of all sorts. Without industry, for instance, we would not have the products we need to perform our everyday activities or the services that allow us to travel from place to place. It is therefore important that we have an industry sector that provides for all of our needs.

There are many different kinds of industries, each specialising and providing us with different services and products. It is important to realise that industry provides services as well as products.

The term 'industry sector' is frequently used to categorise or label different industries and their functions. Some are labelled as industries, even though we think of them as services; for instance, the 'entertainment industry' and the 'health industry' provide services. Others, such as engineering, motor vehicle and textile industries, are manufacturers, as they all make products. The term 'manufacturer' is therefore used to describe those industries that produce goods of different sorts. Some of the major industry sectors (manufacturing and services) are listed below.

Major industry sectors

- Transport
- Energy supply
- Building and construction
- Leisure
- Food and confectionery
- Hospitality
- Agriculture
- Textile, clothing and footwear
- Pharmaceutical
- Engineering
- Tourism
- Music
- Retail
- Chemical
- Telecommunications
- Automobile

Manufacturing

When we hear the term 'manufacturing' we correctly think of things being made or produced in factories or in production plants. Motor vehicles, dishwashers, clothes, tools, furniture, cosmetics, telephones, musical instruments and more are all examples of manufactured goods. The range of manufacturing industries is even more diverse than these examples suggest. What these industries actually do is convert raw materials by processing them into useful products, just as systems do.

Manufacturing system

Lean manufacturing

Manufacturers continually strive to maintain or increase profits. By increasing overall efficiency this is usually the end result. The term 'lean manufacturing' is one that is applied to this task. Lean manufacturing was initially practised by the automotive industries but has now become common throughout all industrial sectors.

Manufacturers attempt leanness by designing components and products that are easy, quick and cheaper to produce. They attempt to standardise component parts and reduce the amount of components needed to complete a product. Products are increasingly made with minimal production processing and a limited range of materials, therefore reducing production costs. Lean manufacturing relies increasingly on 'lean design and planning'. Designing parts and components so that they can be made with as little machining or human labour as possible decreases the cost of production. If parts are lean designed they will have little or no production or machining materials waste. Processes such as vacuum forming, laser profiling, injection moulding and press forming have enabled 'one process, one part' products to be developed on a mass scale. Mass production, automation, continuous assembly line tasks, energy efficiency, materials recycling, effective processing of sourced or raw materials, and packaging for dispatch and transportation all contribute significantly to the concept of lean manufacturing. In other words, the whole process is streamlined.

Components of lean manufacturing

- Lean design – keep it simple
- Information technologies
- Production planning
- Selective materials processing techniques
- Minimal and interchangeable components
- Automated production, reduced human labour
- Production and time management; just-in-time approach
- Outsourcing, lean supply chain
- Energy and materials efficiency and conservation
- Total quality management (TQM) and inspection practices

Manufacturing industries processing raw materials into products

Inputs	Process	Examples of outputs
Materials and components	⟶	Motor vehicles, aircraft, bicycles, watches
Resistant materials, e.g. wood, plastic	⟶	Furniture, houses, musical instruments, gym equipment
Textiles, e.g. linen, nylon, wool, cotton, polyester, etc.	⟶	Clothing, camping equipment
Materials, e.g. metal, plastics	⟶	Machine tools, pens, cutlery
Materials, e.g. electronics	⟶	Mobile phones, televisions
Chemicals	⟶	Cosmetics, petrol, food, drinks, medicines, oils, soap
Vegetables, animals, fish, etc.	⟶	Fresh and frozen foods, fertilisers, cooking oils, cleaning solutions

Levels of production

Products are produced to satisfy market needs and demands. Some products are in high demand from large market sectors. Food, produce and electronic goods, for instance, are items that are in high demand, so they are mass-produced in large quantities. Other products such as outdoor furniture, clothing and camping equipment vary with changing fashions, trends and seasons, so medium-level or batch production methods are often used to satisfy specific or small to large orders. Mass-produced and many batch-produced products are manufactured on assembly lines where the product is assembled in a sequential order. This is often automated with little or no human labour involved. Some products, such as buildings and custom-made cars, are made to suit the needs of individual customers. This is referred to as single or one-off production.

To cater for our needs, modern industry has become more flexible. A great number of manufacturers specialise in producing a limited product range, while others can change their production set-up and diversify to suit the needs of different customers at varying intervals. Automotive manufacturers, for instance, have in the past been regarded as mass producers. However, they have adapted to suit more specific demands from groups or individual customers by introducing batch and one-off production methods.

Major motor vehicle manufacturers now have single-vehicle production platforms that enable them to assemble any type of car on one assembly line. This saves production costs as they have less need to operate individual lines for each model. It also greatly reduces the need to retool for each production run.

Many other producers operate in this way. For instance, food manufacturers are increasingly packaging their food in same-size containers with only the labels and contents differing.

Motor vehicle manufacturing

Shutterstock.com/Nataliya Hora

Supply and demand

In order to stay in business, manufacturers need to ensure continuous production to supply consumers with products. Many factors influence supply and demand. Manufacturers need to be confident that the goods they produce will sell at levels that guarantee enough income to more than cover all their production and distribution costs. In other words, what they produce should be profitable. Production and distribution costs include raw materials, product development, planning, plant and tooling, salaries and transportation. Not all of the profit is retained as such because competitive manufacturers use some of this for future longer-term planning and investment, such as investing in new technology, market research, staff training, and research and development of new ideas and the perceived marketplace.

It is not only the manufacturing sector that needs to consider the above factors, but every other industry sector and business. Whether producing motor vehicles, music, health foods, clothing, travel or sporting events, the producer must know whether or not there is a need for the product or service; otherwise they are taking a major risk with their investment.

What has just been described is a brief overview of a concept known as the marketing mix or the 'four Ps': **product**, **price**, **place** and **promotion**. A product or service needs to be the right one to satisfy a market need, or one for which a need could be generated. It should be offered at a competitive price and be profitable. It should be aimed at the identified marketplace – that is, in terms of people, gender, age range, location and user type. Any promotional methods used (advertising, marketing and so on) should be appropriate and targeted to the perceived consumer or user.

In basic terms, businesses need to have the right product, at the right price for a particular marketplace and the product should be promoted appropriately. As the term 'marketing mix' implies, all four factors are 'mixed' or interrelated. They are frequently adjusted until the mix is just right.

You may occasionally hear this concept referred to as the 'five Ps', the fifth P being 'people'. Sometimes 'people' are discussed as a separate category to 'place'. This seems quite reasonable as people are central to the whole process and, most importantly, the end users!

Product life cycle

Another concept that must be considered by manufacturers is the **product life cycle**. This consists of the life stages of a product. These are:

- introduction – when a product is introduced or released to the marketplace
- growth – when sales increase due to consumer interest and increasing demand
- maturity – when a product is fully accepted and reaches peak sales
- decline – when the product saturates its market sector, is replaced or superseded.

The product life cycle is not as simple as it seems because each stage may increase or decrease in both time/duration and sales, depending on many influencing factors. The concept and its configuration vary from product to product. For instance, furniture tends to

Idealised product life cycle

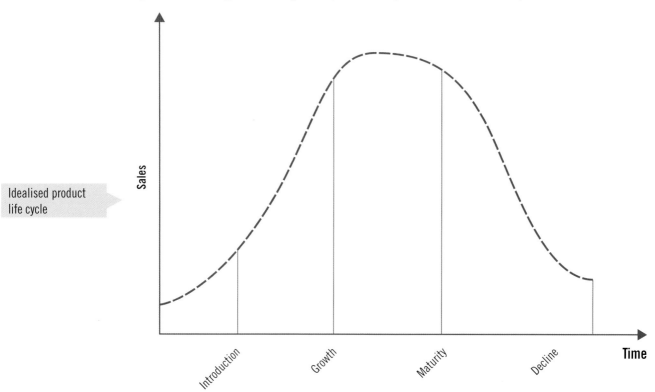

stay around for longer than fashion goods. Some products have shorter lives than others; these include plastic as opposed to longer lasting metal garden furniture. Some products are highly promoted or in demand, so growth and maturity are dynamic.

Many modern-day products have been planned to achieve high sales within a short life cycle. Just take a look at how rapidly items such as mobile phones, fashion wear and music systems have changed in recent times to see evidence of this. Manufacturers often plan for continuous production, high sales and profit margins. They can plan for products to become obsolete so they can introduce replacements. This is known as planned obsolescence.

Planned obsolescence means that a manufacturer plans the decline of a product. This can be either an advantage or disadvantage to both the producer and the consumer, depending on the causes and the effects. Products can become obsolete and replaced, as with clothing, furniture and household items. Some even become antiques!

Items that have a planned obsolescence factored into their design are becoming very common. Fashion items, for instance, tend to have this as styles change rapidly, at least seasonally. Consumers need to ask if they really need to do this, or are they being marketed into following predetermined trends? We could ask the same regarding most major products that we purchase today.

Often items are improved technically and economically with each new version. Electronic goods, computers, mobile phones, digital cameras and cars are all examples of products for which obsolescence has been planned to some extent as manufacturers are continually upgrading the technology involved. By doing this, manufacturers ensure high production and continuity of sales as consumers feel obliged to upgrade, whether or not they need to!

Manufacturers also plan obsolescence for technical and safety reasons. It is good to know that reliability, risk analysis, quality assurance, standards and legislation are concepts considered when manufacturers produce specific items. We purchase food items that have use-by dates, use gas cylinders with disposal dates, and fly on aircraft with maximum flying time and distance specifications. These are features of product planning that benefit the consumer.

As you can see, there are many interrelated factors involved that determine how industry successfully competes in a world of rapid change. Some of these are within industry's control; others are determined by factors such as competition, product appeal, new technology, market trends, legislation and the economy. Some businesses have been around for a long while because they understand the significant influencing factors and know exactly how to survive.

Large- and small-scale producers

The general perception is that large firms are more established and therefore monopolise the industrial sector compared to the efforts being made by small- to medium-size firms. As large firms tend to hold large and existing markets, it is difficult for new and developing producers to compete at this level, so many survive by finding specific market needs and by being flexible in their production processes. Both, however, experience advantages and disadvantages, some of which are listed below.

Advantages and disadvantages of large- and small-scale producers

Production
Large firms can produce large quantities as they have more production resources. Small firms often have limited resources, but they can use this to their advantage by being more flexible.

Marketing
Large firms hold a high degree of market control with greater financial resources. Small firms can react quickly to changing market needs, but within financial limitations.

Human resources

Large firms have greater access to quality personnel and training resources. Small firms often have dynamic and innovative senior personnel who can react quickly to changing needs. They have greater need for experienced trained staff and outsource their training requirements.

Technology

Large firms are able to invest in new and innovative technology, training and support. Small firms have less financial resources to invest so they do this within tight budgets. Upgrading of production technology is less frequent in many small firms.

Products

Large firms can offer a wide range of products at any one time using multiple production lines. Small firms offer a limited range of products. They adapt to new demands and market needs to ensure continuity of production.

Finance

Large firms have good financial resources. They can invest in research and development to maintain market position and expand. Small firms have less capital and are less likely to attract financial investment.

Government regulations

Large firms are more likely to comply with laws and legislation regarding standards, environmental constraints and health and safety. Small firms can experience difficulty in complying with complex legislation due to the high cost factors involved with introducing necessary strategies.

Marketplace

Large firms have greater access to overseas markets. They may be established multinational businesses. Small firms are often local producers who find international competitiveness too costly. Some, however, create a market niche and compete very successfully.

Effects of changing technology

There is probably no better example of seeing changes and the impact of technology than in the modern workplace. Industry has always been a leader in developing and introducing innovative production techniques to improve quality and increase productivity. Industry has become more efficient as a result of better planning, new production processes, modern materials and automation.

Manufacturers are increasingly using production lines, automatic machinery and robots to perform more of the tasks that were previously done by people. This means that fewer people are required in many industries. Some workers are retrenched and have to find alternative employment, while others are retrained for different job roles as new technology also creates demand for new skills and jobs. Automation, computer-aided design, control and manufacturing technology, for instance, require trained computer experts, engineers and technicians to program, operate, maintain and service the array of technical equipment being used for production work.

New technology can offer a cleaner, safer and healthier work environment to employees. People are increasingly freed from doing heavy, laborious jobs with their related dangers. There are fewer health concerns as work environments are increasingly designed to remove people from areas where, for example, sparks, fumes, noise and chemicals are obvious hazards. The automotive industry, for instance, has replaced much human labour with robots that weld and spray-paint vehicles. Some of these changes are a result of technological developments, standards and legislation related to production and health and safety in the workplace. Many industries not only comply with current standards and legislation, but they also lead the way by attempting to predict trends so that they can better plan for the demands of the future.

ISBN 9780170227452

ENERGY SYSTEMS

In this chapter you will learn about energy in its basic forms, and the principles of energy conversion, conservation and supply in manufactured systems. The chapter also explains and analyses renewable and non-renewable energy sources and the effects of energy use on engineered systems and the environment.

Energy is a vital component in any system. To get systems to work we need to provide power, so some source of energy is used. Given that we use such a vast amount of energy in our everyday lives, it is important that we recognise the sources available to us and the forms in which we apply them. Energy sources are either renewable, with an infinite supply, or non-renewable, with a limited supply. We use energy to produce the power that enables us to do many of our everyday activities. We often wake up to an alarm, have a shower, prepare breakfast, use some form of transport to get to school or work, and so on. All of these require the use of energy and systems.

One of the most basic laws of science is the law of conservation of energy. It states that there is a quantity called energy that stays the same when nature undergoes a change. That quantity is the same before the event and after the change. We cannot create or destroy energy. We can only convert it from one form or type to another. On a sunny day, approximately 800–1000 watts of solar power are received at ground level. If we could harness all this energy by converting it to electricity, we would end up with 1000 watts of electrical energy, never more than that. Such a conversion is said to be 100% efficient.

Different types of energy

You are probably familiar with and use many different energy forms: electrical, solar, kinetic, potential, elastic, chemical, heat, nuclear, wind and even mass energy. Some energy types are in fact a combination of, or a different manifestation of, some other energy type or types. Heat energy is the kinetic energy of molecules within a material. Chemical energy, released in a chemical reaction, is a combination of kinetic energy and electrical energy. Conservation of energy is useful only if we know the types of energy involved, the factors that affect each type and, better still, how to calculate quantities of energy.

Potential energy: the energy due to position

Potential energy is energy that exists because of the position or configuration of a system. For example, a sprinter on the starting blocks or a spring in compression has the potential to do useful work. The most common form is **gravitational potential energy**. Any object above ground level will have gravitational potential energy pulling it down to Earth. A diver on a diving board or water at the top of a waterfall will have gravitational potential energy. The higher and heavier the body, the greater the amount of potential or stored energy it has. Hydroelectric power is derived from the potential energy of water.

Another type of potential energy is **elastic potential energy**. This is the energy stored whenever a material is stretched or compressed. The energy stored in a spring is a good example of elastic potential energy. The stiffer the spring and the longer the extension or compression, the greater the amount of energy stored in the spring.

Kinetic energy: the energy due to motion

Moving bodies or systems possess **kinetic energy**. Examples are moving vehicles, a spring as it performs its task in either compression or tension, or a lever as it moves into location. The faster the object moves, and the greater its mass, the more kinetic energy it has. Increasing speed increases the kinetic energy. This is why the braking distance required increases when cars move at higher speeds. The effects of impact are also much greater when vehicles crash at high speed than when they do so at low speed because much more energy is available to deform the vehicle.

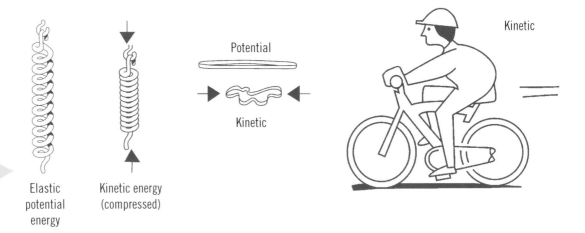

Potential and kinetic energies

Elastic potential energy

Kinetic energy (compressed)

Potential

Kinetic

Kinetic

Mechanical energy: potential plus kinetic

Mechanical energy relates to the use of mechanisms. Mechanisms include levers, pulleys and gears and some of them have been used in one form or another for thousands of years. Simple household systems that use mechanisms include can openers, door handles and water taps. Machines often use more than one mechanism. Bench presses, sewing machines and gym equipment are examples of these. We refer to potential and kinetic energy when we are talking about mechanisms or machines. Mechanical energy is the combination of these two energies.

ISBN 9780170227452

These machines have kinetic energy while being used.

Electrical energy

Moving electric charges, such as electrons flowing through an electrical device, carry electrical energy. The amount of energy depends on the electric current, the voltage across the device and the time for which the current flows. More energy is involved if we use larger currents and higher voltages, and leave the device switched on for a longer period.

Another form of electrical energy does not involve motion; this is stored energy. We find this type in batteries and in charged capacitors. These devices both store electric charge, but the charges are just sitting at the terminals ready to provide an electric current when needed. Electrical energy is useful for the following two reasons.

It can be transmitted efficiently over long distances by using **AC (alternating current)** electricity at high voltages. The voltages are stepped down to a lower value for home use. In Australia our domestic supply is 240 volts. Appliances can just be plugged into a power socket which provides a continuous source of power.

Batteries supply us with stored electrical energy. The current from batteries is DC (direct current), where electrons move in one direction only. An advantage of using batteries is that the device is portable and can be used in places where there is no mains supply, or where mains electricity is difficult to access. A disadvantage is that the power in batteries will run out, so they need to be either recharged or replaced. Disposal of batteries also creates an environmental hazard due to the chemicals inside them.

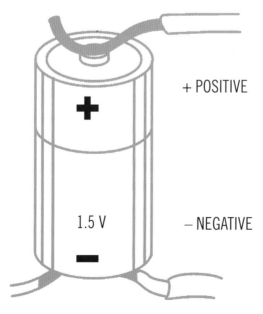

+ POSITIVE

1.5 V

− NEGATIVE

Electrical energy stored in a battery

Heat energy

If we heat water in an electric kettle, electrical energy is converted to heat energy. What happens is that the molecules of water move faster because they have more kinetic energy, which results in increased temperature. In fact the heat energy here is simply kinetic energy. The amount of heat energy is related to the kind of material being heated – its mass and the temperature increase. Materials that are easy to heat, like metals, cannot store large amounts of heat energy. Water is about 10 times harder to heat up than most common metals, but can store or remove 10 times more energy. This is one of the reasons why water is used extensively in cooling systems.

Another type of heat energy, called **latent heat**, occurs when matter changes state from, for instance, liquid to gas and vice versa. This is made use of in air conditioners and refrigerators. We rely on heat energy for many of our everyday needs such as heating systems, car engines and cooking.

Sound energy

Noise, talking and music are examples of sound energy. They are transmitted as sound waves through solids, liquids or gases. Sound energy is the kinetic energy of the molecules as they vibrate to produce sound. The amount of energy is related to the loudness or volume, in decibels, of the sound. Sound energy can be useful, such as in television transmission, radio, alarms, cars and machines. It can also be an environmental health problem if too loud or unwanted, causing noise pollution and hearing loss.

Light or radiant energy

Light energy is vital to plant growth and allows us to see. Light is emitted when electrons change orbits in atoms and molecules, and is transmitted as a wave. The amount of energy carried by light depends on its frequency only. Blue light has more energy than red light because its frequency is higher. Visible light is only a small part of what is called the electromagnetic spectrum, which also contains infrared, ultraviolet, microwaves, radio waves and X-rays. All these are forms of **electromagnetic** (radiant) energy and many systems make use of this energy, mostly as inputs or outputs. Examples are solar heaters, microwave ovens, lasers and simple desk lamps.

Heat, sound and light energies

Chemical energy

Chemical energy is stored within chemicals and released in reactions. Examples include petrol used in engines, coal, gas and the chemicals used in batteries and fuel cells. Human energy comes from the chemicals in the food we eat. Chemical energy is closely related to

ISBN 9780170227452

the electrical energy that binds the molecules of a chemical together. The equation below represents how heat is obtained when burning a fuel:

$$C + O_2 \rightarrow CO_2 + H_2O + heat$$

Fuel + oxygen → carbon dioxide + water + heat

When carbon-based fuels burn they may also produce oxides of sulfur and nitrogen, as well as carbon monoxide. These cause pollution to our environment and related health problems.

Nuclear energy

An atom is made up of a nucleus at the centre and electrons in orbits around it. If the nucleus of an atom of, say, uranium is split, an incredible amount of energy is released in the form of heat and gamma radiation. The energy released by a single **fission** comes from the fact that the total mass of the fission products and the neutrons released is less than that of the original uranium atom. The mass (m) that is 'lost' has been converted directly to energy (E) at a rate governed by Einstein's equation $E = mc^2$ (where c is the speed of light). About 200 million electron volts (MeV) are released by the decay of one uranium atom. This is more than a million times the energy released by burning an atom of a fossil fuel.

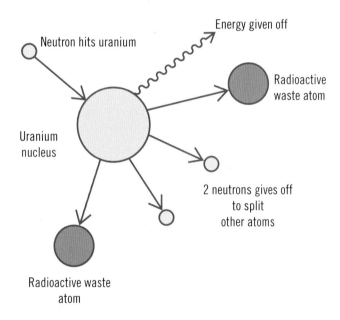

Neutron hits uranium

Energy given off

Radioactive waste atom

Uranium nucleus

2 neutrons gives off to split other atoms

Radioactive waste atom

Nuclear energy: splitting the atom

If the neutrons released are not totally absorbed they can cause other atoms of uranium to split and thus more particles are released; these in turn split other atoms, producing a chain reaction. A nuclear bomb deliberately uses the effect of a chain reaction to produce an explosion. In a nuclear reactor the reaction is controlled.

Another type of nuclear energy is fusion energy. This happens when two light atoms (atoms of low atomic mass) of, say, hydrogen merge or fuse together to form a bigger atom, in this case helium. Energy is released in the process because the mass of the combination will be less than the two masses of the individual nuclei – mass has been converted to energy. Nuclear fusion is the process powering the sun and other stars. In the core of the stars, hydrogen is converted into helium by fusion – providing enough energy to keep the stars burning.

LEARNING ACTIVITY 3.1

1 List five types of energy and give an example of each type.

2 List the types of energy or energies that you would associate with:

    a a gas fire

    b a motorised scooter travelling at speed

    c a microwave oven

    d a toaster

    e the force of friction

    f the sun.

3 In terms of energy, explain why water is used in cooling systems.

4 Give two examples of stored electrical energy.

5 Give two examples of electromagnetic radiation. Which one carries more energy and why is this so?

6 Name the two types of nuclear energy and describe their main differences.

Energy conversion in systems

Energy in its raw form is generally not easily usable. Energy such as direct heat from the sun or wind has uses in appropriate environments, but we usually need to convert energy into a more usable form. While this conversion means that we are more easily able to access and use different forms of energy, there is always some energy waste that occurs through the conversion. Every system can be described in terms of its **input**, **process** and **output**. We often use a systems block (IPO) diagram to show this. The following example is for a car engine where we look at the input and output in terms of energy.

IPO (input, process, output) diagram of a car engine

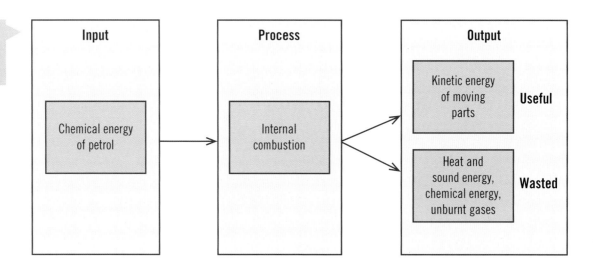

ISBN 9780170227452

The output energy consists of about 60% useful energy and 40% wasted energy. The conservation of energy principle means that the total input energy equals the total output energy. The engine in this case is said to be 60% efficient. All systems convert energy and are less than 100% efficient. There is always an amount of wasted energy or an unwanted energy form in the output. One of the challenges faced by systems manufacturers is to reduce this wasted energy.

In more complex systems many different forms of energy are involved. These systems also produce unwanted energies that make them less efficient. The following table outlines the energy conversions in some common systems.

Input energy	System	Output energy
Electrical	CD player	Sound, light, mechanical and heat
Electrical	Television set	Sound, light and heat
Chemical/electrical	Gas/fan heater	Heat, mechanical and sound
Human/chemical	Bicycle	Mechanical, heat and sound
Wind/kinetic	Wind turbine	Electrical, mechanical and sound
Solar	Solar vehicle	Mechanical, heat and sound

LEARNING ACTIVITY 3.2

1 List the type of energy that would be the input energy to the following.

   a Corkscrew

   b mp3 player

   c Solar garden light

   d Car jack

   e Automatic watch

   f Digital multimeter

   g Bench vice

2 List the types of energy that would be the output energy or energies of the following systems.

   a Television

   b Lawn mower

   c Car jack as it lifts a car

   d Refrigerator

   e Toilet cistern as it is flushed

3 List three systems that may have different energy inputs, but the same output.
Name the inputs and outputs.

4 Draw and label an IPO diagram to show the input, process and output of a bicycle.

5 What factors do you think affect the efficiency of a braking system?

6 What is the undesired energy output of each of the following?

   a DVD player

   b Television

   c Gas heater

   d Computer

Sourcing and distributing energy

Sources of energy

Energy needs

We need some type of energy to operate a technological system whether it is mechanical, electrical or integrated. Many basic mechanical systems, such as bicycles, can openers and car jacks, use human energy as the input source. We are, however, increasingly using other sources such as electrical energy to power not just electrical systems but also mechanical systems. The can opener now has a motor. The motor uses electrical energy that, in Australia, comes mainly from the chemical energy of coal burnt in power stations.

When we are designing products, consideration always needs to be given to the type of energy source being used and whether it is renewable or non-renewable. Individuals and organisations should consider the effects of using these energy sources on the environment and on their longer term sustainability before making a decision about what type of systems to design.

We need to be constantly looking for more efficient ways of using energy, and ways in which we can use renewable rather than non-renewable sources. The next section looks at what renewable and non-renewable sources are available to us and how they are used.

ISBN 9780170227452

Renewable energy

Renewable energies are those that we will continue to have a fairly constant supply of. Examples are energies derived from the sun, the wind, the tides, biomass, running water (hydro power) and geothermal energy from the Earth's core. Essentially all energy originates with the sun. The sun is a massive nuclear energy converter. A tiny fraction of that energy is captured by the Earth. Even then about 30% is radiated back into space. The rest is absorbed in some way or other. The sun provides the light and heat that affects all of the other sources that provide us with energy. For instance, green plants require light (and heat) to grow.

These plants can be converted into usable energy such as wood and into biofuels such as ethanol from sugar cane. The decomposition of plants over time forms fossil fuels such as coal, which can be used to create chemical energy. Many power stations use coal as a source of fuel.

Wind is formed by convection currents that result when the warm air (from the sun) rises and cold air moves in to take its place. The wind also affects the seas, turning still waters into waves.

The sun evaporates water from oceans and lakes. The water vapour rises and cools to eventually fall as rain or snow to feed mountain streams. As the water runs down to the sea it carries motion energy, which can be converted to other forms.

Energy direct from the sun: solar energy

Solar energy comes directly from the sun. It can be used directly to provide heat and light, but in order for it to be most useful it needs to be stored in some way, as people will want to access the power at night and at times when there is relatively little sun (such as on cloudy days).

Solar panels can be used to trap heat that can then be used to, for instance, heat water. These solar panels are called heat collectors and vary in their sophistication, but essentially are a set of pipes through which water or air runs. The pipes are heated by the sun, which in turn heats the water (or air) running through them. Regular and intense sun will provide the best results, which means that this is not a viable option for all climates.

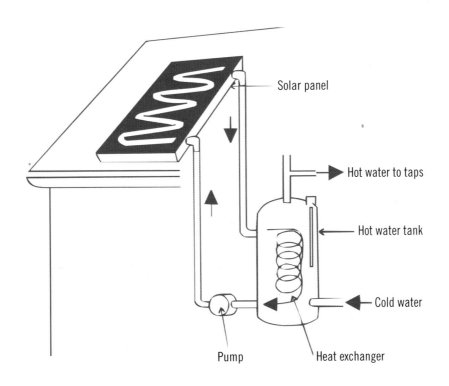

Solar panel

Hot water to taps

Hot water tank

Cold water

Pump

Heat exchanger

Solar collector used for heating water

ISBN 9780170227452

Many features in the design of the heat collectors affect the efficiency of heat collectors:

1 The material used for the pipes should be a good heat conductor and the coating should be a good absorber of heat. Copper, steel, stainless steel and aluminium are commonly used. Copper and stainless steel are better because they do not rust and are better conductors of heat, but they are more expensive. Black paint can be used for coating the pipes as black surfaces absorb radiation well.

2 The shape and layout of the pipes should capture as much radiation as possible. Round pipes soldered onto a panel are the most common. A pillow-shaped structure is more efficient but more expensive to manufacture. The pipes can be housed inside glass tubing and the air between the two removed to form a vacuum. This stops heat being lost through any flow of air. Mirrors and lenses above and around the pipes collect more sun rays and increase efficiency.

3 The insulator used for housing the piping system prevents heat being lost once the water or air has been heated. A good insulator should be used. A double layer of glass (double glazing) above the piping system provides both protection and a reduction of heat loss.

Solar energy is often most useful when it is converted into another form. Solar cells have been developed to convert and store energy. They are photovoltaic cells that convert light to electrical energy. While there have been great improvements made to the design of these cells they still rely on exposure to a great deal of sun. Solar cells are now being used to power calculators, telephones, parking meters and even cars, although this technology is still in the experimental stage. We have yet to see a solar-powered car parked in a suburban garage. An array of solar cells can be connected to make up a power plant.

A semiconductor material called silicon is used to make a single solar cell. You can read more about semiconductors in Chapter 5, 'Electrotechnology'. Basically a very thin layer of N-type silicon lies on top of a thicker layer of P-type silicon. When light from the sun falls on the N-type layer it becomes the negative terminal and the P-type layer becomes the positive terminal of the cell. The cell is now ready to provide electricity with a voltage just under 1 volt. Not all the sunlight available is converted to electricity, making the device less than 100% efficient. Only short-wavelength light has enough energy to dislodge electrons within the silicon to provide electricity, reducing efficiency to about 20%.

Solar cells are relatively expensive to manufacture as only very pure silicon can be used. Single-crystal silicon cells are the most efficient. Other forms of silicon such as polycrystal

Solar panels contain many solar cells

Shutterstock.com/Elena Elisseeva

ISBN 9780170227452

and amorphous silicon have recently been developed. These types of silicon are cheaper to produce. In a crystal the atoms are arranged in a perfect lattice formation, whereas in amorphous materials the atoms are bound together in a haphazard way. Technologists are now experimenting with other types of materials to make cheaper and more efficient solar cells. Thin-film cells using cadmium telluride and gallium arsenide cells are examples of such cells.

Heat, solar towers and solar ventilators

Solar towers and solar ventilators use the energy from the sun. A solar tower uses heat from the sun to heat the air. The force provided by the rising hot air can be used to drive turbine blades (see the illustration on page 47). The turbines operate generators and electricity is produced.

The efficiency of a solar tower can be improved by including a network of tubing filled with water. The hot water can be distributed to local users, as in combined heat and power generation (CHP).

Other similar technologies that use and recycling waste heat for generation purposes are being developed. These are based on the Brayton and Rankine (thermodynamic) cycles of converting waste heat and pressure into useful work and electricity generation. Instead of using the waste for heating or hot water distribution (CHP), it is recycled to further generate electricity, therefore completing a **closed loop cycle**.

Solar ventilators use panels to collect solar energy to generate power for non-passive ventilation systems to emit heat from roof cavities and living spaces. This reduces the need for air conditioning and lowers electricity supply costs.

The above technologies are discussed in Chapter 2 (pages 21–51).

Energy from the wind

Wind is an energy source that has been used for many years. For instance, it has been used to power transport, such as sailboats (often along with another source of energy) and to drive windmills. Windmills are an example of systems that convert energy. They convert kinetic wind energy into a more usable form, such as mechanical energy. That energy can be used to pump water, grind grain or power an electricity generator. The blades of modern-day wind turbines are similar to aeroplane wings. The difference in air pressure on either side of the blade results in a force that causes motion.

In a number of countries (including Australia) wind farms, or wind power plants, are being developed, generally to create electricity. Wind farms are seen by many people to be a viable way of generating power using a renewable energy source. There remain some concerns about their visual impact, the noise they make and their effects on wildlife. Some countries have overcome these issues by building wind farms off-shore in isolated areas where tidal energy systems may also operate, minimising the total area required for the plant.

Wind turbines

Shutterstock.com/Andy Z.

Energy from running water: hydro power and tidal power

Falling or moving water has been used for many years as a source of energy for turning paddles and turbines, which in turn create power. Kinetic energy from water was used in industries such as mills in past years as a primary source of power. Water is now used to generate electricity; the force of the water moving under the influence of gravity turns turbines that create electricity.

Energy from the core of the Earth: geothermal energy

Natural heat energy lies beneath the surface of the Earth. Volcanoes and hot springs are evidence of this energy. The greatest challenge to using this energy is accessing it. There have been a number of methods used, but they tend to be expensive and some believe that they may be detrimental to the environment in terms of noise and the possible impact on land pollution and underground earth movement if this energy source is used.

Energy from the waves and the tides

Waves have been recognised as a source of energy, but it is quite difficult and expensive to use the energy in practice. While there are several working tidal power stations around the world, research to find ways we can more easily access and use this resource continues.

Waves are a recognised source of energy.

Getty Images/Environment Images/UIG

ISBN 9780170227452

Energy from organic matter: biomass energy

We have used bioenergy, the energy created from biomass, for thousands of years for warmth and cooking. Biomass is essentially organic matter. Today, wood is still our largest biomass resource but many other sources can now also be used for bioenergy, including plants, residues from agriculture or forestry, and the organic component of municipal and industrial wastes. Even the fumes from landfills can be used as an energy source.

When juice is extracted from sugar cane the organic waste produced can be burnt to provide heat and generate electrical power. Only around 40% of a tree is used for timber production; the rest provides a resource for biomass technology. There are moves to use forest waste alongside coal in power stations. Technologies using biomass help protect the environment by making use of renewable plant material such as sawdust, tree trimmings, rice straw, alfalfa and grass. Other sources include poultry litter, other animal wastes, industrial waste and the paper component of municipal solid waste.

Biomass (renewable, raw materials) processing plant

Shutterstock.com/nostal6ie

The table below summarises some of the advantages and disadvantages of using renewable energy to generate power.

Source of energy	Advantages	Disadvantages
Solar	Will not run out	Cloud cover reduces output
	No air pollution	No power at night
	No cost for fuel	Difficult to store power
	Ideal for isolated areas	Huge solar panels needed
Wind	Will not run out	Depends on steady winds
	No cost for fuel	Visual pollution
	No air pollution	Noise pollution
		Effects on wildlife
Hydro	No cost for fuel	Limited locations
	No air pollution	Construction may damage environment
Tidal	No cost for fuel	Needs large waves
	Will not run out	Hazard to shipping
	No air pollution	
Geothermal	No cost for fuel	Not widely available
	Long-term supply	Costly to obtain
Biomass	Uses waste material	Labour-intensive

LEARNING ACTIVITY 3.3

1 List six renewable energy sources.

2 List four ways in which the sun provides energy.

3 Explain the three factors that affect the efficiency of heat collectors, and discuss ways of increasing that efficiency.

4 Explain how a solar cell produces electricity.

5 Name three uses of wind energy and two disadvantages of using wind for power generation.

6 Make a list of materials that can be used for biomass energy.

Non-renewable energy

Non-renewable sources are those that are in limited supply. Wood and fossil fuels are examples of these. They take many thousands of years to form, which means that if we continue to use them at the current rate they will eventually run out. Uranium for nuclear energy is plentiful at present, but it will eventually run out as well.

Energy from fossil fuels: coal, oil, gas

Fossil fuels provide us with a range of sources of energy. The most common of these are coal, oil and natural gas. Fossil fuels release their energy when they are burnt. In a coal-fired power plant a boiler produces steam that turns a turbine. The turbine then turns a generator to produce electricity. The processes also generate a lot of by-products, such as carbon dioxide,

ISBN 9780170227452

carbon monoxide, sulfur oxides, hydrocarbons and solid particles. Many of these have a detrimental effect on the environment, such as a build-up of greenhouse gases and the production of acid rain.

Efforts are being made to reduce these emissions. Gas can be used, for instance, to power vehicles with internal combustion engines, heat buildings and cook food. There are additional uses for these materials, such as using coal to produce plastics and fertilisers. While fossil fuels have been used a great deal in the past, and are still a key source of energy, they are a limited source as it takes many thousands of years for them to form. Extracting and transporting them can also have a detrimental impact on the environment.

LEARNING ACTIVITY 3.4

1   Explain briefly how coal is used to produce electricity in a power plant.
2   What are the by-products when coal is burnt and what are their effects?

Energy from the atom: nuclear fission and fusion

Uranium is used to produce nuclear energy. Energy is contained in the nucleus of the atom and combining or splitting atoms releases this energy. While we are aware of the potentially destructive nature of nuclear energy, it can also be used to produce electricity. In one type of nuclear power plant the fission of nuclei of uranium-235 atoms contained in fuel rods releases energy to make steam or heat up carbon dioxide. The steam or heated gas is then used in a way similar to that in a coal-fired power plant to generate electricity.

Nuclear power station

Shutterstock.com/SpaceKris

ISBN 9780170227452

The greatest issue with nuclear energy is safely disposing of the waste. Many of the smaller atoms left after the fission of uranium are radioactive. They are called radioisotopes and emit radioactive particles that are very dangerous to any life form. Some isotopes die away after a short time and are dealt with on site. Others last for hundreds of years and need to be disposed of safely. One method is to store them in solid canisters deep underground. There are concerns that the waste can leak out and contaminate soil and water.

Some countries with low reserves of coal and gas have turned to nuclear energy to generate much of the electrical power they use. Nuclear reactors using fusion instead of fission would use deuterium (an isotope or form of hydrogen) to produce energy. Practical fusion reactors are yet to be built. There are three main factors that first need to be addressed:

1 The temperature needed for fusion to take place is very high: of the order of millions of degrees Celsius.

2 The gas of charged particles called plasma, within which the reaction takes place, needs to be confined long enough to release energy.

3 This energy must be converted into a useful form, such as electricity.

Distributing and storing energy

Once a power plant has produced electricity, this form of energy has to reach consumers, who can be a long way away. This is done along very-high-voltage transmission lines and using **AC electricity**. High voltages are used to reduce heat loss in the transmission cables. Electric currents produce heat in conducting wires because of the resistance of the conductors used. Superconducting materials with virtually no resistance would increase the efficiency of transmission, but these materials are still under development and expensive. AC is used instead of **DC electricity** as the voltage can easily be stepped up or down using transformers.

The storage of energy is vital in allowing us to access and use energy when and where we want it. As you can see from all of the sources of energy discussed in this chapter, there is a great deal of energy around us.

The goal of engineers and designers has been to develop systems and products that allow us to store energy. Large amounts of energy are not easily stored. Systems such as batteries and large capacitors can store only limited amounts. Rechargeable batteries have been a very important development for storing energy because they have allowed us to easily transport electrical energy wherever we want. This has allowed us to use more sophisticated cameras when we go on a holiday, digital music players and mobile phones when we are on the move, and torches to see when we are walking at night.

Weblinks

www.renew.org.au

www.energyquest.com.au

www.energyquest.ca.gov/projects

www.csiro.au

www.whitehat.com.au/Australia/Inventions/InventionsA.html

www.howstuffworks.com

LEARNING ACTIVITY 3.5

1 Explain how uranium is used to produce electricity in a power plant.

2 What kinds of waste material are produced in a nuclear reactor and why are we concerned about them?

3 Draw up a table showing what you think are the advantages and disadvantages of coal-fired and nuclear power generation.

END-OF-CHAPTER ACTIVITIES

1 Explain in your own words the law of conservation of energy.
2 Gravitational potential energy on Earth depends on two factors. What are they?
3 Two factors affect kinetic energy. What are they?
4 Mechanical energy is the sum of which two types of energy?
5 When a pendulum swings or oscillates kinetic energy and potential energy are involved. Indicate on a diagram or diagrams where you think each type of energy is at a maximum.
6 What are the advantages and disadvantages of using batteries to power electrical systems?
7 What three factors affect heat energy?
8 Name two systems that use latent heat energy.
9 What are fossil fuels and how do we make use of each of them?
10 What type of nuclear energy is associated with the sun?
11 Search the CSIRO website **www.csiro.au/Outcomes/Energy/Renewables-and-Smart-Systems.aspx** and find out about at least one wind farm being developed in Australia.
12 Investigate and note the benefits and possible disadvantages of utilising wind as an energy source.
13 Develop a poster or PowerPoint presentation that addresses the above issues.
14 Find out which countries in the world are the biggest users of nuclear power.
15 Investigate and write a short description of a disaster that occurred recently at a nuclear power plant.
16 Organise a debate about the pros and cons of nuclear power generation in Australia.
17 Search the Internet for information on solar towers, and if and where the technology may exist in Australia.

CASE STUDY 3

Solar house

This case study by Rex Candy (natural resources engineer) gives an overview of why and how he chose to install a 'stand alone' electricity system in his home using solar renewable energy. Rex follows a process of analysing the situation, deciding on a project brief, researching options and technologies, planning the task, installation, testing and evaluating the project on completion.

Note how Rex uses the process to arrive at a best solution. He moves back and forth through the process, considering further options and modifying the system throughout its lifetime based on changing needs and new technological developments. This is a process similar to that prescribed in this book and followed by you as a student with your project work.

When you read through the material, you should note how the system works, the input, the process and output components, and the advantages and disadvantages of the system.

Situation: why renewable energy?

In the 1980s my family and I were establishing a house on a rural property in Gippsland, Victoria. The property is more than 10 kilometres from the nearest small town, and accessed only by a minor gravel road. It is reasonably remote, on the edge of a large tract of forested public land. The property has significant exposure to bushfire risk.

Planning for the house included planning the supply of all necessary services such as electricity, heating, water, waste water disposal and telecommunications.

Electricity supply options

Two options were identified for supply of electricity to the house:
1 connection to the power grid
2 'stand alone' electricity system, using renewable energy.

Research

Investigation of the grid connection option indicated that:

- the nearest existing power line was more that 3 kilometres distant, but had no spare capacity
- the nearest possible power connection point was a further 2.5 kilometres distant
- the initial capital contribution required for connection to the power grid was $48 000 (in 1985)
- no cost sharing was possible with neighbouring properties
- reliability of service would not be guaranteed (long single wire/earth return, through bushland).

Selection and justification

The two options were evaluated as follows.

	For	Against
Grid connection	Possible to use higher energy consuming appliances and tools (e.g. toasters, dishwashers, welders)	$48 000 initial capital cost Quarterly bills Unreliability Need for backup systems
Stand alone	Reliability Low initial capital cost Anticipated lower operating costs (?) Capable of upgrades in response to future increases in demand Skills were available to design, construct and operate the system	Time required for monitoring, operation and maintenance

Considering all of the above factors, it was decided to establish a 'stand alone' power system. The unreliability of the grid connection would have required that a backup (stand alone) electricity system be installed as well, particularly for times of emergency such as during bushfires or severe weather events.

Design of our 'stand alone' electricity system
Selecting the most appropriate energy source

We decided to use renewable energy because the environmental and cost impacts of a fossil fuel-based system were unacceptable. A fossil fuelled system, based on a mechanical generator, would have required either 24 hours a day operation or the addition of batteries to supply electricity when the generator was not running.

The renewable energy sources we considered are summarised below.

Energy source	Comments
Hydro	Insufficient availability and reliability of water supply
Wind	Site is sheltered from the prevailing winds by nearby hills
Solar (photovoltaic)	Good solar access, sun hours per day adequate in all months

As a result, we decided to build a solar electricity supply system based on photovoltaic cells charging a battery bank, with a generator as backup.

Solar panel array

Specific requirements: system size

Initially, the size of our system could be kept small by limiting the demand for electricity. Low energy lighting was used and alternative energy sources were used where feasible; for example:

- We used a wood fuelled 'slow combustion' stove (for cooking, home heating and hot water).
- We used bottled gas (for refrigeration, supplementary cooking and toasting).
- Appliances with high electricity demand (for example, electric iron and washing machine) were run during short periods of generator operation.

Our initial system capacity was 0.13 kilowatt, which was sufficient only to sustainably run up to five low powered lights or appliances. This has been progressively increased over 25 years to the current capacity of 1.1 kilowatt.

Planning installation: equipment and infrastructure

The major components of our electricity system are:

1 battery and solar panel shed:
   - photovoltaic cell array
   - battery bank (12 V DC)
   - control system, battery charge regulator, switchboard, circuit breakers
   - inverter (converts 12 V DC to 240 V AC)
   - battery charger

2 generator shed:
   - generator
   - backup generator
   - fuel store

3 house and sheds:
   - control/display panel
   - system wiring, including 12 V lighting circuit and 240 V power circuit.

Solar panel shed

Battery bank

Generator system

Living with the 'stand alone' electricity system

Operation

Our electricity system supplies 12 V DC and 24 V AC to the house and sheds. The 12 V DC circuit supplies almost all lighting, as well as low powered appliances such as a small sound system. The 240 V AC supply is used to meet all other demands such as television, computers, power tools, supplementary lighting and, more recently, a freezer/refrigerator. The 240 V supply is provided from the inverter for most of the time.

The generator is operated usually for only a few hours per week, except during extended cloudy periods, or periods of sustained high demand. During periods of generator operation, all 240 V electrical demand is transferred to the generator, including the house, the sheds and a battery charger, which provides supplementary input to the battery bank.

Redesign and modifications: system augmentation

Our electricity supply system has been progressively augmented over its 25-year life in response to:

- growth in demand (for example, teenagers using computers, TV, additional lighting)
- improved technology (for example, more efficient solar panels, availability of energy efficient fridge/freezers, energy efficient lighting)
- system components (such as batteries) reaching the end of their service lives.

The system infrastructure was designed and constructed to provide for future upgrades. Solar cell capacity has been increased by 8.8 times, with all other key system components (battery bank, inverter and battery charger) capacities increased by around 2.5 times.

Evaluation: how has it worked out?

Positives

- System has been reliable and cost-effective.
- Good for the planet (low carbon emissions).
- Motivation for others (an example that one can live a comfortable life without grid electricity).

Negatives

- Ongoing requirement to manage demand (for example, the use of energy-efficient lighting and appliances, and switching off unnecessary demand), and avoiding the use of appliances, which are not vital (such as hair dryers).
- Inability to use some tools and equipment (such as welders).
- Time is consumed in system monitoring, operation and maintenance.

Estimated costs

Capital costs	Estimated total capital cost over 25 years has been approximately $23 000. This includes the capital cost of the energy system components, as well as a highly efficient fridge/freezer to reduce demand.
Operating costs	Current approximate costs are $5 for generator fuel per week, and an annual cost of $80 for generator servicing.

ISBN 9780170227452

4

MECHANICAL SYSTEMS

In this chapter you will learn about the concepts and principles related to the design, configuration and applications of operational mechanical systems. Some of the areas and topics explored are motion, forces, related calculations, component assembly, hydraulics and pneumatics, friction, machine design and methods of describing basic to more complex systems and their uses.

A **mechanism** is a device that is used to produce useful force and motion. When we join or group sets of mechanisms for a particular purpose we have what is called a mechanical system. These are often referred to as machines. Mechanisms can convert a small **force** into a larger one to make things move more easily with less effort and greater efficiency. They can change the direction of motion and their speed can also be determined and controlled. We use mechanical devices frequently, from simple mechanisms like switches, door handles and water taps to more complex systems such as video players, elevators, machine lathes and car engines.

Mechanisms are important in specialised areas such as the manufacturing industry. While many modern technological systems are electronically controlled they often operate mechanical devices to move parts and perform various production processes. In the motor vehicle industry car bodies are formed and moved to assembly points. Many thousands of car parts are produced using machines and then delivered to different locations for assembly by hand or by machine.

With modern design and technological developments we probably have less physical contact with mechanisms than we did in the past although this still occurs. Electronic control of systems using sensors eliminates the need for switches and the actual mechanical parts of the system are hidden from view. We experience this with increasing use of **automatic circuits**, such as in automatic doors, electronic central locking systems and automated production lines in industry. It is only when we look around us and observe our daily movements and activities that we realise how much we depend upon mechanical systems to make our lives easier.

Motion and force

Mechanisms are designed and configured to do different tasks and they all have certain common characteristics. Mechanisms have inputs of energy and force to make them work and processes that convert energy and change motion so they can achieve the required output movements.

There are two kinds of mechanical energy:

1 Potential energy is energy that is stored and released to create power.

2 Kinetic energy is energy that is associated with movement.

Different types of motion

Mechanisms change the speed and direction of motion. They also change motion from one type to another. The four basic kinds of motion are **rotary**, **linear**, **reciprocating** and **oscillating**.

Rotary motion, the most common kind, is circular motion or spinning in one direction, either clockwise or anticlockwise. Wheels, gears, fishing reels, fans and propellers all rotate.

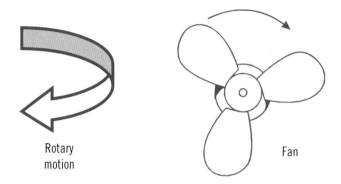

Rotary
motion

Fan

Linear motion is straight-line motion in one direction, on any axis; vice-jaws, steering racks and elevators are examples of this when they are moving.

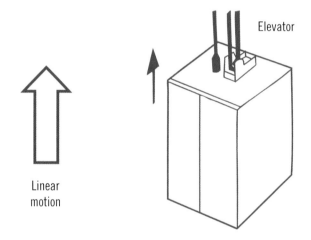

Elevator

Linear
motion

Reciprocating motion is continuous two-way straight-line motion, on any axis. Pistons, sewing machine needles, powered jig saws, industrial press tools and compressors all reciprocate. We refer to each return movement of a reciprocating device as a cycle.

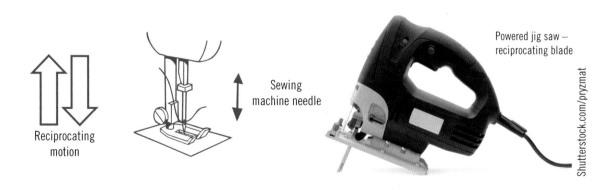

Reciprocating
motion

Sewing
machine needle

Powered jig saw –
reciprocating blade

ISBN 9780170227452

Oscillating motion is a swinging back and forward motion and is the least common kind. Swings and pendulums oscillate.

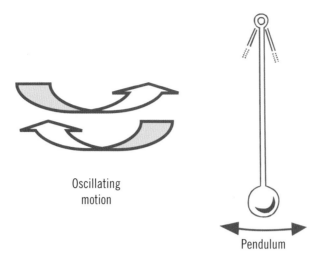

Oscillating
motion

Pendulum

Combining different types of motion

The four basic types of motion are often used separately, as the swing and fan demonstrate. Other individual devices have one kind of motion as input and another as output. For example, turning a woodscrew so that it moves forwards into the wood converts rotary into linear motion. Turning a hexagonal nut on a bolt will also move the nut along the thread of the bolt in linear motion.

Mechanical systems are often designed to change motion by combining different types of mechanisms. The rotary motion of a car steering assembly pinion makes the steering rack move in a linear motion, left or right. Reciprocating and rotating motion occur with an engine piston and crankshaft.

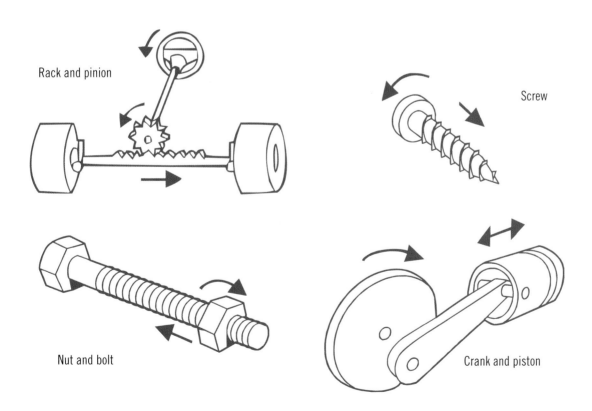

Rack and pinion

Screw

Nut and bolt

Crank and piston

LEARNING ACTIVITY 4.1

1 List five practical applications for each kind of motion.

2 Sketch and describe three systems that change motion from one kind to another.

3 Use kit components to build a model system that has two kinds of motion.

4 Search the website **www.technologystudent.com** for information on motion and mechanisms. Familiarise yourself with the site as it contains a wide range of systems knowledge.

Forces

When something is being moved, the movement is the result of an applied push or pull force. When a body is motionless it is said to be in **equilibrium**. This occurs when the force acting on a body is equal and opposite to the body's reaction force. Equilibrium is therefore a state of balance.

When designing mechanical systems to create movement, we need to consider force and its effects on the various parts of the system. We attempt to design an effective configuration that needs the least possible force to achieve a desired output motion.

Forces act in different ways and have different effects on stationary and moving parts. There are five basic types of force; these are compression, tension, shear, torsion and bending.

Compression forces

Compression forces tend to compress (or squash) an object.

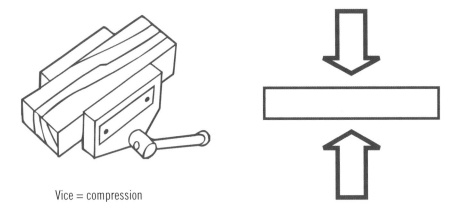

Vice = compression

Tension forces

Tension forces occur when something is being stretched.

Tension forces

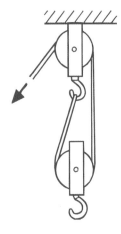

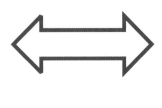

Pulley system = tension

ISBN 9780170227452

Shear forces

Shear forces are cutting or slicing forces. For example, shear forces occur because the two handles, such as a pair of scissors, apply force in different directions.

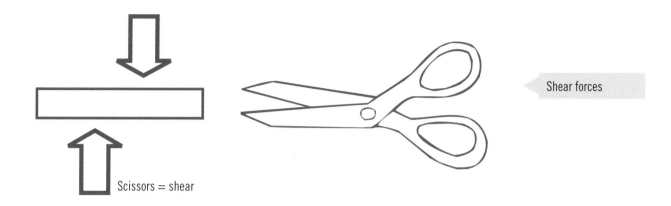

Scissors = shear

Shear forces

Torsion forces

Torsion forces twist an object.

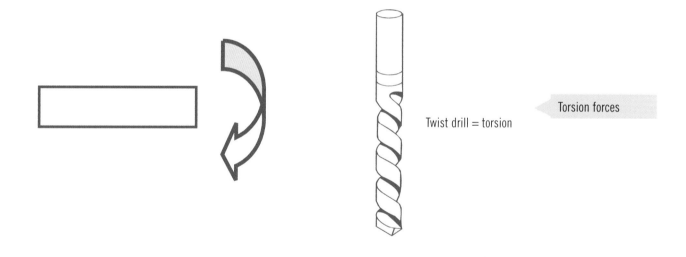

Twist drill = torsion

Torsion forces

Bending forces

Bending occurs when something is under both tension and compression.

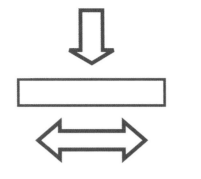

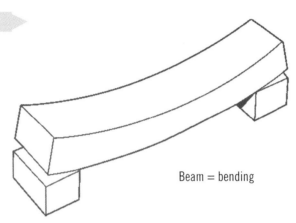

Bending forces

Beam = bending

Shutterstock.com/Lian Deng

Compression and tension springs

Compression and tension springs are common mechanical components. They work in opposite mode to each other, in that a compression spring presses or squeezes as force acts on it. The spring attempts to react against the force, as with pliers, lever arms, press tools and suspension systems. Tension springs stretch when operational and likewise attempt to resist the force acting on them, as with spring return devices on doors and machine guards.

Springs under tension (top) and under compression (bottom)

iStockphoto/© camilla wisbauer

Shutterstock.com/Pokpong

ISBN 9780170227452

Calculating force

The behaviour and control of a mechanism is what designers and engineers attempt to achieve by planning and calculating known information and data into their designs. Newton's three laws of motion govern the behaviour of objects, including mechanisms. These are:

1 Every object in a state of uniform motion tends to remain in that state of motion unless an external force is applied to it.

2 The relationship between an object's mass m, its acceleration a, and the applied force F is $F = ma$.

3 For every action there is an equal and opposite reaction.

You will find these laws useful in this section when we perform calculations and examine concepts such as levers, mechanical advantage, acceleration and equilibrium.

When an object is moving due to an applied force it is said to be changing velocity – it is accelerating. This is Newton's second law of motion and can be represented by the following formula:

$$\text{Force} = \text{mass} \times \text{acceleration}$$
$$F \ = \ m \ \times \ a$$

Force is measured in newtons (N), mass in kilograms (kg) and acceleration in metres per second per second (m/s^2). **Acceleration** is the rate of change of velocity and the acceleration due to Earth's gravitational force is measured at 9.8 m/s^2.

From this, for example, we can calculate the force due to gravity on a mass of 20 kg:

$$F = m \times a$$
$$= 20 \times 9.8$$
$$= 196 \text{ N}$$

When we need to move objects we attempt to do so as easily as possible. We use hoists to lift loads and spanners to tighten nuts and bolts. What we are actually doing is using a small force to apply a larger force to the load. The longer the handle (greater distance), the smaller the force required. The term **moment** is used in describe this action of force and distance.

A moment (Nm) is the product of force (N) and distance (m):

$$\text{Moment} = \text{force} \times \text{distance}$$

If a force of 20 N is applied to a lever measuring 0.5 m, we calculate the moment (force applied to the work) as 10 Nm. By increasing the length of the lever we can apply less input force; this makes the task easier. If the length of the lever is doubled to 1 m and the force required remains 10 N, only 10 Nm need be applied to the lever.

Try to open a vice or loosen a nut by holding the handle or spanner at mid-length, and then at the end. The calculation and diagram below should explain this.

$$\text{Input force} = \text{moment} \div \text{distance}$$
$$= 10 \div 1.0$$
$$= 10 \text{ N}$$

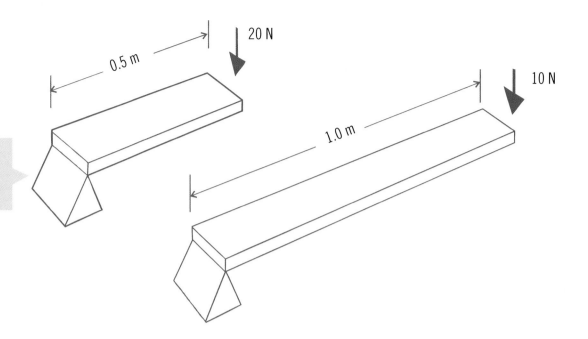

Increasing the length of the lever reduces the size of the force required.

We can use this formula to measure equal and opposite forces. If a body such as a set of weighing scales or a model crane needs to be in a state of balance (equilibrium), then the clockwise (CW) and anticlockwise (ACW) moments must be equal.

Anticlockwise moment $10\,N \times 1.5\,m = 15\,Nm$

Clockwise moment $10\,N \times 1.5\,m = 15\,Nm$

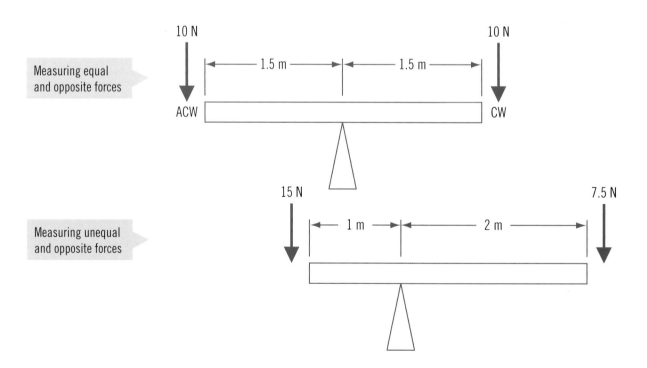

Measuring equal and opposite forces

Measuring unequal and opposite forces

ISBN 9780170227452

When the arm or jib is moved on the pivot, altered in length, or the load is changed, equilibrium can still be maintained by changing the input force or by moving it along. This action is called counterbalancing and is how cranes operate without falling over.

A simple calculation will show this:

Anticlockwise moment $15\,N \times 2.0\,m = 30\,Nm$
Clockwise moment $10\,N \times 3.0\,m = 30\,Nm$

When the turning effects of both moments are combined (both clockwise or both anticlockwise), for example when using a wheel brace to loosen a wheel nut and change a tyre, we add both moments. This turning effect is known as **torque**.

Torque (N) = moment A + moment B

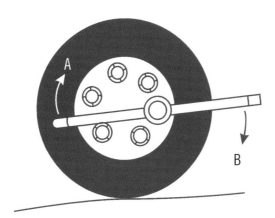

A wheel brace loosening a car wheel nut

LEARNING ACTIVITY 4.2

1 Using diagrams, name and describe two examples of each kind of force.
2 Using the formula $F = m \times a$, calculate the mass of a body if it requires a force of 50 N to accelerate at a velocity of 4 m/s^2.
3 What does the term 'equilibrium' mean?
4 a Define the term 'moment'.
  b Write a worked example using the formula:
    Moment = force × distance

Levers

Levers were some of the earliest mechanisms developed by humans. They were used to shift heavy loads such as rocks and trees. We use them today for similar tasks and in various forms, such as spanners to tighten nuts and bolts and crowbars to lift or open boxes. Sometimes we use them without realising it. For instance, door handles, knives, water taps, gear sticks and **brakes** are all levers.

We design levers for different and quite specific jobs and their configuration is based on the task. Crowbars and spanners are single levers, pliers and tweezers are pairs, and **linkages** may be connections of multiple levers. All of these levers work differently to one another, and they are classified in one of three basic categories or classes.

The most common levers are class 1 and class 2 levers; they can be used to move a large **load** (L) using a small **effort** (E). This is called **mechanical advantage** (MA). The effort can be applied further from the pivot or **fulcrum** (F) than the load, giving greater leverage.

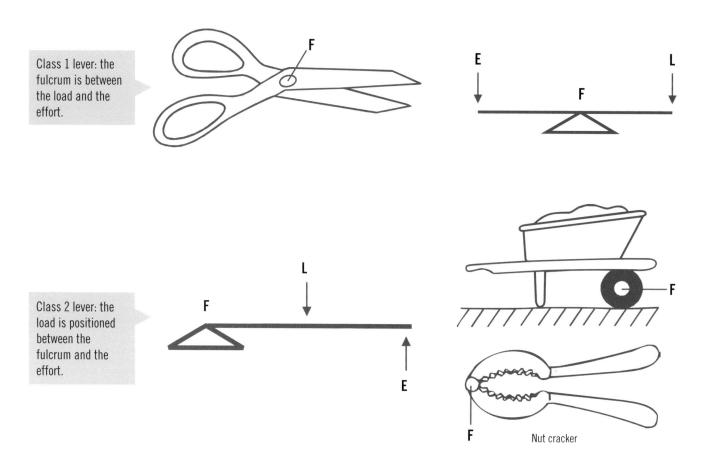

Class 1 lever: the fulcrum is between the load and the effort.

Class 2 lever: the load is positioned between the fulcrum and the effort.

Nut cracker

Class 3 levers such as tweezers require a greater effort than the load they are moving, and the effort is applied closer to the fulcrum than the load. We use class 3 levers when only a small force is needed or where a short lever is required.

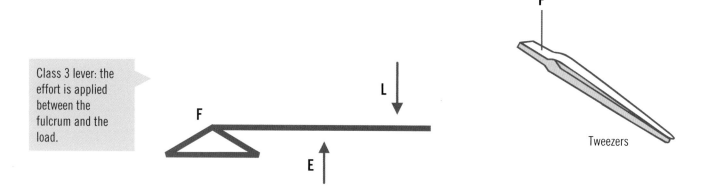

Class 3 lever: the effort is applied between the fulcrum and the load.

Tweezers

ISBN 9780170227452

Calculating mechanical advantage, velocity ratio and efficiency

Calculating **mechanical advantage** (MA), velocity ratio (VR) and efficiency are important in systems design as they allow us to compare machines and predict their actual performance. We can do this for all sorts of mechanisms, including gears, pulleys and levers.

Mechanical advantage

To calculate the mechanical advantage of a lever such as a wheelbarrow, we use the formula:

$$MA = L \div E$$

If a lever lifts a load of 200 N with a effort of 100 N, the mechanical advantage would be:

$$200 \div 100 = 2 \div 1$$
$$= 2$$

We can calculate load when only the effort and the distance of the effort and load from the fulcrum are known:

$$\text{Load} \times \text{distance} = \text{effort} \times \text{distance to fulcrum}$$

For example, the effort required to move a load is 200 N; if the load is positioned 0.5 m and the effort 1 m from the fulcrum we can calculate:

$$\text{Load} \times 0.5 = 200 \text{ N} \times 1$$
$$\text{Load} \times 0.5 = 200$$
$$\text{Load} = 400 \text{ N}$$

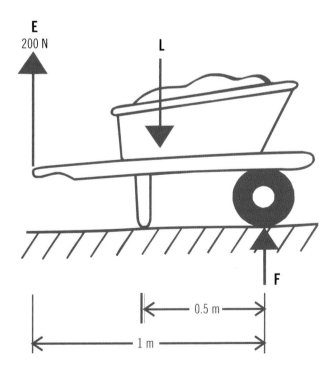

Load × distance = effort × distance

Velocity ratio

When large loads are lifted using a small effort, we can see that this is mainly due to the greater distance the effort is from the fulcrum. This also means that the distance moved by the effort is greater than that moved by the load. When the two distances are compared, we get the velocity ratio. We use the formula:

VR = distance moved by effort ÷ distance moved by the load

If effort distance is 400 mm and the load is lifted 100 mm, VR = 400 ÷ 100, or 4:1.

> Velocity ratio (VR) = distance moved by effort ÷ distance moved by the load

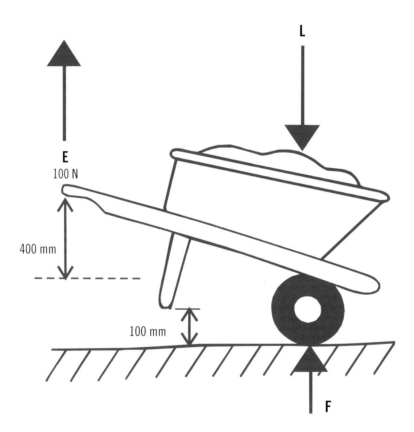

These calculations assume that the lever is correctly used and in good order. The efficiency of the wheelbarrow can be calculated using the formula:

$$\text{Efficiency} = \text{MA} \div \text{VR}$$
$$= 2 \div 4 \times 100\%$$
$$= 50\%$$

Efficiency

Mechanisms can be inefficient due to poor design, incorrect assembly, uneven loading, friction, wear and deformation. If a mechanism had a MA = 3 and a VR = 5, its efficiency would be 3 ÷ 5 = 60%.

ISBN 9780170227452

1 Find and describe to your class group one example of each kind of lever. Produce a poster for this.

2 Define the terms 'fulcrum', 'effort' and 'load'. Plan a PowerPoint presentation to explain your definitions.

3 Using the formula VR = distance moved by effort ÷ distance moved by load, calculate the velocity ratio if the effort distance is 500 mm and the load is lifted 400 mm.

Work and power

When machines are performing tasks they are using energy, in the same way a pedestal drill or an electropneumatic pump would use electrical and mechanical energy. When energy (measured in joules, J) is used, **work** is being done.

Power is a measure of how quickly work is done. Knowing this is important to us when making decisions on which machine to purchase or use to perform tasks effectively and efficiently. We tend to describe a machine as 'powerful' if it is working harder and faster. Power is measured in **watts** (W).

The formulas for calculating work and power are:

$$\text{Work} = \text{force (N)} \times \text{distance moved (m)}$$
$$\text{Power} = \text{work done} \div \text{time taken}$$
$$= \text{energy used (J)} \div \text{time taken}$$

For example, we can find the power of a small mechanical hoist when lifting a 100 kilogram load (980 N) 2 metres off the ground in 10 seconds by performing the following calculations.

$$P = W \text{ (work)} \div t \text{ (time)}, \text{ where work} = \text{force (N)} \times \text{distance moved (m)}$$
$$= 980 \text{ N} \times 2 \text{ m} \div 10 \text{ s}$$
$$= 1960 \div 10$$

The required power of the hoist = 196 watts

$$1000 \text{ watts} = 1 \text{ kilowatt (kW)}$$
$$1\,000\,000 \text{ watts} = 1 \text{ megawatt (MW)}$$
$$746 \text{ watts} = 1 \text{ horsepower (hp)}$$

Mechanisms and their uses

Linkages

Linkages are very common mechanical devices that are used to provide motion and forces in the direction needed for specific tasks. They are best described as a collection of levers that are linked or connected together. Linkages can also change the direction of movement and the amount of force to different locations simply by changing the length of the link or by moving the link pivot or fulcrum. Some linkages that we use are toggle clamps, windscreen wipers, bicycle brakes and folding tables.

Parallel linkages are used to make two or more parts move together or stay parallel to each other as they move. They can be single sets or multiple linkages that need to reach further distances.

Reverse action linkages can be used to change the direction of movement from the input to the output. Linked steering rods on go-karts and emergency exit fire doors use these.

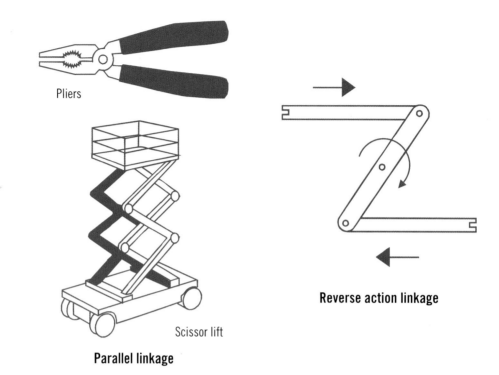

Pliers

Scissor lift

Parallel linkage

Reverse action linkage

Treadle linkages convert oscillating and rotary motion. Car windscreen wipers use a form of treadle and parallel linkages to gain oscillating motion of the wipers. Foot- or treadle-operated machines also use these to change the oscillating motion of the foot pedal to drive the rotating mechanisms.

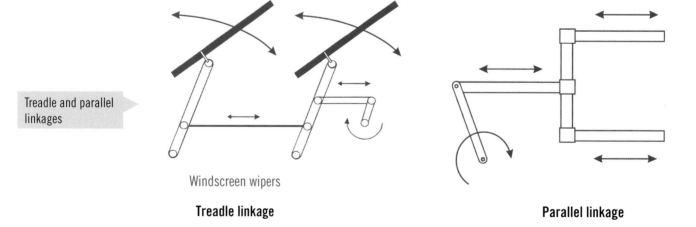

Windscreen wipers

Treadle linkage

Parallel linkage

Bell crank linkages are used to change the direction of movement. They are connected together and formed to the required shape for applying loads. Bicycle brakes are good examples of these.

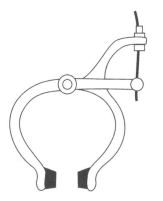

Bell cranks as bicycle brakes

LEARNING ACTIVITY 4.4

1 Using basic line diagrams, describe each type of linkage below.

   a Parallel

   b Reverse action

   c Treadle

   d Bell crank

2 Construct a linkage that converts rotary motion to reciprocating motion.

3 Find three different examples of linkages that are not shown in this section and use diagrams to describe each.

Rotary motion

The most common kind of motion in mechanical systems is rotary motion. Most machines that we come into contact with use rotary motion as their only form of movement, or as an input that will be changed to a different output motion. For instance, washing machines and bicycles use only rotating parts to gain output motion. Cars use rack-and-pinion steering to convert rotary into linear motion, so the vehicle turns left or right, and the reciprocating motion of the engine pistons rotates the crankshaft.

Engines and electric motors are frequently used to provide the input force and movement to machines. The input motion and speed is rarely what is required so we use different mechanical components to change speed and direction. To do this we use **pulleys**, **chains** and **sprockets**, and **gears**, or a combination of these.

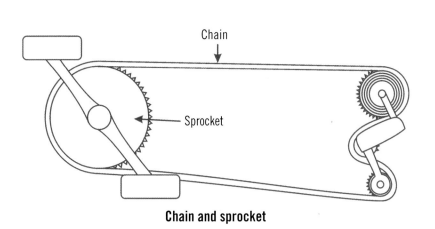

Chain

Sprocket

Chain and sprocket

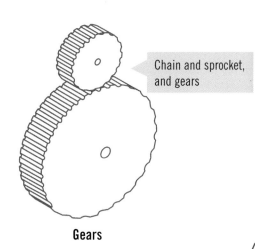

Chain and sprocket, and gears

Gears

It is important that we choose the right mechanism when designing mechanical systems. All three types of rotary mechanisms perform the same function, but each has its advantages and disadvantages and is suited to different uses.

Gears are used most often when large forces are needed: they are stronger and do not slip as belts sometimes do. Pulleys and belts are used when the load is light, when minimal force is needed, and when there is some distance between the input and output shafts, so they can be connected by belts of different lengths. Chain and sprockets combine the advantages of gears and pulleys as they are quite strong and can span greater distances between inputs and outputs without slipping.

Pulleys and belts

Pulleys and **belts** are used to transmit movement and force. To do this efficiently and without slipping, they rely on friction between the wheel and belt, so they need to be in tension. A number of different belt types have been developed to cope with situations in which larger than usual forces are needed or to prevent the belt from slipping. These include multiple belts for large forces, toothed belts to prevent slipping, and round belts that are used when the spindles are at different angles to one another. Belts are also made of different materials. They can be reinforced with fibre or nylon strands and come in different shapes, the most common being the V-belt.

Drilling machines in workshops frequently use belt drives. The machine has an electric motor (input) with a pulley wheel attached. As the motor spindle or shaft rotates, the belt moves and drives the output wheel and shaft (process), so the drill chuck rotates (output). On pulley systems, the driver and the driven wheels rotate in the same direction. Belts are also used to drive wood lathes, washing machines and fans for engine cooling systems.

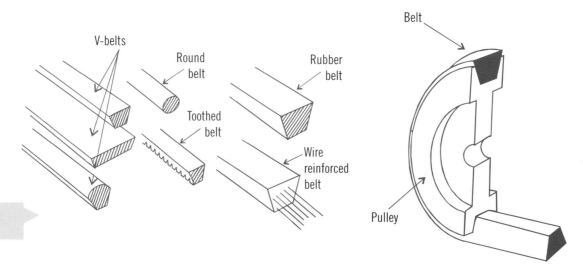

Pulley and belts

The **V-belt** is the type most used. Its section shape and size varies, but the typical V is basically the same. The belt fits into pulley wheel grooves of the same profile.

Round belts are rarely needed. As they can be twisted, they are useful when small forces are involved and this force has to be transmitted to a different axis.

Toothed belts are used when it is essential that slip does not occur and an accurate output speed is needed. Both the pulley and the belt are toothed, similar to gear wheels. Plotters and printers use these, as do motor vehicle engines as part of their valve timing devices.

ISBN 9780170227452

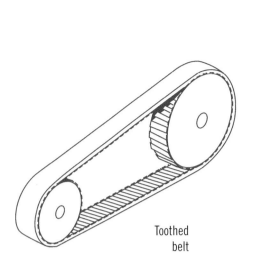

Toothed
belt

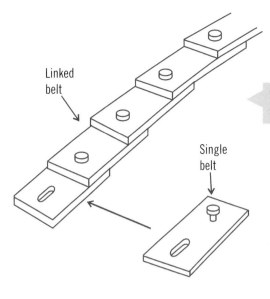

Linked
belt

Single
belt

Toothed and linked belts

Linked belts are not as widely used because most machines are designed to allow a continuous belt to be fitted with ease. When belt fitting is difficult because other machine parts are in the way or the required belt size is not available, a belt can be assembled using links.

To ensure that adequate tension is applied to the rotating belt, pulley systems are usually designed so that one of the shafts is adjustable. On drilling machines, for example, the motor and its shaft can be adjusted and locked in position to stretch the belt and increase tension. Another way of doing this is to use a spring-loaded jockey wheel positioned against the running belt.

Lifting devices

Lifting pulleys and chains can be very effective as lifting devices. We often use chains on hoists to lift large loads, such as car engines, and on industrial conveyor systems. Ropes are frequently used to lift light loads. The lifting task can be made easier by adding pulley wheels to the system so that less effort is required. As both diagrams below show, if one wheel is used the effort must be equal to or greater than the load in order to lift the load. If a second wheel is added the effort needed is halved, giving a mechanical advantage of 2:1. For example, with four wheels the advantage is 4:1; with six wheels, it is 6:1; and so on.

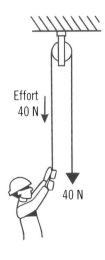

Effort
40 N

40 N

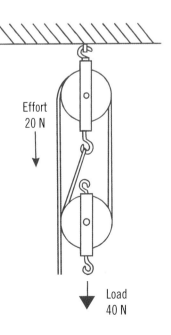

Effort
20 N

Load
40 N

Lifting pulleys and chains

With hoist and lifting systems the load must be lifted safely without dropping. To prevent this from occurring, a **ratchet and pawl** is added as a safety device; this allows the pulley to rotate in one direction only. As the pawl rotates, the spring-loaded ratchet positions itself between the pawl teeth, like a wedge. This is the clicking sound heard when one is being used.

Spring

Pawl

Ratchet

Ratchet and pawls or similar devices are used on socket wrenches, screwdrivers, fishing reels and boat winches.

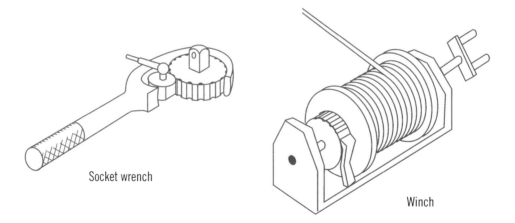

Socket wrench

Winch

Chains and sprockets

Chains and sprockets, like pulleys and belts, are used to transmit rotary motion between input and output shafts on machines. Both wheels rotate in the same direction. Sprockets are toothed driver and driven wheels. Chains are usually metal links; they are strong and do not slip as they mesh with the sprocket teeth. We use chain and sprockets to provide motion and to drive machines, motor bikes, go-karts and bicycles.

ISBN 9780170227452

Like pulley and belt systems, chains need to be in tension or they may become loose. The correct tension can be applied by adjusting the distance between the shafts, or by using a spring-loaded jockey wheel to push against the moving chain.

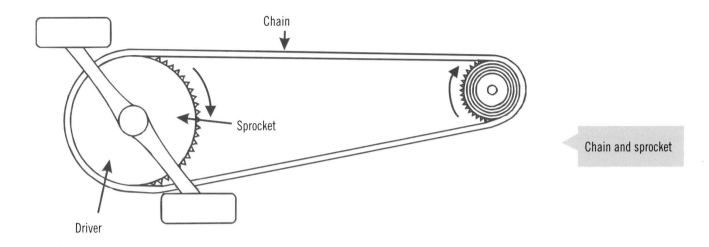

Chain

Sprocket

Driver

Chain and sprocket

Calculating pulley and sprocket speeds

The output speed of a pulley when the driver (input) pulley = 400 mm diameter, the driven (output) pulley = 100 mm diameter and the input speed = 1000 revolutions per minute (rpm) can be calculated using the following formula:

$$\text{Output speed} = \text{input speed} \div \text{velocity ratio}$$

where VR = driven pulley diameter ÷ driver pulley diameter.

$$VR = 100 \div 400$$
$$= 1:4 \text{ (this can also be expressed as } \frac{1}{4} \text{ or 0.25)}$$
$$\text{Output speed} = 1000 \div 0.25$$
$$= 4000 \text{ rpm}$$

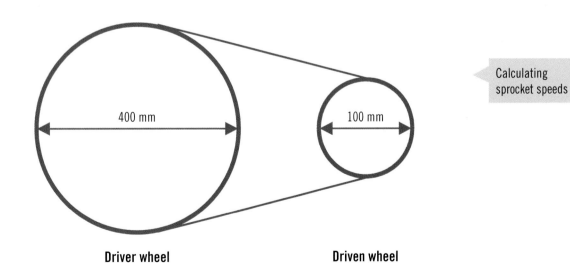

400 mm

100 mm

Calculating sprocket speeds

Driver wheel

Driven wheel

ISBN 9780170227452

Calculating the speed of chain and sprockets is similar to working out pulley speeds. Instead of using diameter, we use the number of teeth on the sprockets to calculate the velocity ratio. For example, if input speed = 1000 rpm, teeth on driver = 50 and teeth on driven = 25:

$$\text{Output speed} = \text{input speed} \div \text{velocity ratio}$$

$$VR = \text{teeth driven} \div \text{teeth driver}$$
$$= 25 \div 50$$
$$= 1:2 \text{ or } 0.5$$
$$\text{Output speed} = 1000 \div 0.5$$
$$= 2000 \text{ rpm}$$

Put simply, if a driver (input) wheel is greater in diameter, or has more teeth than a driven (output) wheel, the output speed is greater than the input speed. When the input wheel is smaller, or has fewer teeth, the output speed is less than the input speed. As the sprocket calculation shows, the driver sprocket has twice the number of teeth of the driven sprocket and the output speed is twice that of the input speed. This concept also applies to gear systems.

Gears and movement

Rotary gears are toothed wheels that are fixed to driver (input) and driven (output) shafts and meshed together to transmit rotary motion. Cars, workshop machines, power tools, and audio and video players are some of the many systems that use gears to transmit energy and change speed.

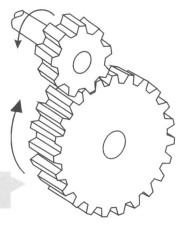

Simple gear chain

Gears are strong and they do not slip, so they are very efficient. They are made of metal for strength and reliability. Plastics are also used. Nylon is used, for example, as it is strong, lightweight and less expensive than metal.

When gears are meshed, the direction of motion changes; the driver gear rotates the driven gear in the opposite direction. Two gears meshed together form a simple **gear train**. If they have a different number of teeth, the ratio determines the output speed. This can be calculated in the same way as for sprockets, by counting the number of teeth on each wheel.

When a number of gears are meshed we have what is called a gear train. These are used when a number of outputs are needed, or when the output shaft has to rotate in the same direction as the input shaft. To get both shafts rotating in the same direction, an **idler gear** is fitted between them. Idler gears have no effect on the speed of the gear train.

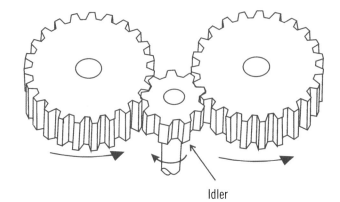

Gear train

Idler

ISBN 9780170227452

When large speed changes are needed or a number of outputs are required to rotate at different speeds, we use **compound gear trains**. These may have any number of shafts with multiple gears on each, depending on the number of outputs, the direction and the speed required for each output. The diagram below shows a basic compound gear train with two output shafts and two output speeds. These systems can be designed so that gears can be disengaged, allowing for sliding shafts to move and engage different-sized gears to get a range of output speeds. Motor car gearboxes are based on this type of system.

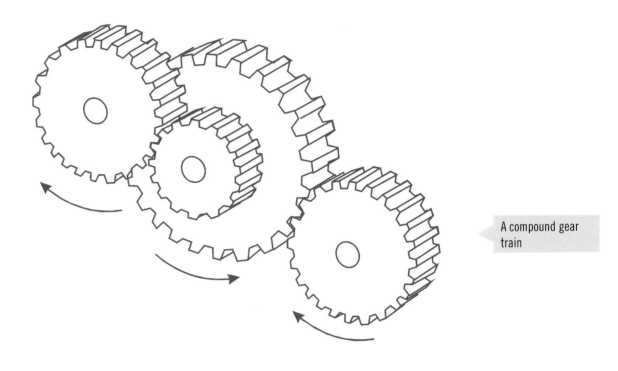

A compound gear train

Bevel gears are used to change the axis of rotary motion through 90° and, by using gears of different sizes, to change speed. The teeth on bevel gears are cut accurately at 45° to ensure that both wheels are exactly 90° to each other.

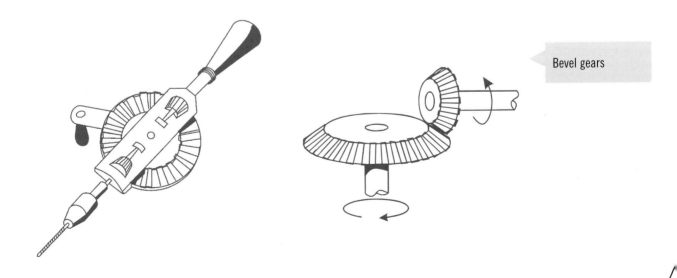

Bevel gears

Another method of changing direction and making large speed reductions is to use a **worm gear** and worm wheel. The worm in the diagram below has only one tooth and looks like a screw thread or spiral. As the worm rotates through one revolution it rotates the worm wheel by one tooth, so a high ratio is achieved. If the worm wheel has 40 teeth, the velocity ratio would be 40:1.

Worm gears

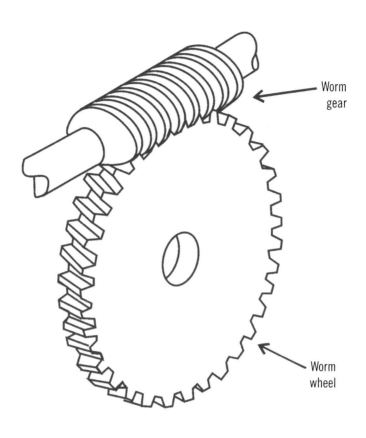

Worm gear

Worm wheel

Calculating gear speeds: example

Calculate the output speed of a pedestal drill when the input speed from the motor is 1200 rpm. The driver wheel has 40 teeth and the driven wheel has 60 teeth.

$$\text{Output speed} = \text{input speed} \div \text{velocity ratio}$$

$$\text{VR} = \text{teeth driven} \div \text{teeth driver}$$
$$= 60 \div 40$$
$$= 3{:}2 \text{ or } 1.5$$
$$\text{Output speed} = 1200 \div 1.5$$
$$= 800 \text{ rpm}$$

At a glance we can see that the input wheel is smaller than the output wheel, so the output speed is reduced. Each revolution of the 40-toothed driver gear rotates the 60-toothed driven wheel by 40 teeth, or $\frac{2}{3}$ of a revolution. This means the output speed will be $\frac{2}{3}$ of the input speed (1200 rpm), which is 800 rpm.

ISBN 9780170227452

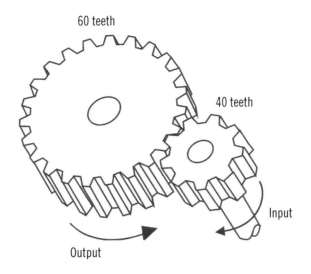

60 teeth

40 teeth

Input

Output

The output wheel is reduced when the input wheel is smaller than the output wheel.

LEARNING ACTIVITY 4.5

1 Name and briefly describe each of the following.

   a Pulleys

   b Chains and sprockets

   c Gears

2 List two applications for each of the systems described in Question **1**.

3 Construct working examples of the three rotary systems using kit components and explain each to your class group.

4 Calculate the output speed of a motorised gear train that has an input speed of 6000 rpm, a driver gear of 150 teeth, an idler gear of 40 teeth and a driven gear of 50 teeth.

Changing motion

Motion often has to be changed from one type to another; for example, rotary to reciprocating or reciprocating to oscillating. If we look at machines and their operating manuals, we should find many different devices and variations of these that create change in movement and perform specific tasks.

Motor vehicle steering systems, for example, convert rotary motion to linear motion using a steering **rack and pinion**. Drilling machines also use this to move the chuck spindle when drilling.

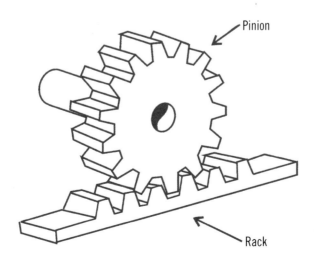

Pinion

Rack

Rack and pinion gears

The rack and pinion is a configuration of a rotary gear and a linear gear. The rack is categorised as a linear gear.

A **crank and slider** converts rotary motion to reciprocating motion. A typical use for this mechanism is on machine hacksaws to drive the saw blade back and forth. Car engine pistons and crankshafts operate in a similar way, and in this case the pistons reciprocate to drive and rotate the crankshaft.

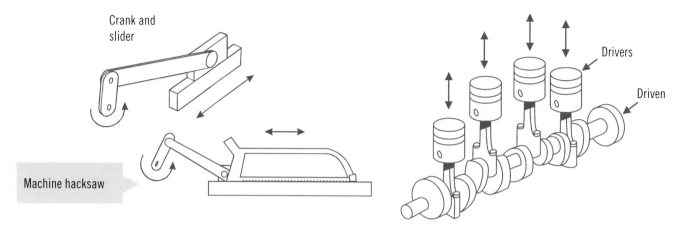

Crank and slider

Machine hacksaw

Drivers

Driven

Cams (irregular-shaped disks or cylinders) rotate to move **cam followers** (which rest on the cam surface) through reciprocating or oscillating motion. Cams can be adapted to a range of applications. They can move components into position and open and close machine parts, and are useful timing devices. Engine camshafts are good examples of this as they rotate to open and close the inlet and outlet valves and to control the timing and firing sequence of each valve. Oscillating fans use simple cam mechanisms to direct and control their movement.

Cams can have many shapes or profiles depending on what output movement is needed. If a cam has a profile that rises and falls steadily (that is, the distance from the shaft centre increases and decreases to a point), the follower will rise and fall, or reciprocate, once per revolution of the cam. Eccentric or circular cams are like this as they are circular disks with the drive shaft fitted off-centre. Pear-shaped cams are profiled so the follower reciprocates once during each revolution of the cam. Apple-shaped cams reciprocate their follower twice per revolution.

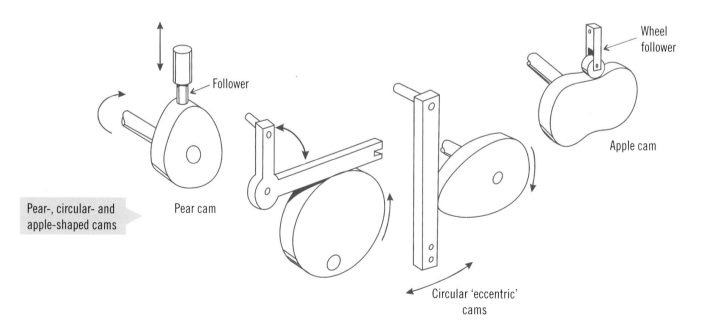

Wheel follower

Follower

Apple cam

Pear-, circular- and apple-shaped cams

Pear cam

Circular 'eccentric' cams

ISBN 9780170227452

1 Sketch and describe three systems that convert rotary motion to linear motion.

2 Sketch and describe three systems that convert rotary motion to reciprocating motion.

3 Describe three different cams and applications for these.

4 Name and describe three systems that use linear gears.

Friction and lubrication

Friction is the force that attempts to stop surfaces sliding over each other. Friction can have advantages and disadvantages. It prevents us from sliding when we walk and provides grip to keep our cars on the road. Friction also creates heat and wear on moving surfaces; this is why we have to replace our shoes, car tyres and machine parts.

High-friction surface

Low-friction surface

Dry ground

Slippery ground

Frictional variations are a result of:

- forces acting on both surfaces

- type of materials used (hard or soft)

- material surface finish (wet or dry, rough or smooth).

Mechanical systems experience friction, heat and wear due to movement and surfaces making contact with each other. Some devices are designed to use friction to their advantage. Car and bicycle brakes need friction to operate safely. Pulley belts also use it to grip the surface of the pulley wheels. This is why belts are made of soft materials with rough or notched gripping surfaces. Others, such as cams, cranks and sliders, need less friction; they are designed with smooth surfaces so that they can slide easily.

When friction exists in mechanical systems, we need to apply greater forces to get things moving. This wastes energy and is inefficient, so good mechanical design and appropriate material selection are very important.

Friction cannot be eliminated totally. Where it remains a problem, we can attempt to reduce it by using **bearings** or lubricants such as oil or grease. Thin oils are used in light machinery to lubricate precision parts. These oils are said to be of low **viscosity** as they are thin and flow easily. Medium- to high-viscosity oils are thick and used for large machinery, gearboxes and engines.

The viscosity grade of oil is set by the Society of Automotive Engineers. SAE 20 oil is a low-viscosity oil, SAE 40 is a medium-viscosity oil, and SAE 70 a high-viscosity oil. Oils get less viscous as they get hotter; that is, they get thinner and flow more easily. This can be a problem when machines operate in both hot and cold conditions. Car engines and gearboxes use SAE 20–50 multigrade oil because its viscosity changes to suit actual working temperature changes.

Where mechanical systems need to be lightweight and free from lubricants, plastic components are often used. Nylon is frequently used for gears, rollers and bearings as it is strong, lightweight and quiet, and has self-lubricating properties. Plastic components are used for light machinery and to operate devices such as audio and video systems.

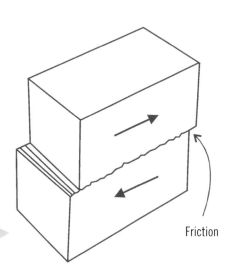

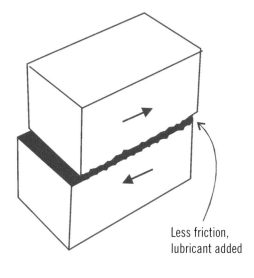

Cars need more friction than skiers.

Friction

Less friction, lubricant added

Alamy/eddie linssen

Shutterstock.com/Ilja Mašík

ISBN 9780170227452

Pneumatic and hydraulic systems

Pneumatic and hydraulic systems are used to produce force and movement. They are similar in a number of ways as they both use cylinders to produce motion and their speed and force can be controlled. The difference is that **pneumatic systems** use compressed air and **hydraulic systems** use fluids, such as oil.

We come into contact with pneumatic systems when we walk through automatic doors in buildings, inflate bicycle tyres or experience the dentist's drill. Train and bus doors are often operated by pneumatic systems as are the air-assisted brakes of vehicles. Pneumatic systems are very common in industry where they are used to carry out a range of tasks. They move parts and components around assembly lines, hold or clamp components to machines and spray-finished products such as cars and washing machines.

Shutterstock.com/Rob Kemp

A bicycle pump is a pneumatic system.

Hydraulic systems are used to do more demanding tasks than pneumatic systems. They can be used to move heavier loads and apply greater force with less chance of failure. This is because hydraulic oil cannot be compressed and it is less likely to escape than compressed air. We use hydraulic systems to operate car brakes and lifting devices such as car jacks and mechanical diggers.

How pneumatic systems work

Pneumatic systems use **compressors** to compress and feed air through them. As the air leaves the compressor, it is regulated before it enters the cylinders and moving parts of the system. Regulators are important devices in any pneumatic system as they keep the compressed air at a constant pressure. When compressed air enters the **cylinder** it pushes the piston forwards, creating linear movement of the piston rod.

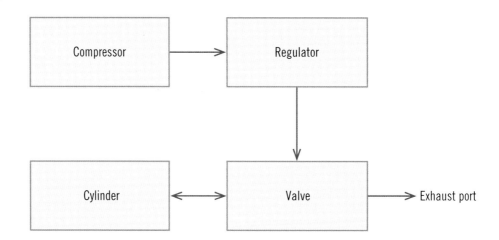

Cylinders can be single or double acting. Single-acting cylinders use air to move the piston outwards; an internal spring returns the piston. On the return stroke the air is sent back through the three-way valve and released through the exhaust port.

The formula for measuring pressure is:

$$\text{Pressure (Pa)} = \frac{\text{force (N)}}{\text{area (A) m}^2}$$

The **SI unit** for pressure is the pascal (Pa), equal to the newton (N) per square metre (N/m²). Hence, $1\,\text{Pa} = 1\,\text{N/m}^2$.

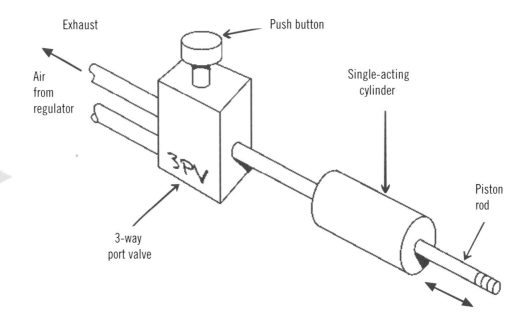

Single-acting cylinder in a pneumatic system

Double-acting cylinders are air powered in both directions, so springs are not required. Their movement, force and speed can be controlled more accurately than for single-acting cylinders. This is why they are used to provide force and movement to high-speed drills and automated machines in the manufacturing industry.

ISBN 9780170227452

There are many types of cylinders, pistons, valves and regulators, each of which are used for different applications. In systems design, diagrams and symbols are used in the same way as for electronic circuits.

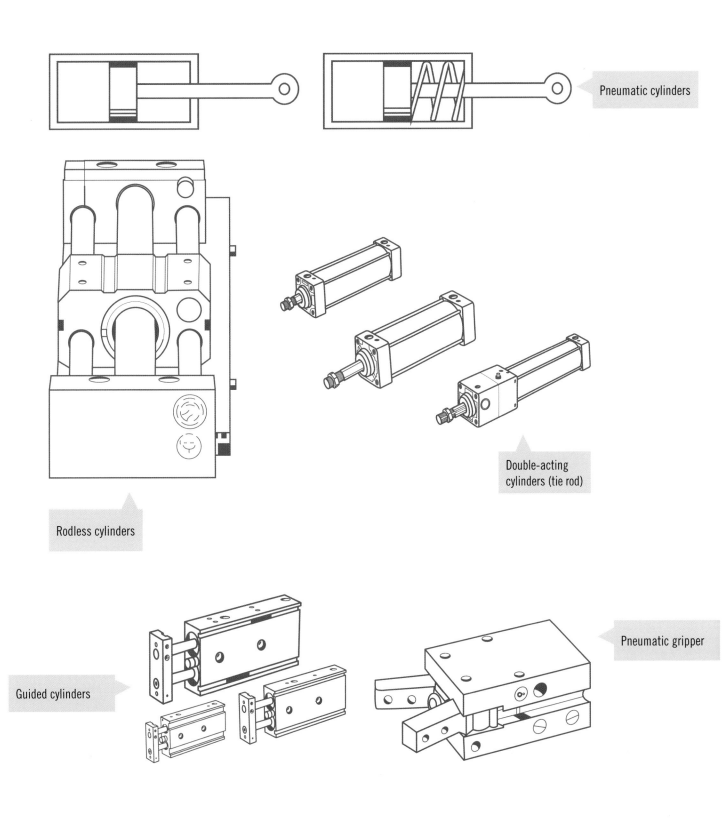

Pneumatic cylinders

Double-acting cylinders (tie rod)

Rodless cylinders

Pneumatic gripper

Guided cylinders

How hydraulic systems work

Hydraulic systems use fluids such as hydraulic oil to create movement. To operate, hydraulic oil is pumped by the input piston through a one-way valve to the main cylinder, where it forces the output piston to move. To reverse the output piston, the one-way valve is released and the oil flows back into the reservoir. This is shown in the diagram below. Some systems use hand levers to pump the oil, others use electric pumps.

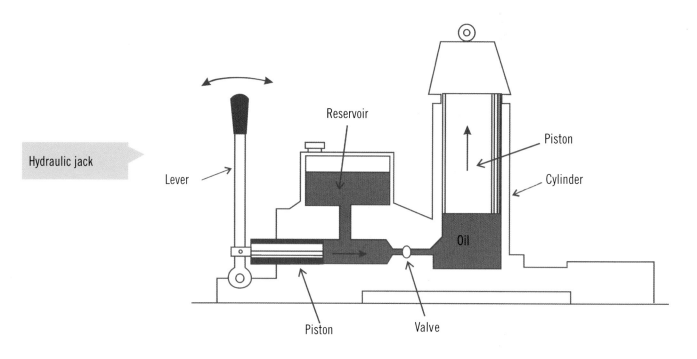

Hydraulic jack

Lever

Reservoir

Piston

Cylinder

Oil

Piston

Valve

Hydraulic system on a mechanical digger

Shutterstock.com/Scruggelgreen

ISBN 9780170227452

1 Complete the table below to indicate the type of motion, force and energy form. *Note*: Some of the devices listed are open loop systems, so their only form of control is manual (not automatic). The first row has been completed for you.

System/device	Input	Process	Control	Output
Bicycle brakes	Tension on brake lever	Cable tension	Human	Brake pad compresses on wheel rim – friction
Automatic doors				
Car window wipers				
Hydraulic lift				
Rack and pinion				
Corkscrew				
Scissors				
Sewing machine				
Treadmill				

2 Discuss your answers to Question 1 with your teacher and class group.

Understanding and describing working systems

This section brings together a number of mechanisms, devices and related concepts examined in this chapter to show how they are used in real working systems. We then develop methods of describing operational systems.

In systems engineering you need to describe the systems you are working with as this helps you to plan projects and to show your understanding of how they work. Chapter 1 examined systems design and how to describe working systems. By doing this, you can break systems down into subsystems and explain how they actually work, step by step. You should always attempt to give detailed descriptions in writing and by using diagrams as a good visual means of communicating your ideas. You can, for instance:

- give written descriptions of the system to explain its purpose and how it works

- use charts and diagrams to identify subsystems and the working sequences of the system

- use other visual representations, such as annotated sketches and drawings.

Example 1: describing a power drill

Note how the three methods used below to describe the electric drill complement one another. The written description is quite detailed as it tells how the drill works. The block diagram identifies the subsystems and related data, such as voltage and output speed. The annotated drawing shows what the system looks like, providing a visual representation of both the written description and the information in the block diagram.

Further detail can be added. For example, the written description could also explain how the motor converts electrical energy into mechanical energy. The output block could include a list of undesirable outputs, such as sound, heat and vibration.

A written description of the system

An electric drill is a powered, hand-held device that is used to hold and rotate a drill bit, to drill holes into various materials. The drill has been illustrated below.

A push switch on the handle activates the motor, which converts electrical energy into mechanical energy. The motor spindle rotates a pair of gears to produce mechanical rotary output motion of the drill chuck.

Block diagram

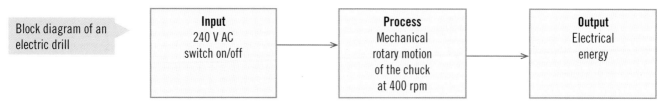

Block diagram of an electric drill

Input	Process	Output
240 V AC switch on/off	Mechanical rotary motion of the chuck at 400 rpm	Electrical energy

Annotated drawing

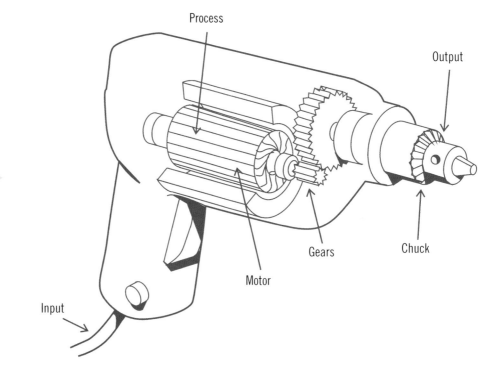

Annotated drawing of an electric drill

Example 2: describing a bench drilling machine

Notice how the three methods used together give a clear description of the machine and how it works. The written description is quite detailed; however, it is in two parts in order to explain two different operational features, or subsystems, of the machine. Block diagrams have been used to describe the transmission and drill feed subsystems. The illustration provides a visual representation, and should be referred to when describing the system.

Further details can be added. For example, the pulley and belt system relies on friction to operate effectively and this can be explained in the written description. The three belt settings produce three possible output speeds, and these can be added to the detail in the output block.

ISBN 9780170227452

A written description of the system

A bench drilling machine, as its name suggests, is bench mounted. The machine is used to drill holes into and through materials. An electric motor (A) produces rotary motion at the input shaft, rotating the input pulley wheel (B). This drives a pulley belt to transmit motion to the output pulley wheel (C). This rotates the output shaft and drill chuck (D). The machine has three pulley wheels on each shaft, giving three possible output speeds.

Another feature of the machine is that the drill bit can be fed into the material by using a handle. To do this, the machine uses a rack and pinion. By turning the handle, the pinion gear (E) rotates and moves the rack (F) downwards. As the output shaft is fitted to the rack, it moves down with it (G).

The machine also has an adjustable table that can be moved up and down for different material sizes.

Block diagram

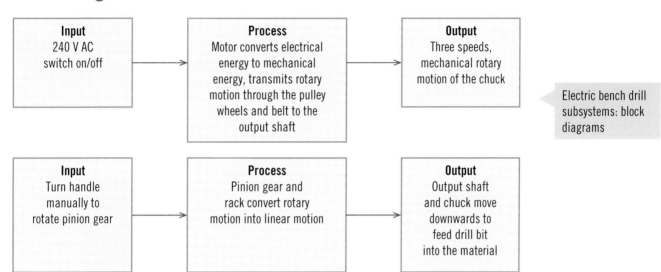

Electric bench drill subsystems: block diagrams

Annotated drawing

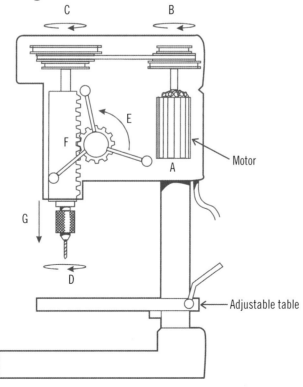

Bench drilling machine

LEARNING ACTIVITY 4.8

1 Give a brief written description of a machine in your workshop. Include details of how the mechanical parts work.

2 Construct a block diagram for a drilling machine that includes all measurable values, such as input voltage, ratios and output speeds.

3 Diagrams **a–f** on pages 114–16 are a selection of systems and subsystems from a motor vehicle.
   - Research each and name and label them.
   - Do a basic IPO diagram for each.
   - Indicate if/where 'control' exists.

Car steering system

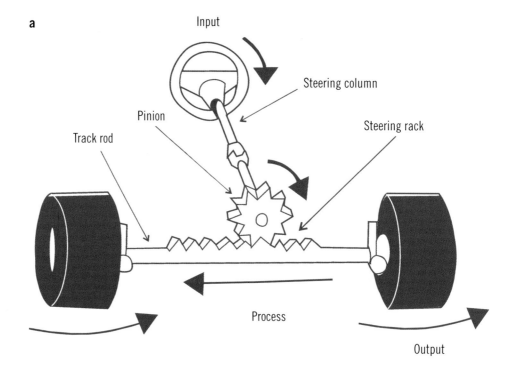

Four-stroke engine cycle

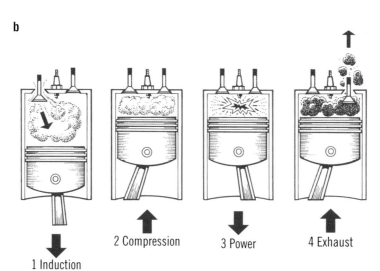

ISBN 9780170227452

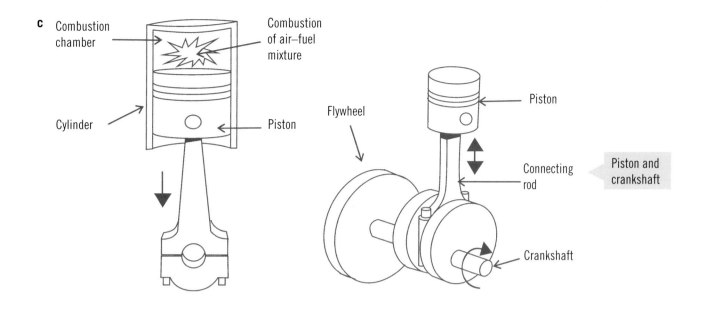

c

Combustion chamber

Combustion of air–fuel mixture

Cylinder

Piston

Flywheel

Piston

Connecting rod

Crankshaft

Piston and crankshaft

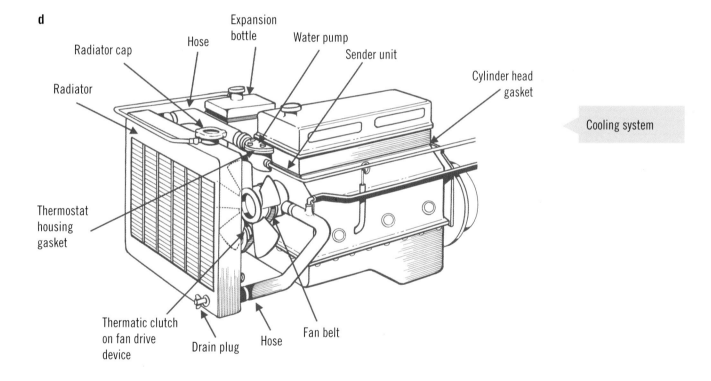

d

Radiator cap

Hose

Expansion bottle

Water pump

Sender unit

Cylinder head gasket

Radiator

Thermostat housing gasket

Thermatic clutch on fan drive device

Drain plug

Hose

Fan belt

Cooling system

Wheel and gears

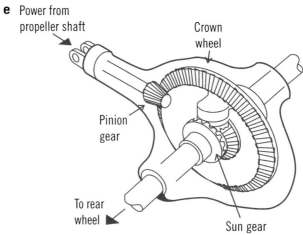

e Power from propeller shaft

Crown wheel

Pinion gear

To rear wheel

Sun gear

Typical braking system

f

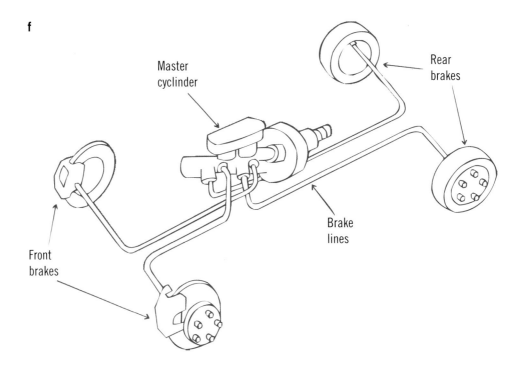

Master cyclinder

Rear brakes

Front brakes

Brake lines

END-OF-CHAPTER ACTIVITIES

1 Find and list three practical applications for each kind of motion.
2 Build a model system that converts rotary motion into reciprocating motion.
3 Using diagrams, give three examples of each kind of force.
4 Define Newton's three laws of motion.
5 Use the formula $F = m \times a$ to calculate the mass of a body if it requires a force of 150 N to accelerate at a velocity of 3 m/s^2.
6 Define the term 'moment' and calculate this if a force of 60 N is applied to a lever measuring 2 m.
7 Describe three situations in which we use counterbalances.
8 A lever 3 m long is to rest balanced on a pivot placed 1 m from one end. Calculate the counterbalance force (N) if 40 N are applied to the 2 m end. What are the clockwise and anticlockwise moments, in Nm?
9 What is meant by the term 'mechanical advantage'?
10 Use the formula below to calculate the velocity ratio if the effort distance is 550 mm and the load is lifted 250 mm.

$$VR = \text{distance moved} \times \text{effort} \div \text{distance moved by load}$$

11 A lever 2 m long is to rest balanced on a pivot placed 0.5 m from one end. Calculate the counterbalance force (N) if 50 N is applied to the 1.5 m end. What are the clockwise and anticlockwise moments (in Nm)?
12 Write the formula for calculating efficiency and show how this can be found, using your own set of values.
13 Find the power required by a mechanical hoist to lift a 200 kg load 3.5 m off the ground in 8 seconds.
14 Use a suitable material such as card, plastic rod and pins to model three different linkages. Show and explain each to your class.
15 Name and describe the three types of rotary systems explained in this chapter.
16 List five uses for each component below.
   a compression spring
   b tension spring
17 Construct a complex model of a rotary system using kit components and explain this to your class.
18 Calculate the output speed of a motorised gear train when the input speed is 5000 rpm, the driver gear has 60 teeth and the idler gear has 20 teeth, while the driven gear has 90 teeth.
19 Friction depends on _____ acting on both surfaces, the type of materials used (hard or soft) and the surface finish.
20 Look at the diagram of the single-acting cylinder pneumatic circuit on page 108. Use a poster or PowerPoint presentation to describe briefly how this works.
21 What is the difference between single- and double-acting cylinders?
22 Explain the difference between pneumatic and hydraulic systems.
23 List and briefly describe three pneumatic and three hydraulic systems.
24 Explain why machines are inefficient.
25 Sketch a mechanism that can be used to steer a vehicle. Give a brief description of how it changes the direction of movement.

Weblinks

www.technologystudent.com

www.designcouncil.org.uk

www.engineersedge.com

www.howstuffworks.com

5

ELECTROTECHNOLOGY

In this chapter you will learn about the concepts and principles related to electrical and electronic systems, electronic components, basic circuit theory and how to build circuits. You will also examine a range of design concepts for electrotechnology design and production tasks and some useful construction details for electronic projects.

Unlike mechanical systems that have been used for thousands of years, **electricity** and systems that use electricity are much more recent. Alessandro Volta invented the first battery in 1800 and by the middle of the 19th century, generators could produce an electric **current**. One of the first useful electrical systems in 1838 was the Morse code method of communication. By the early 20th century there were systems that converted the electric current into light, heat and mechanical energy. Later scientists and engineers discovered ways of controlling the movement of electrons in a circuit, and the field of electronic engineering was created. Recently engineers have combined light and electronics to develop optoelectronic systems such as DVD players. At the beginning of the 21st century we see and use many electrical and electronic systems every day. When you switch on the light in a room you are using a very large electrical system. The GPS, blood-pressure monitor and iPhone are examples of electronic systems. Other common systems include railways and tramways, room heaters, television transmitters and receivers, digital cameras, hair dryers and computers.

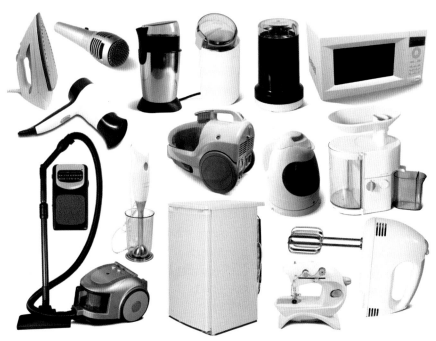

Electrotechnology systems

Shutterstock.com/Iakov Filimonov

ISBN 9780170227452

Electrotechnology systems

Electrical, electronic and microelectronic systems make up what we call electrotechnology systems. They all need electricity to operate, with the main differences being the size, amount of electricity required and the components used.

An electrical system: a heater

Heaters, motors and generators can all be classified as electrical systems. They use or produce relatively high electric currents. A basic example would be a bar heater with an indicator lamp. The mains socket, power lead and switch can be considered as being out of the system and are therefore not included in the process box. The system is made up of two main components: the heater element and the indicator lamp.

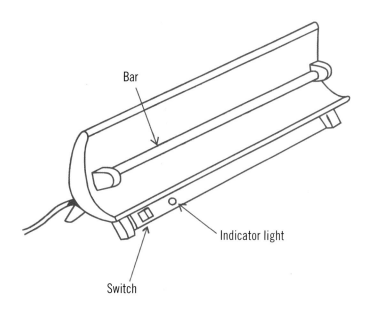

Bar

Indicator light

Switch

Basic bar heater

An electrical system uses relatively large currents and at times high voltages.

Open and closed loop systems

The words 'open' and 'closed' are used to describe the way the output is achieved in a system. The heater in the example of the electrical system would be an open loop system because there is no feedback. The heater will continue to provide heat and heat the air until it is switched off manually.

If we add a temperature sensor we can control the system by feedback. The system then becomes a closed loop system. The sensor senses the output (heat) and adjusts the input to provide just the amount of heat required. A simple bimetallic switch reacts to heat by bending when it gets hot. This sensor will switch the heater off if it gets too hot and switch it back on again as the air cools to a set temperature. A complex sensor will use electronic components such as thermistors, transistors and integrated circuits to give better control. Better control here would mean more precise temperature control and also less time delay in reacting to temperature changes. This delay is called lag and can be found in all closed loop systems. A good feedback electronic control unit will have very small lag.

The output of the system is not monitored and the input is not affected by the output in an open loop system.

The output of a closed loop system is monitored in some way and controls the input. You should clearly define both input and output before deciding whether a system is an open or closed loop. A garden solar light is not a closed loop system and yet needs no human intervention.

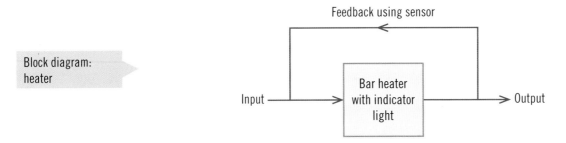

Block diagram: heater

An electronic system: alarm circuit

Electronic components such as resistors, transistors, capacitors, diodes, thermistors and integrated circuits are used to control the flow of electrons in the circuits of electronic systems. The electric current in these systems is relatively small. A simple alarm is a good example of an electronic system. A sensor, such as a pressure pad, is connected to the input of the electronic circuit. A buzzer produces a beeping sound when a person walks on the pad.

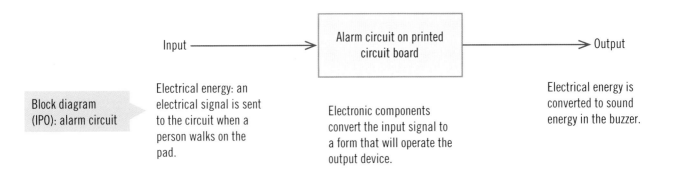

Block diagram (IPO): alarm circuit

Electronic and microelectronic systems use small currents and low voltages.

Flow charts

Flow charts and block diagrams can be used to explain the operation of a system. The chart below shows the operation of a basic bar heater used to heat a room. Note the symbols used.

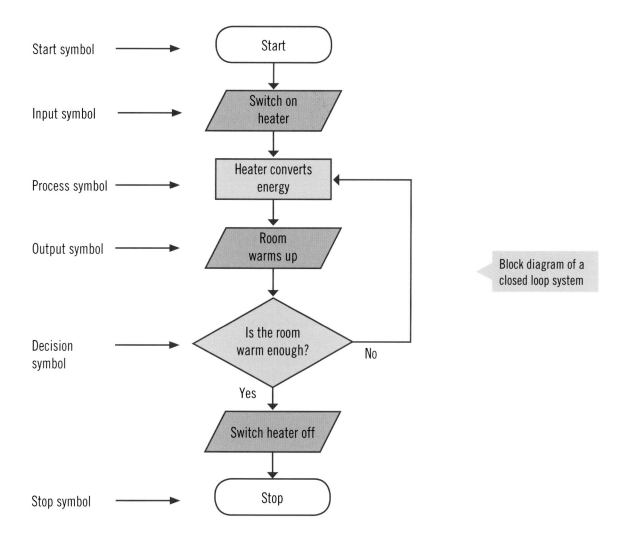

LEARNING ACTIVITY 5.1

1 Use block diagrams to describe the input, process and output of the following.

   a Hair dryer

   b Alarm system for car

   c Electric fish-tank pump

   d Garden solar light

2 Explain the difference between open loop and closed loop electronic systems, giving an example of each.

3 **a** A modern electric kettle is an example of an electrical system. Sketch a diagram of such a kettle.

    b Explain its operation in terms of input, process and output.

    c Explain whether the system is open or closed loop.

4 A battery-operated alarm clock radio is an example of an electronic system. Terms such as 'radio waves', 'light energy', 'sound energy', 'electrical energy' and 'electronic components' would be used to describe its operation. Draw a block diagram and explain the operation of the system as it wakes you up in the morning.

5 When you load a washing machine and switch it on, it fills with water to a certain level. The machine then turns off the inlet tap and goes through its washing cycle. At the end of the cycle, dirty water is pumped out and fresh water is taken in for a rinsing cycle. The rinse water is eventually pumped out and the machine spins the load and stops, completing the whole process. Draw a flow chart to explain the operation of a washing machine from start to stop.

Components and their uses

There are a large number of electronic components. A basic circuit for a flashing light can be made up of only three different types of components, whereas a more complex circuit for an infra-red receiver would contain many more components. Details about components can be found in the catalogues of major suppliers of electronic equipment and on their websites. Information such as uses, operating temperature, power rating and tolerance can be obtained. This section will outline such information about the following basic components: resistors, capacitors, inductors and semiconductors.

Resistors

Resistors have three main purposes:

1 They limit the electric current in circuits. The greater the resistance, the smaller the current is going to be. A common example is the use of a resistor next to a light-emitting diode (LED) to reduce the current and protect the LED from damage.

2 They control the current in a circuit. A variable resistor can be used to control the current in, say, a motor to increase or decrease its speed.

3 They divide voltage. For instance, 9 volts can be divided into 8 volts and 1 volt by using two selected resistors or a variable resistor. This is how the volume control in an amplifier works.

A narrow rectangle or a zigzag line is used to represent a resistor. The rectangle symbol is most widely used nowadays.

Resistor symbols

Types of resistors

There are many types of resistors and each has its advantages and disadvantages. The five main types are:

1 **carbon-composition resistors**, which contain graphite, ceramic and resin, are cheap, but can be affected by heat and be unreliable

2 **carbon-film resistors**, which use carbon deposited onto a ceramic core, are more accurate than carbon-composition resistors, and are normally pale yellow with four colour bands

3 **metal-film resistors**, which have metal coated onto a ceramic core, are more accurate than either type mentioned above, and are normally blue with five colour bands

4 **wire-wound resistors**, which use windings of nickel–chromium wire round a central core, are accurate and can handle large currents

5 **foil resistors**, which have a thin foil of nickel–chromium that is bonded to a ceramic base, are very accurate and are not greatly affected by heat.

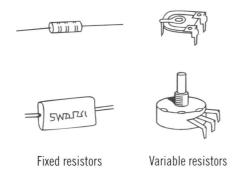

Fixed resistors   Variable resistors

Resistor types

Resistor values: the ohm

A resistor has an electrical property called resistance. Resistance values are given in ohms (or Ω, the Greek letter 'omega'). These range from a fraction of an ohm to millions of ohms. Not every single value is available commercially. Only 'preferred' values are made and sold because in the values of the resistors most basic circuits are not critical. Also, resistors can be placed in series or in parallel to obtain other values.

There are many ways resistance values can be written. The following table gives some examples of resistor notation used in circuit diagrams.

Resistor value (Ω)	Notation
12	12R, 12 Ω
500	500R, 500 Ω
1 000	1K (K = kilo/thousand)
1 200	1K2
12 200	12K2
560 000	560K
1 200 000	1M2 (M = mega/million)

Colour code

The colour of the band and its position make up a code. Most resistors will have four colour bands, but some will have five. Each colour is given a number, as shown in the table below.

Colour	Number	Multiply by
Silver		0.01
Gold		0.1
Black	0	1
Brown	1	10
Red	2	100
Orange	3	1 000
Yellow	4	10 000
Green	5	100 000
Blue	6	1 000 000
Violet (purple)	7	
Grey	8	
White	9	

For instance, red is given the number 2, green the number 5 and blue the number 6. If the first three colours (for a four-colour band resistor) are green, blue and red, the resistor will have a value of 5600 ohms.

1 The first band colour is green, which gives us the first number (5).

2 The second band colour is blue, which gives us the second number (6).

3 The third band colour is red, which gives us number 2, but we do not write down 2; instead we write 00 (two zeros). The third colour gives us the number of zeros we need.

4 So the number indicated by the colour bands is 5600. This is the same as 5.6K or 5K6. A common mistake is to write down 562.

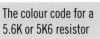

The colour code for a 5.6K or 5K6 resistor

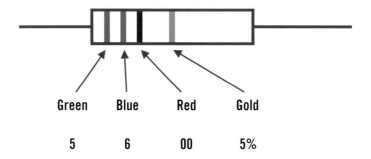

Green	Blue	Red	Gold
5	6	00	5%

Tolerance

The band gap is wider between the last two bands; in this case, the third and the fourth bands. We use this to read the colours in the right order. The fourth or last band gives us a percentage (for example, 2%) rather than a number. A gold band, which is the most common, is 5%. This is called the tolerance of the resistor.

A 5600 ohm resistor rarely turns out to be exactly this value. If a tolerance value of 5% is quoted for this resistor, its true value can be anywhere between 5320 ohms and 5880 ohms.

ISBN 9780170227452

Tolerance is the estimated range the resistor value falls within ±5% of the quoted value. This is explained below:

1 5% of 5600 is 280.

2 5600 minus 280 is 5320 ohms, the minimum value acceptable.

3 5600 plus 280 is 5880 ohms, the maximum value acceptable.

Testing resistors

The resistance value in ohms of a resistor can be measured with an analogue or digital multimeter. This should be done before the resistor is in a circuit. If you have to do this when the resistor is in a circuit, you should switch the power off so as not to damage the multimeter. You should also consider the fact that other components will affect the reading.

Analogue meter

1 Set the dial to the ohms position. Choose a scale just above the resistance value. For example, '× 10' means that the reading will have to be multiplied by 10.

2 If you are not sure, choose the biggest scale, such as '× 1000'.

3 Touch the tips of the test leads together and adjust the control (this is a knob on some meters). The reading should be zero ohms. This is called zero-adjust. Your eye should be straight above the pointer to avoid error. If the pointer does not move, the fuse inside the meter needs to be replaced.

4 Connect the test leads to the terminals of the resistor. If the pointer does not move, change to a lower scale until the pointer is in a position where the scale is easy to read. Recheck the zero-adjust if you have had to change the scale. You should not forget the scale multiplier (such as '× 10') when noting the value.

Digital meter

1 Set the dial to the ohms position; select the largest value if you are not sure. Check the zero reading by touching the test leads. There is no adjusting knob, but if the reading is not zero, the meter could be faulty or the battery needs to be replaced.

2 Measure the resistance by touching the terminals of the resistor with the test leads. If the display shows 20, you need to check the dial position to decide whether or not it is just 20 ohms, 20K or 20M.

3 The dial position specifies the maximum resistance measurable in that particular position. Most meters will display the number 1 if the resistor value is higher.

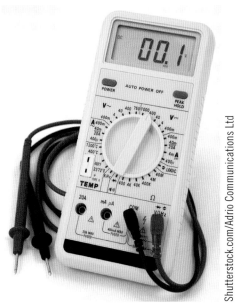

A digital multimeter

Resistors in series

Two or more resistors can be placed in series to obtain a higher value resistor. The term 'series' means that the same electric current goes through each resistor.

A 100 ohm resistor in series with a 560 ohm resistor gives a total of 660 ohms. We add the values to find the total resistance:

$$R_{(total)} = R_1 + R_2 \ldots$$

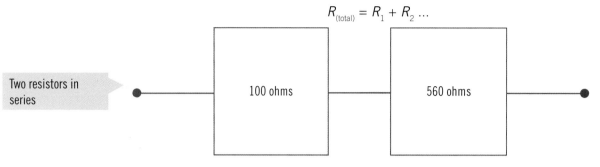

Two resistors in series

Take care if the two resistors use different notation, such as 100 ohms and 10K. The total will be 10 100 ohms, not 110 ohms.

Resistors in parallel

When resistors are connected in parallel, the total resistance decreases. Parallel connection means that the ends of the resistors are connected together.

Two 100 ohm resistors in parallel will give a total of exactly half the resistance – 50 ohms. If the resistors are not the same, this equation can be used:

$$R_{total} = \frac{R_1 \times R_2}{R_1 + R_2}$$

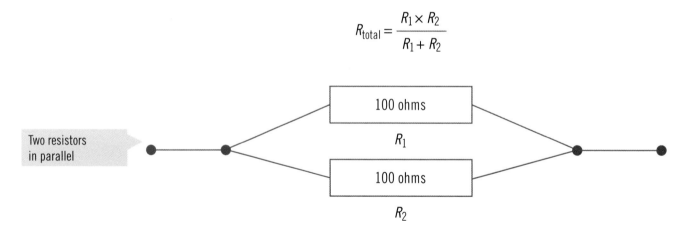

Two resistors in parallel

LEARNING ACTIVITY 5.2

1 Name five types of resistors.

2 A 2700 ohm resistor can be written in two other ways. What are they?

3 List the colours of the following four-band resistors of 5% tolerance.

  a 1K

  b 68K

  c 2.2M

  d 10R

 ISBN 9780170227452

4 Calculate the minimum and maximum values acceptable for a 680 ohm resistor with a tolerance of 5%.

5 Write down the values for each of the resistors with the first three colours shown.

   a Orange white red

   b Brown red orange

   c Green blue yellow

   d Brown green black

6 Draw and calculate the total resistance of the following resistors.

   a Two 680 ohm resistors in parallel

   b Two 560 ohm resistors in series

Capacitors

A capacitor is an electronic component that stores electric charge, namely electrons. It has two terminals connected to two thin metal plates, with an insulator (called a dielectric) in between. The capacitor has an electrical property called **capacitance**.

The structure, symbols and types of capacitors are shown in the diagrams and photographs that follow.

Structure of a capacitor

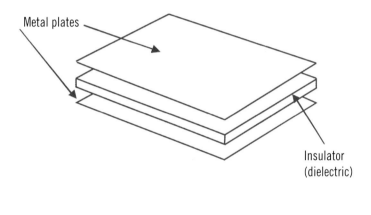

Metal plates

Insulator (dielectric)

Capacitors: structure, symbols and types

Types of capacitors

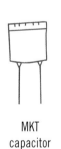

MKT capacitor

Greencap capacitor

Capacitor symbols

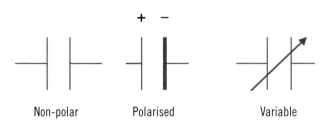

Non-polar   Polarised   Variable

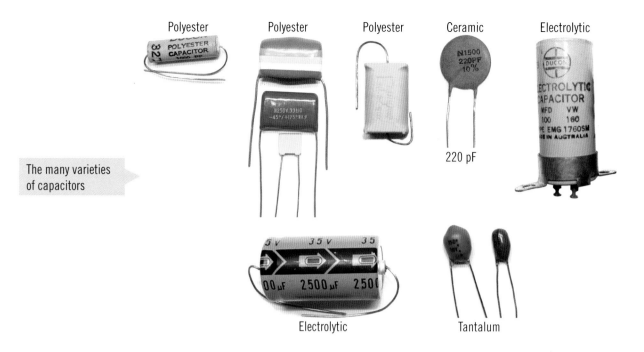

The many varieties of capacitors

Polyester Polyester Polyester Ceramic Electrolytic

220 pF

Electrolytic Tantalum

Charging and discharging capacitors

The plates of the capacitor are neutral until they are connected to a source of electricity, such as a battery. The battery will remove electrons from one plate and add electrons to the other so that they become positive and negative respectively. This happens very quickly if there is no resistance in the circuit. There is a quick flow of electrons (a sudden current) until the plates are fully charged. Once this happens, the electrons stop flowing and the current stops. If the capacitor is now disconnected from the battery, the charge will remain on the plates, but with time it will leak away and the capacitor will be discharged. A quicker discharge can be achieved by simply making the terminals touch each other.

Very large capacitors should be handled with care when fully charged as they can give an electric shock if discharged through the human body.

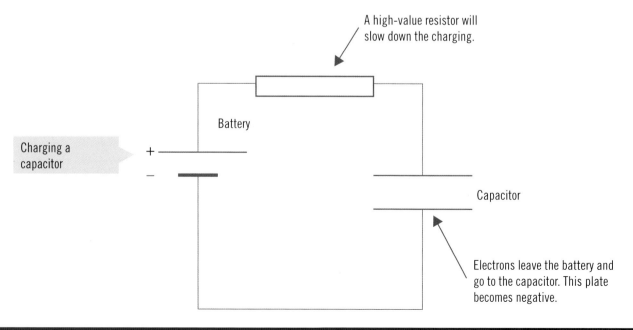

A high-value resistor will slow down the charging.

Battery

Charging a capacitor

+

−

Capacitor

Electrons leave the battery and go to the capacitor. This plate becomes negative.

ISBN 9780170227452

Capacitor values: the farad

A capacitor connected to a battery of V volts will store a charge of Q coulombs. The ratio Q/V is called the capacitance C of the capacitor (just like the ratio V/I = resistance).

The letter C is used for capacitance. Capacitance is measured in farads (F); for example, C = 0.001 farad, or 0.001 F.

A large-value capacitor will store more charge than a small-value one if they are connected to the same battery. As capacitor values are generally very small, other units with prefixes such as 'milli–', 'micro–', and 'pico–' are more convenient.

> 1 millifarad = 1 mF = 0.001 F (1 farad divided by 1000)
> 1 mF is 1/1000 F, just like 1 mm is 1/1000 m or 0.001 m
> 1 microfarad = 1 µF (pronounced 'mu F' and sometimes written as simply uF)
> 1 µF = 1 farad divided by 1 million
> 1 nanofarad = 1 nF = 1 farad divided by 1000 million
> 1 picofarad = 1 pF = 1 farad divided by 1 000 000 million

Types of capacitors and their uses

Capacitors are generally named after the insulating material used between the plates or the special use they have. The three most common are ceramic, polyester and electrolytic capacitors. There are fixed capacitors and variable capacitors.

- **Ceramic capacitors** are mainly disc-shaped, and values range from 1 pF (picofarad) to 100 000 pF. The plates consist of a deposit of silver on a thin sheet of mica or ceramic. These capacitors are non-polar, which means they have no positive and negative terminals and can be connected either way in a circuit. They should, however, be placed so that any writing on the body is easy to read.

- **Polyester capacitors** are also known as greencap capacitors. They are non-polar and values range from 0.001 µF (microfarads) to 4.7 µF. Ceramic and polyester capacitors are used as bypass and coupling capacitors. This has to do with allowing AC electricity through while blocking direct current (DC) electricity. Speaker systems use them to channel high-frequency signals to the tweeter.

- **Electrolytic capacitors** are typically used where large values for capacitance are required. The most common is the aluminium electrolytic capacitor. The negative plate is in the shape of a can and the positive plate is a roll of aluminium foil inside the can. The space between the plates is filled with a semi-liquid material called an electrolyte. Aluminium oxide deposited on the foil forms the insulator required. Electrolytic capacitors are polarised (that is, they have positive and negative terminals), and care should be taken when placing them in circuits. If connected the wrong way, they may explode due to the chemical reactions inside. Electrolytic capacitors are used in power supplies and timing circuits.

- Other types of **fixed capacitors** are polycarbonate, MKT, polypropylene, polystyrene and tantalum.

- **Variable capacitors** are capacitors that can be adjusted to give different values from around 2 pF to 500 pF. Rotary or compression types are also made. In the rotary type the amount of overlap between the plates determines the capacitance value. In the compression type (also called a trimmer capacitor), the spacing between the plates is changed. Air or mica is used as the insulator between the plates. Variable capacitors are used in tuning circuits, as you would find in a radio.

- **Supercapacitors** are similar in size to electrolytic capacitors, though they have a much larger capacity and energy density.

Supercapacitors are better than traditional capacitors as they not only cope with higher surges, but also react faster. Supercapacitors use a carbon surface to store electric charge. The surface area is much greater than in traditional capacitors that use metal surfaces. Supercapacitors can be charged and recharged much faster and they do not deteriorate over time, so they last longer. You can find more information on supercapacitors in Chapter 2, page 46.

Capacitor data

The numbers and letters found on a capacitor give information about the capacitor. The amount of information depends both on how much can be printed on the body and on the manufacturer, who will provide more in the catalogue. Three important quantities are usually found: the capacitance value, the voltage rating and the tolerance.

Polarised capacitors have indicators to show which leg is positive and which is negative. The shorter leg will be negative, or the arrow sign will point to the negative leg. The capacitor value is printed on most electrolytic capacitors, such as 100 µF. Ceramic and polyester capacitors use a coding system.

Coding system

1 If there is a decimal point in the code (such as 0.01) the value is in microfarads; for example, 0.01 µF.

2 If there are three numbers and a letter (such as 472 J), the value is in picofarads. The code is 472, giving a value of 4700 pF. The first two numbers are written down (47), and the last number is the number of zeros that should be added. In this case we should add two zeros. The letter J indicates a tolerance of 5%.

3 If there are only two numbers (such as 33), the value is just in picofarads, such as 33 pF.

Capacitor markings

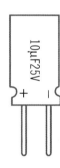

Tolerance

Capacitors, like resistors, have tolerance percentages.

> The tolerance letters and values used are F = 1%, J = 5%, K = 10%, L = 15% and M = 20%.

Voltage rating

The voltage rating is printed on most capacitors. If a capacitor has a rating of 50 volts, it can be used up to this voltage, but never beyond that value. If it is used beyond the value, the capacitor will overheat and be permanently damaged.

ISBN 9780170227452

Capacitors in series

Similar to resistors, capacitors can be connected (two or more) in series. The total capacitance will be reduced. This is the opposite effect to that obtained when resistors are connected in series. For example, two 100 μF capacitors in series will be equivalent to just 50 μF (which is half the value). If the capacitors are polarised, the positive end of one should be connected to the negative end of the other.

$$C_{series} = \left(\frac{C_1 \times C_2}{C_1 + C_2} \right)$$

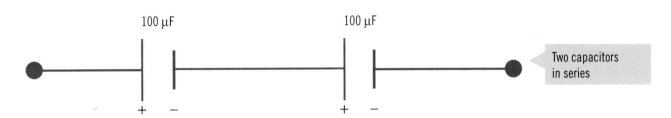

100 μF   100 μF

+   −   +   −

Two capacitors in series

Capacitors in parallel

When capacitors are connected in parallel the total capacitance will increase. The total capacitance will be equal to the sum of the two (or more) capacitances. For instance, two 100 μF capacitors in parallel will be equivalent to a 200 μF one. The two positive ends of the capacitors must be joined up, as shown in the diagram below.

$$C_{parallel} = C_1 + C_2$$

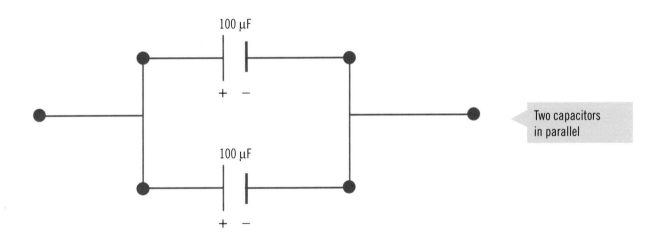

100 μF

+   −

100 μF

+   −

Two capacitors in parallel

Inductors

An inductor is a coil of wire with either an air core (the space inside the coil) or a core made of a magnetic material, such as iron. Air-cored inductors are used in radio tuning circuits, and iron-cored inductors can be found in power supplies and fluorescent lamps. Electromagnets, relays, solenoids, ignition coils, electric motors and transformers all contain coils and can be thought of as inductors.

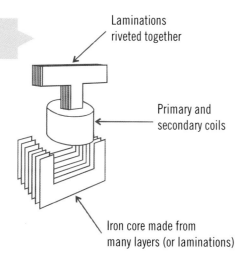

A transformer

Laminations riveted together

Primary and secondary coils

Iron core made from many layers (or laminations)

The main property of inductors in basic electronic circuits is their ability to generate electricity. This can be put to good use in an ignition coil, but can be harmful to circuit components if protective devices are not used. A good example is the inclusion of a diode across a relay coil. When a relay is switched on or off, a high voltage is produced for a fraction of a second. This voltage can harm the transistor used to switch the relay. If a diode is connected across the relay coil, it will stop that high voltage reaching the transistor.

An electric motor actually produces electricity as the coil spins, but that electricity effectively reduces the current in the coil and stops it overheating. If, for some reason, the motor coil stops spinning while the motor is still connected to the power source, the current in the circuit remains high and the coil overheats and can burn out. You should always switch off the power if a motor is jammed and cannot spin.

LEARNING ACTIVITY 5.3

1 a Draw a diagram showing the structure of a capacitor.

  b Explain how you would charge and then discharge the capacitor.

2 Capacitance can be indicated in millifarads. Name three other possible units.

3 Name four types of capacitors.

4 What advantages do supercapacitors offer?

5 Explain why you should take care when using electrolytic capacitors.

6 Write down the value and tolerance of the capacitors with the following markings.

  a 392J

  b 474K

  c 105J

7 Draw and calculate the total capacitance of the following electrolytic capacitors.

  a Two 470 µF capacitors in parallel

  b Two 1000 µF capacitors in series

8 Explain what makes up an inductor and give four examples of inductors.

9 Explain why a diode is needed across a relay coil in a circuit.

10 Explain why power should be cut off if a motor is jammed and does not spin.

Semiconductors

In a conductive material such as copper, electrons can move almost freely within the material. These are called 'free' electrons. In an insulator such as plastic, electrons are bound to the atoms and are not free to move, except at very high voltages. A semiconductor is somewhere between a conductor and an insulator. Two commonly used semiconductors are silicon and germanium; both are used to make components such as diodes and transistors.

ISBN 9780170227452

A material can be a conductor, an insulator or a semiconductor.

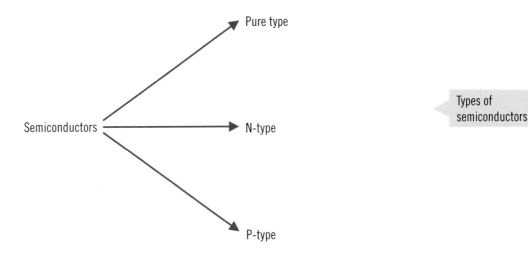

Types of semiconductors

Types of semiconductors and their uses

Semiconductors are classified as pure, N-type or P-type.

- A pure semiconductor is one to which no foreign atoms are added. They are poor conductors at low temperatures, but will conduct at higher temperatures as electrons break free and move. A pure semiconductor makes a good temperature sensor.

- In an N-type semiconductor, atoms of one selected element such as phosphorus are added to a bit of pure semiconductor. This is called 'doping' and results in extra electrons being available to produce electric currents. The current is cause by the flow of negative (hence, N) charges.

- In a P-type semiconductor, another element such as boron is used in the doping process. This results in an opposite effect. Instead of providing extra electrons, the boron atoms create what are called 'holes' ready to accept electrons. When an electron moves to fill a hole, it creates a hole in the space it has left behind. Another electron may move in to fill the new hole. The hole has 'moved'. As a hole can be considered as positive (electron missing), the current in this case is caused by the flow of something positive (hence, P).

Semiconductor devices

Diodes

There are four main types of **diodes**: junction diodes, zener diodes, light-emitting diodes and photodiodes.

Junction diodes

When a P-type and an N-type semiconductor are joined together we have a P–N junction (see illustration on page 134). This is how junction diodes are made. A junction diode has a positive (also called the anode) and a negative terminal (or cathode).

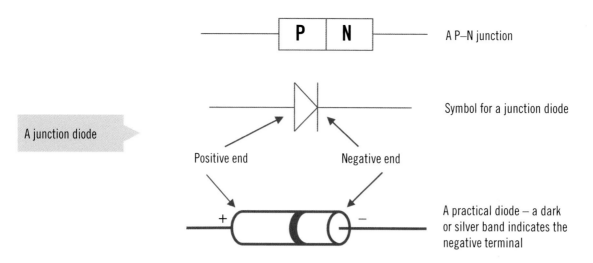

A P–N junction

A junction diode

Symbol for a junction diode

Positive end

Negative end

A practical diode – a dark or silver band indicates the negative terminal

The diode acts as a one-way valve in a circuit by allowing current to flow in one direction only. When this happens, the diode is said to be forward-biased. When the diode is connected so that it stops the flow of electricity, it is said to be reverse-biased. This works only up to a certain voltage. The arrow in the symbol tells us in which direction the diode will allow current to pass.

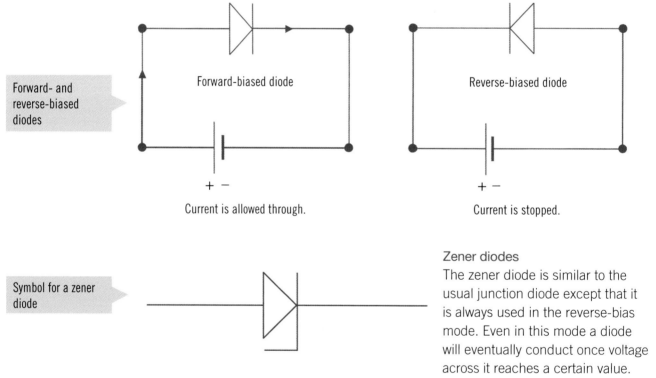

Forward- and reverse-biased diodes

Forward-biased diode

Reverse-biased diode

+ −

+ −

Current is allowed through.

Current is stopped.

Zener diodes

Symbol for a zener diode

The zener diode is similar to the usual junction diode except that it is always used in the reverse-bias mode. Even in this mode a diode will eventually conduct once voltage across it reaches a certain value. This voltage remains fixed regardless of any changes that may take place in the circuit. The supply voltage may increase for some reason, but the voltage across the zener diode will not. This makes the zener diode very useful in voltage regulation, giving a fixed reference voltage over a range of input voltages.

ISBN 9780170227452

Light-emitting diodes

The light-emitting diode (LED) is simply a junction diode that emits visible light when it conducts in the forward-bias mode. LEDs are available in different sizes and colours and are used mainly as indicators, but they can also be found inside components called optocouplers. Infra-red-emitting diodes are used in remote control systems.

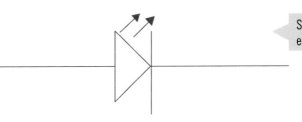

Symbol for light-emitting diode

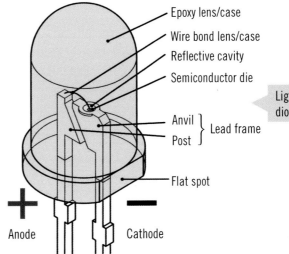

Epoxy lens/case
Wire bond lens/case
Reflective cavity
Semiconductor die

Anvil }
Post } Lead frame

Light-emitting diodes

Flat spot

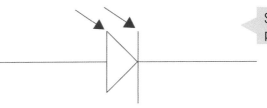

Anode   Cathode

Photodiodes

The operation of a photodiode depends on the amount of light (mainly infra-red) falling on the P–N junction. The more intense the light, the greater the current will be. Photodiodes make good light sensors. These diodes are used in the reverse-bias mode.

Symbol for a photodiode

Care when using diodes

As with all electronic components special care is needed when selecting and using diodes, especially LEDs. Identify the positive (also called anode) and the negative terminals and insert the diode the right way in the circuit. Manufactures quote the maximum reverse voltage that the diode can handle. This is important with LEDs, as this voltage can be quite low. If an LED is connected the wrong way to a 9 volt battery it will be damaged as the maximum reverse voltage allowed is only about 3 volts for most LEDs.

Manufacturers also quote the maximum current that can pass through a diode. Using a resistor next to it can protect a diode. An LED will operate well with a current of about 20 mA. It will overheat with larger currents. A resistor of about 1 kV next to the LED will protect it in most basic circuits.

Testing diodes

A diode can be tested using a multimeter. This is best done when the component is not in a circuit and with an analogue meter, although a digital one can also be used.

1 Set up the multimeter to measure resistance (in the low ohms range, such as × 1). Place the leads across the terminals of the diode and note the reading.

2 It will be either high (the needle will not move) or low (about 600 ohms, depending on the diode).

3 Reverse the leads and note the new reading. It should be the opposite of that obtained previously. If both readings are the same, the diode is faulty.

4 Other components may affect the readings if the diode is in a circuit, but the power should be switched off if this method is attempted. Power should always be off when measuring resistance; otherwise the multimeter would be damaged.

5 With the power on, the voltage across a diode can be measured to check for correct operation. This should be about 0.6 volt for most diodes when they are conducting (forward-biased). If it is known that the diode should be conducting and a much higher or lower voltage is obtained, the component is faulty.

LEARNING ACTIVITY 5.4

1 Explain the difference between a conductor and a semiconductor. Give two examples of each.
2 There are three classifications for semiconductors. What are they?
3 Explain the main difference between a P-type and an N-type semiconductor.
4 List the four main types of diodes.
5 What is the basic function of a junction diode?
6 What do the letters 'LED' stand for?
7 What is the maximum reverse voltage for an LED?
8 What test instrument can we use to test a diode?

Transistors

Transistors are still the most common and important devices in basic electronics. Many types of transistors are available, but there are two main classes: junction transistors and field effect transistors.

Junction transistors

There are two kinds of junction transistors: NPN and PNP, where N stands for negative and P for positive. In the NPN transistor a very thin slice of P-type semiconductor is sandwiched between two thicker slices of N-type semiconductor. The layers are called the **emitter** (E), **base** (B) and **collector** (E), and each is connected to a terminal or pin so that the transistor has three legs or terminals.

ISBN 9780170227452

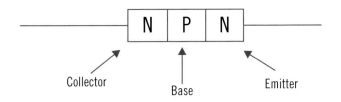

An NPN transistor

Collector

Base

Emitter

Symbol for an NPN transistor

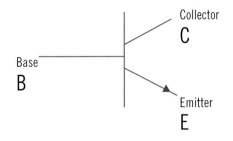

Collector
C

Base
B

Emitter
E

The arrow shows that current goes from the base (+) to the emitter (–).

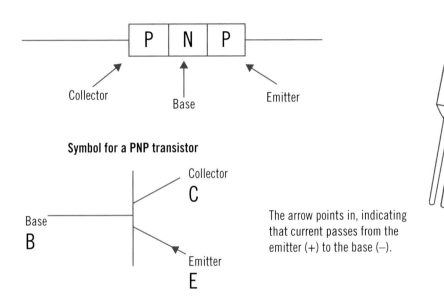

A PNP transistor

P N P

Collector

Base

Emitter

Symbol for a PNP transistor

Collector
C

Base
B

Emitter
E

The arrow points in, indicating that current passes from the emitter (+) to the base (–).

BC 548

Field effect transistors

Field effect transistors (FETs) look the same as junction transistors – they both have three terminals (B, C and E) – but their construction and mode of operation are different. There are two types of FETs: N-channel and P-channel and the terminals or pins are labelled source S, gate G and drain D (see illustration on page 138). A FET can be a junction FET (JFET) or an insulated gate FET (IGFET). A popular variation of the latter is the MOSFET, where MOS stands for metal oxide semiconductor. MOSFETs are used extensively in integrated circuits and amplifiers. They are better converters of energy than junction transistors. Another advantage of FET transistors is that they are less affected by heat. A disadvantage, however, is that they are very sensitive to electrostatic discharge (ESD).

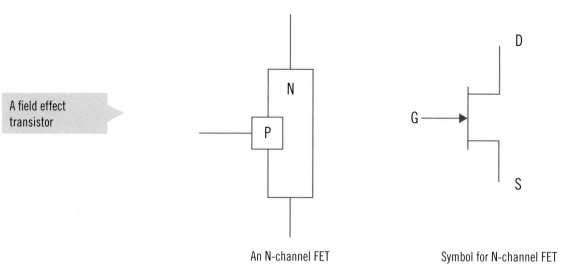

A field effect transistor

An N-channel FET

Symbol for N-channel FET

The following precautions will prevent damage to components (especially integrated circuits) made up of MOSFETs:

1 Do not touch the leads if possible.

2 Do not remove the component from its packaging until it is ready for use.

3 Wear an antistatic strap, which may be earthed using the earth pin on a DC power supply. This prevents the build-up of static electricity on the person. Do not connect the strap directly to the mains socket earth pin.

4 Use an earth-tipped soldering iron.

Transistor identification

Transistors are identified by a number of codes. In one common code, the first letter printed gives the semiconductor material used: A for germanium and B for silicon. The second letter indicates the most suitable use. For example, a transistor coded C is for audio-frequency use. Printed numbers often relate to voltage and power ratings for the transistor:

• A BC 548 transistor is a silicon audio-frequency one, with a voltage of up to 30 volts allowed and a power rating of 0.5 watt.

• A BC 546 transistor is similar except that the maximum voltage allowed is 60 volts. In a circuit with a 9 volt supply, either transistor can be used.

Transistors come in a variety of shapes and sizes or packages. Each package has its own pin configuration and this information is essential as it tells us where the base, emitter and collector are located.

Some transistor packages

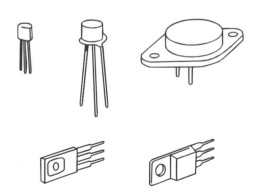

ISBN 9780170227452

The junction transistor as a switch

A transistor can be used as an electronic switch. A finger or a lever (or some other kind of action) activates a mechanical switch; a transistor switch is activated by voltage. If the voltage (between the base and the emitter) is below about 0.6 volt, the transistor acts as an 'off' switch. There is no connection between the emitter and the collector. When this voltage is increased to above about 1 volt, the transistor conducts and the emitter and collector act as an 'on' switch. The switch is not perfect as there is a small voltage loss (0.1 volt) across it. A perfect switch is a short circuit with no voltage loss.

Measuring the voltage across the base and the emitter is a good way of testing whether a transistor is fully on or off. A reading of less than 0.6 volt indicates the transistor is off and one of more than 1.0 volt indicates the transistor is on. These values depend on the type of transistor, but they should not vary much.

Measuring the voltage between the collector and the emitter is also another way of checking the transistor. A low value (0.1 volt) means that the transistor is fully on, and a high value (a few volts) means that the transistor is off.

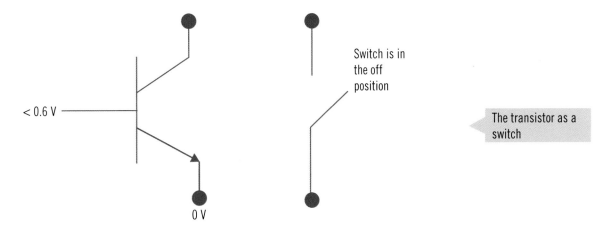

Switch is in the off position

The transistor as a switch

The junction transistor as an amplifier

The output current from, say, a microphone is very low and not strong enough to operate a loudspeaker. It needs to be made bigger (amplified) before entering the speaker coils. This is done by a number of transistors in an **amplifier**. A transistor can be set to **amplify** current.

The voltage values set at the three terminals of a transistor are critical for correct performance. If they are too low the transistor will be off, and might as well not be there as no amplification takes place. If they are set too high, many things can happen, such as overheating and distortion. The trick is to set the transistor so that it is neither on nor off, but partly on. The voltage between the base and the emitter should not be allowed to fall below 0.6 volt or rise above a certain value. This is achieved mainly by using resistors, capacitors and regulators. The transistor acts as an amplifier over a limited voltage range. A small change in the base current (the input) is amplified to a larger change at the collector current (the output).

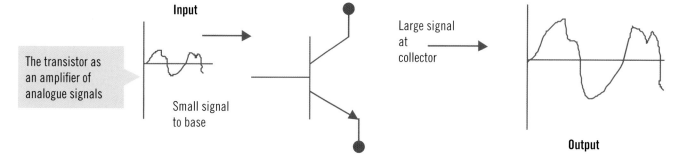

The signal being amplified is in analogue form. Voltage values can assume any value including positive and negative ones.

Input

Small signal to base

Large signal at collector

Output

The transistor as an amplifier of analogue signals

Integrated circuits

An **integrated circuit** (IC) is a complete circuit that is manufactured as a single package. It contains a number of transistors and at times resistors, diodes and capacitors, all made on a single chip or wafer of silicon semiconductor. There are two different types of integrated circuits:

1 Transistor-transistor-logic (TTL) integrated circuits require a supply voltage of 5 volts.

2 Complementary metal oxide semiconductor (CMOS) integrated circuits require between 1 and 3 volts. These chips are easily damaged by static electricity and must be handled carefully.

There are also two main groups of ICs: linear ICs and digital ICs.

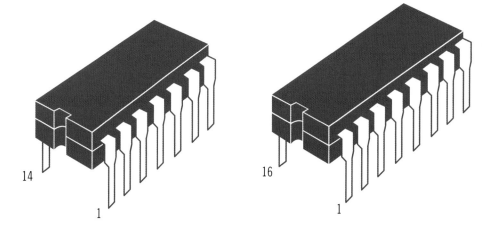

Integrated circuits (14-pin and 16-pin)

14

1

16

1

Linear ICs

Linear ICs include amplifier-type circuits and deal mainly with analogue signals. These are electrical signals that change over a range of values. The signal from a microphone is analogue, as it can range from zero volts when there is no sound to pick up to a few millivolts for a loud sound. The LM 384, a 5 watt audio amplifier IC, is a good example of a linear IC.

ISBN 9780170227452

Digital ICs

Digital ICs contain switching-type circuits and handle digital signals. These signals have only two values: high (H) or low (L). In voltage terms, H would be somewhere near the supply voltage (a few volts) and L would be zero volts. Another way of indicating H is to write the number 1 and L is then 0. Calculators, CD players and computers are designed to deal with digital signals. An analogue signal can be converted into a digital signal and vice versa using converters. Integrated circuits come in different packages, like transistors. The dual in-line (DIL) types have 8, 14 or 16 terminals or pins, and the orientation of the pins should be well understood before they are used.

Programmable integrated circuits

A **programmable integrated circuit** (PIC) is basically a digital IC with input, process and output. The process part is programmable. A computer program is used to decide what happens to the input signals as they enter the chip. The output of the IC will depend on the instructions programmed in. This could be a simple two states on/off or high/low output, and a LED will flash on and off if it is connected to this type of output. The timing and sequencing of the on/off sequences can be changed by reprogramming. Electric motors and other output devices can be programmed to turn on and off at predetermined times and sequences. PICs are good control devices to use in robot construction and in similar projects.

The number of inputs and outputs vary according to the type of PIC used.

PICAXE and STAMP chips are examples of programmable ICs.

LEARNING ACTIVITY 5.5

1 What are the two main classes of transistors?

2 Name the two types of junction transistors. What do the letters stand for?

3 Draw the symbol for a PNP transistor. Label the terminals or pins.

4 Which of the following forms the middle layer in a transistor: the base, the collector or the emitter?

5 What are the types of field effect transistors and what are the pins called?

6 Draw the symbol for an N-channel FET.

7 What are the advantages of FET and MOSFETs over junction transistors?

8 What is the disadvantage of FET and MOSFETs over junction transistors?

9 Give an example of a code used in labelling a transistor.

10 State two uses for transistors.

11 What are the two types or families of integrated circuits?

12 Why should CMOS ICs be handled with care?

13 Which type of IC deals mainly with analogue signals?

Transducers, sensors and switches

Transducers are devices that convert one form of energy into another. Microphones, loudspeakers, motors and generators are good examples of transducers. They are often used as input and output devices in electronic and electrical systems, as shown in the table below. A transducer itself has an input, a process and an output.

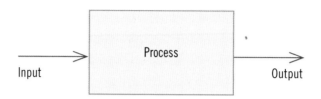

The input, process and output of some transducers

Transducer type	Input	Process	Output
Electric motor	Electrical energy	Force on a conductor	Motion energy
Electric generator	Motion energy	Electromagnetic induction current is produced if a wire moves through a magnetic field.	Electrical energy
Solar cell	Solar (light) energy	Photovoltaic effect in semiconductors	Electrical energy
Loudspeaker	Electrical energy	Force on a conductor. A coil with a current through it rotates if it is placed in a magnetic field.	Sound energy
Microphone	Sound energy	Electromagnetic induction. Electric current is produce if a wire cuts a magnetic field.	Electrical energy

Examples of transducers

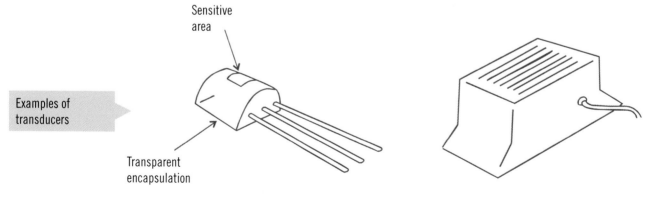

Phototransistor

Buzzer

ISBN 9780170227452

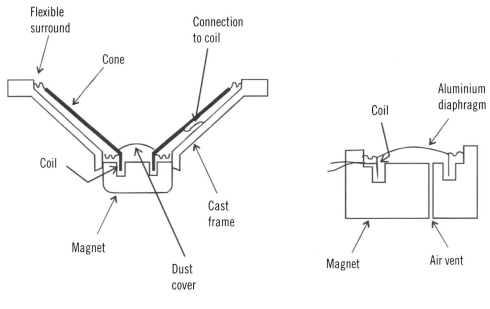

Loudspeaker

Microphone

Motors

Electric motors convert electrical energy into mechanical kinetic energy, together with some unwanted (inefficient) heat and sound energies. They can operate on DC or AC electricity depending on the design. DC motors are most commonly used in kits and project work; they can be continuous or stepping:

- In a **continuous motor** the shaft will rotate as long as the power is connected.
- In a **stepping motor** the shaft will rotate a few degrees and then stop. Power needs to be pulsed to the motor, which will repeat the rotate-and-stop cycle. Special electronic circuitry is needed to provide the power pulses.

Servo motors are continuous motors, but have a feedback loop. This helps in the accurate positioning of the shaft. These motors also need some electronic circuitry for proper operation.

Electric motor operation is based on electromagnetism. A current-carrying conductor generates a magnetic field; when this is placed in an external magnetic field, it will experience a force proportional to the current in the conductor, and to the strength of the external magnetic field.

Opposite (north and south) polarities attract, while like polarities (north and north, south and south) repel.

The internal configuration of a DC motor is designed to harness the magnetic interaction between a current-carrying conductor and an external magnetic field to generate rotational motion.

Motors are rated by their operating voltage and torque or turning force. Small DC motors are generally rated somewhere between 1.5 and 9 volts. They spin fairly fast at a few thousand revolutions per minute (rpm) and have low torque. A gear train can be used to reduce speed and at the same time increase torque.

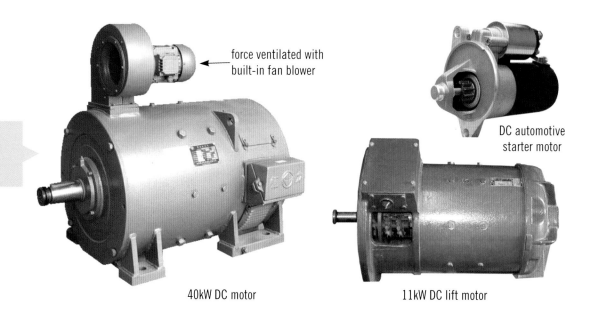

Examples of DC motors, both industrial and automotive

force ventilated with built-in fan blower

DC automotive starter motor

40kW DC motor

11kW DC lift motor

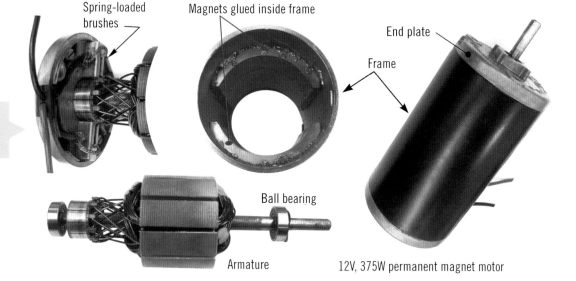

12V 375W permanent magnet motor

Spring-loaded brushes

Magnets glued inside frame

End plate

Frame

Ball bearing

Armature

12V, 375W permanent magnet motor

Generators

An electric generator is a device that converts (input) mechanical energy into (output) electrical energy. A generator forces electric charge (carried by electrons) to flow through an external electrical circuit. Typical sources of mechanical input energy may be petrol or diesel motors (portable) for small to medium scale use, or steam turbines (plant) as used in large scale electricity generation. The reverse conversion of electrical energy into mechanical energy is done by an electric motor. Generators and motors have a number of similar features and functions.

Sensors

Sensors convert quantities such as temperature, light, pressure, force, motion, displacement and flow into electrical signals. Something in the sensor, at times a physical property such as resistance, changes as conditions change. For example:

- The resistance of a light-dependent resistor (LDR) changes as light intensity changes.

- The resistance of a thermistor changes as its temperature changes.

ISBN 9780170227452

Types of sensors

What is sensed	Sensor type
Light	LDR Phototransistor Photodiode
Heat	Thermistor Thermocouple Silicon semiconductor
Motion	Optoelectronic Hall effect
Pressure	Switch Strain gauge
Sound	Microphone Ultrasound receiver

Switches

In a switch, metal contacts are made to touch each other to allow electricity to pass through, or they are separated to stop the flow. A switch has a current and a voltage rating. A 1.5 amps, 250 volts switch will work well up to these values, but will overheat if these values are exceeded.

Poles and throws

A switch is named after the number of poles and **throws** it provides.

1 A single-pole (SP) switch will be able to make or break one circuit only.

2 A double-pole (DP) switch will control two circuits.

3 The throws are the number of positions to which each pole can be switched. There are single-throw (ST), double-throw (DT) and even triple-throw (TT) switches.

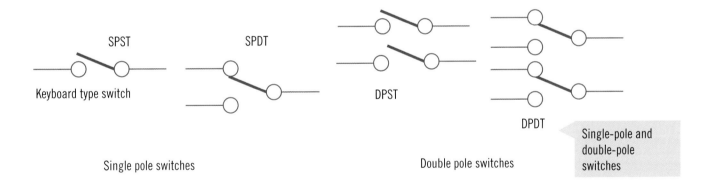

SPST — Keyboard type switch

SPDT

Single pole switches

DPST

DPDT

Double pole switches

Single-pole and double-pole switches

Using switches

Single-pole switches are most commonly used for switching power on and off in a single circuit. The double-throw type will have three terminals and only two of them are used: the centre one and either one of the other two.

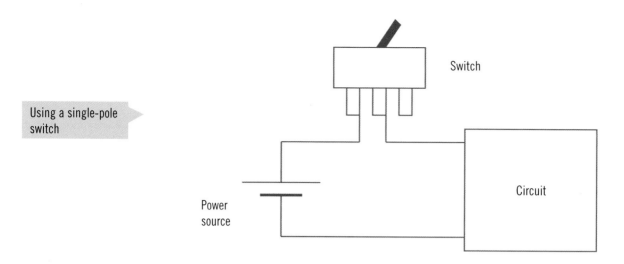

Using a single-pole switch

The double-pole double-throw (DPDT) switch can be used to switch two circuits. In this case one row or pole is used for one circuit and the other for the second one. Another popular use of this type of switch is to reverse the direction of the current in a motor and make it spin the other way.

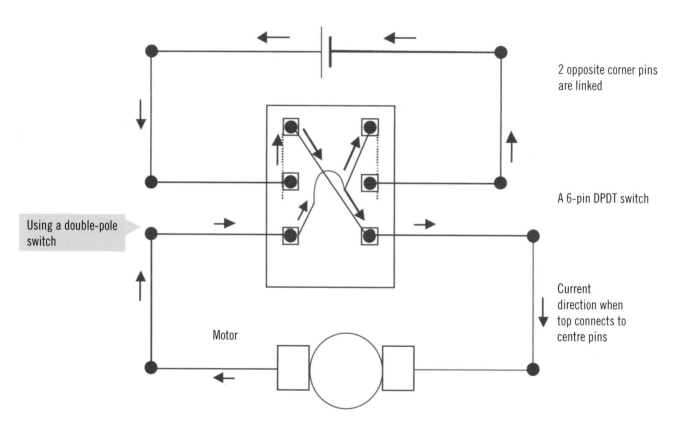

Arrows indicate the direction of the current.

Manual switches

Push-button, toggle, slide, rotary and keyboard type switches are the most widely used types of manual switches. Push-button switches can be of the NO (normally open) type, or the NC (normally closed) type.

ISBN 9780170227452

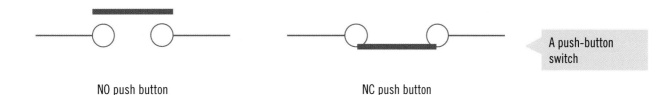

NO push button

NC push button

Reed switches

Reed switches are operated using permanent magnets or electromagnets. The metal contacts of reed switches are made of two strips of magnetic material such as nickel–iron sealed in a glass tube. A magnet or a coil activates the switch.

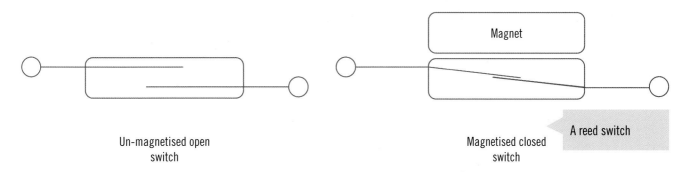

Un-magnetised open switch

Magnetised closed switch

Magnet

A reed switch

Relay switches

A relay is a switch that is activated when an electric current passes through a coil inside it. The switch can then turn on one or more circuits. A relay is used when a small output current from, say, an electronic circuit is not big enough to operate a device that needs a large current. That small current is used to energise the relay, which in turn switches on a separate circuit containing the device. Relays are used in cars to switch on many electrical components such as headlights, fans and windscreen wipers.

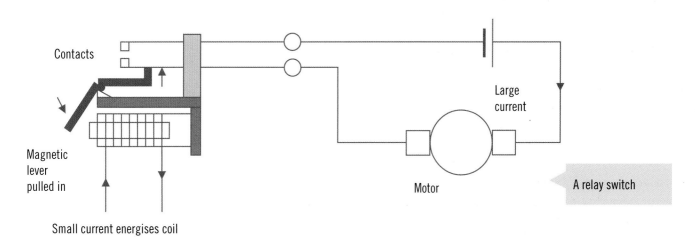

Contacts

Magnetic lever pulled in

Small current energises coil

Large current

Motor

A relay switch

LEARNING ACTIVITY 5.6

1 What are transducers? Give four examples.

2 Name three types of motors.

3 Which type of motor incorporates a feedback loop?

4 Explain why a gear train is needed in some motor applications.

5 Give three examples of sensors, and state the physical or other property that changes in each case.

6 What do the letters stand for in the switches listed below?

   a SPDT

   b DPDT

   c DPTT

7 What are the two main uses of a DPDT switch?

8 What do the letters NO and NC stand for when describing switches?

9 Explain how a reed switch works.

Electrical power sources

Electrotechnology systems need the right power source to operate efficiently. Batteries, solar cells and mains electricity are the most common sources of electric power. The requirements of the system in terms of shape, size, voltage and current dictate the kind of power source that is suitable.

Batteries

An electromotive force (EMF) is the force that is required to move the electrons in the circuit from the negative terminal to the positive one. If this direction does not change the power is from a DC source. The word 'voltage' is commonly used instead of EMF, simply because EMF is measured in volts.

The most popular DC power source is the battery, and batteries or cells can be grouped into two types: primary and secondary cells:

1 A primary cell cannot be recharged.

2 A secondary cell can be recharged.

A cell is the most basic battery. A battery is in fact a collection of cells connected together. The car battery, for example, is made up of six very efficient 2 volt secondary cells connected in series (positive to negative) to give 12 volts.

Six 2 volt cells connected in series produces 12 volts.

Cells in series – a battery

Connecting cells (or batteries) in series will increase the voltage available, but the maximum current that can be drawn from the power source will not increase. In fact, the maximum current that can be supplied will be the same as that supplied by only one cell. This is why you cannot start a car with a lot of torch batteries connected to give 12 volts. The voltage will be high enough, but there will not be enough current to turn the starter motor as a

 ISBN 9780170227452

torch cell is not a very efficient source of current. The motor may need 40 amps, but a torch battery gives out less than 1 amp.

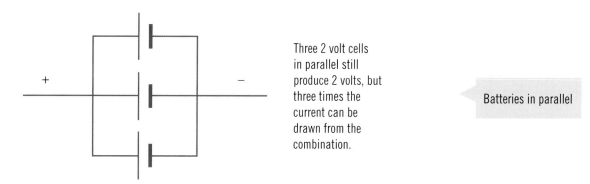

Three 2 volt cells in parallel still produce 2 volts, but three times the current can be drawn from the combination.

Batteries in parallel

If current rather than voltage is needed, the batteries or cells are connected in parallel rather than in series, but this time the current available is increased, although the voltage stays the same. This combination is often used with solar cells.

Wet and dry cells

There are three main parts to a cell: the two terminals made of metal and the chemical between them – the electrolyte. If the electrolyte is a liquid, the cell is called a wet cell. A car battery is a good example. The electrolyte in a torch battery is in the form of a paste and this type of cell is called a dry cell. Batteries are often named after the materials used for making them, such as carbon–zinc, lead–acid, nickel–cadmium and lithium.

Properties of some batteries

Name	Voltage (V)	Wet or dry	Primary or Secondary	Notes
Carbon–zinc	1.5	Dry	Primary	General use; lowest price
Lead–acid	2.2	Wet	Secondary	High current: 6 to 12V
Lithium	3.3	Dry	Primary	Small and light; used in heart pacemakers and computers
Mercury cell	1.35	Dry	Primary	Miniature button type used in cameras and hearing aids
Nickel–cadmium	1.25	Dry	Secondary	Constant voltage; used in power tools

Charging batteries

An electric current normally comes out of the positive side of a battery. If the battery needs recharging, an electric current needs to be passed in the opposite direction, into the positive terminal. Not all batteries can be recharged as the chemical process inside some cannot be reversed.

A battery charger that has a slightly higher voltage than the battery is used. The positive of the charger is connected to the positive of the battery. Nickel–cadmium and other rechargeable batteries can be recharged by inserting them in a mains-powered recharger. The charging current is controlled so as not to overheat the battery. If the cell will not fully charge, it should be discharged until its voltage is about half the rated value before being recharged.

1 Fast charging a NiCad battery shortens its life. It can also cause it to explode as it overheats.

2 A car battery should never be recharged using another battery as this can lead to an explosion.

Charging current goes into positive of battery

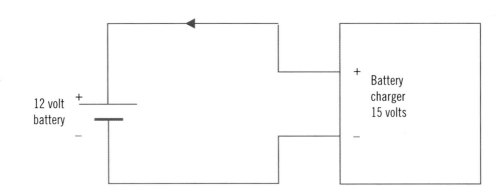

Charging a battery

12 volt battery

+

−

Battery charger 15 volts

+

−

Battery capacity

Apart from the voltage of a battery, another important quantity is its energy rating. Energy rating or battery capacity is quoted in amp × hours or simply amp-hours. A 40 amp-hour (Ah) battery can provide a current of 1 amp over 40 hours. The same battery will supply 2 amps for 20 hours. We get the number 40 when we multiply the amps by the hours:

$$\text{Amp-hours} = \text{amps} \times \text{hours}$$

Other power sources

Other types of power sources are nuclear cells, fuel cells and solar cells. Some of these cells are discussed elsewhere in this book.

1 The **nuclear cell** converts nuclear energy into electrical energy. Nuclear cells are used in spacecrafts and satellites.

2 A **fuel cell** uses hydrogen and oxygen gas. Electricity is produced as the two gases combine to form water. Such cells are still being developed and are not commonly available.

3 The **solar cell** converts light energy into electrical energy. A large surface area is required to produce useful output power, but small cells can be used in calculators and similar devices.

LEARNING ACTIVITY 5.7

1 What does EMF stand for?

2 What are the two types of cells and what is the main difference between them? Give an example of each type.

3 Explain what changes and what stays the same when batteries are connected in series.

4 Explain what changes and what stays the same when batteries are connected in parallel.

ISBN 9780170227452

5   Explain the difference between a wet and a dry cell. Give an example of each.

6   What can we say about the electric current when a battery is being recharged?

7   A 40 amp-hour battery is connected to a 2 amp electric motor. For how long will the battery last?

8   Apart from the common battery, name three sources of electric power.

9   What are the gases used in fuel cells?

Understanding circuits

There are many quantities associated with electricity – current, voltage, resistance, charge, power, capacitance and inductance, to name a few. The next section explains the meaning of the four that are most widely used in circuit calculations and how we can work out their values in simple circuits.

Summary of voltage, current, charge and resistance symbols and units

Quantity	Symbol for quantity	Measurement unit	Symbol for unit
EMF	E	Volt	V
Voltage	V	Volt	V
Current	I	Ampere	A
Charge	Q	Coulomb	C
Resistance	R	Ohm	Ω

Source: Table 1.2, Peter Phillips, *Electrical Principles,* 2nd Edition, Cengage Learning, 2012, p. 12.

Current, *I*

Electric current is a measure of the flow of electric charge. If there is a lot of charge and it is flowing very fast, the current will be high. Electrons carry the charge and these move round the circuit, leaving the battery at the negative end. They then go through the components and devices to finally return to the battery at the positive end. Electrons flow from negative to positive. The direction of the current is the opposite (see the illustration on page 152).

Current is measured in amperes (also called amps or A). The Italicised letter *I* denotes current in equations.

Current is always shown by an arrow going from positive to negative. Electric current was discovered first and it was given that direction. Many years later it was found that small atomic particles called electrons made up electric current. It was decided to leave things as they were. Current goes in one direction and electrons go the other way.

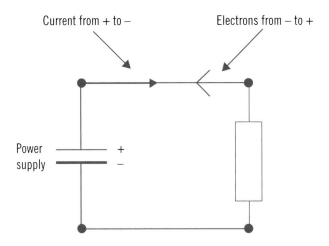

Current from + to −   Electrons from − to +

Movement of electrons and current direction in a circuit

Power supply   +   −

Voltage, V

Voltage is a measure of how much energy is being converted by a given number of electrons as they move round the circuit. In a resistor this energy is converted from electrical energy into heat energy. A large voltage will mean that a lot of energy is being converted. In a car battery the energy conversion is from chemical energy to electrical energy.

Voltage is measured in volts or V. The italicised letter V denotes voltage in equations.

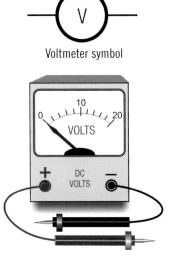

Voltmeter symbol

Multimeters

Analogue multimeter set to read voltage

Simplified voltmeter drawing

Digital multimeter set to read voltage

Resistance, R

Resistance is a measure of how the flow of electrons is being resisted. A large-value resistor will reduce the flow and hence the electric current. A connecting wire or speaker cable needs to have a very low resistance to allow the electrons to flow easily and not waste their energy. We want all that energy to go to a component or a speaker. A low-resistance wire will be short, thick and made of a good conductor. When circuit calculations are made we assume that all connecting wires have zero resistance.

ISBN 9780170227452

Resistance is measured in ohms (Ω). The italicised letter R denotes resistance in equations.

Power, P

Power is a measure of not only the amount of energy converted, but also of how fast it is being converted. Power is the rate of conversion of energy.

Power is measured in watts (W). The italicised letter P denotes power in equations.

Basic circuit theory

A circuit is made up of a power source, such as a 9 volt battery, connected to electrical and electronic components and devices. The name we give to the circuit depends on the way in which the components are connected. Apart from the very simple circuit in which the battery is connected to a single component, there are two basic circuit types: series circuits and parallel circuits.

An understanding of circuit theory will enable you to use technological principles to work out the power P in watts, current I in amps, resistance R in ohms, and voltage V in volts, in a circuit, and where relevant compare with specifications as published by manufacturers. You will also understand the tests that need to be done if a circuit is not working and be able to modify circuits so that you can improve them. You may even be able to design your own circuits if you have a good knowledge of component behaviour.

A simple circuit

The simplest circuit is made up of the power source connected and a **load**. The load could be a resistor, a buzzer, a motor, a heater, and so on. In the diagram on page 154 the power source has a voltage of 9 volts. A resistor of 12 ohms (12 Ω) is connected to it. We can work out two other important electrical quantities for the circuit: the electric current I (the amps), and the power P (in watts).

Ohm's law

Ohm's law gives the relationship between the voltage V, the current I and the resistance R. If we know or can measure two of them we can work out the third one.

$$V = I \times R$$

$$I = \frac{V}{R}$$

$$R = \frac{V}{I}$$

The diagram below shows visually Ohm's law at a glance – that is, using the Ohm's law triangle to derive equations for power, current, voltage and resistance.

Ohm's law at a glance – Ohm's law triangle

Ohm's law triangle

$V = IR$

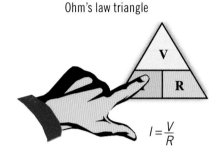

$I = \dfrac{V}{R}$

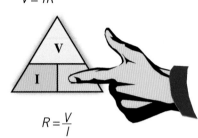

$R = \dfrac{V}{I}$

Ohm's law equations

1 Write the equation.

$$I = \frac{V}{R}$$

2 Multiply both sides by R.

$$I \times R = \frac{V}{R} \times R$$

3 Cancel out the Rs on the right-hand side.

$$I \times R = \frac{V}{\cancel{R}} \times \cancel{R}$$

$$I \times R = V$$

4 Rewrite the equation with V on the left-hand side (V is now the subject).

$$V = I \times R$$

1 Write the power equation.

$$P = V \times I$$

2 Write Ohm's law for V.

$$V = I \times R = IR$$

Ohm's law – power, current and resistance equations

3 Replace V in equation 1 with IR.

$$P = IR \times I$$

4 Multiply $I \times IR$ to give I^2R.

$$P = I^2R$$

1 Write the power equation. $\boxed{P} = \boxed{V} \times \boxed{I}$

2 Write Ohm's law for I. $\boxed{I} = \dfrac{\boxed{V}}{\boxed{R}}$

3 Replace I in equation 1 with $\dfrac{V}{R}$. $\boxed{P} = \boxed{V} \times \dfrac{\boxed{V}}{\boxed{R}}$

Power, voltage and resistance equations

4 Multiply $V \times \dfrac{V}{R}$ to give $\dfrac{V^2}{R}$. $\boxed{P} = \dfrac{\boxed{V^2}}{\boxed{R}}$

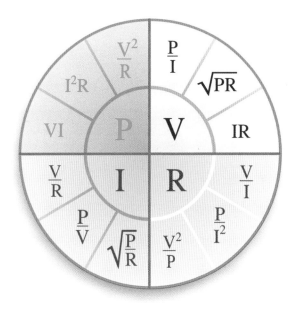

Summary of equations – the equation wheel (V, I, R and P)

Working out the current in amps

If $V = 9$ volts and $R = 12$ ohms we can use Ohm's law to work out the electric current in the circuit.

1 Ohm's law: $V = I \times R$.

2 This means the current $I = V \div R$.

3 $I = V \div R$, so I equals 9 volts divided by 12 ohms, which is 0.75 amp.

4 This can be converted into milliamps by multiplying by 1000. The current in the circuit is 750 milliamps or 750 mA.

Working out the power in watts

To work out electrical power we multiply the voltage by the current.

1 Power equation: $P = I \times V$.

2 $P = 0.75 \times 9 = 6.75$ watts (Note that we always use amps and not milliamps in equations.)

3 This means that 6.75 joules of energy are being converted every second from one form into another. In a resistor, electrical energy is converted into heat energy.

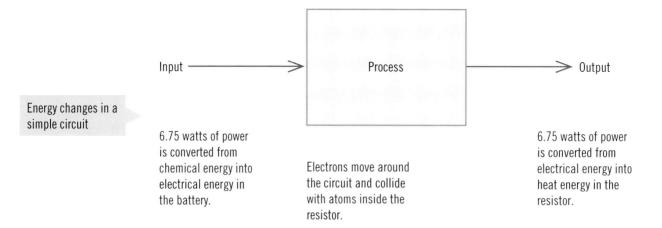

Input ⟶ Process ⟶ Output

6.75 watts of power is converted from chemical energy into electrical energy in the battery.

Electrons move around the circuit and collide with atoms inside the resistor.

6.75 watts of power is converted from electrical energy into heat energy in the resistor.

Lost volts and internal resistance

The calculations above assume one important thing: the battery is perfect and 100% efficient. All the chemical energy is converted into electrical energy. This is not the case for practical batteries. A good car battery is a good energy converter; however, some of the chemical energy available is converted into heat inside the battery and whatever remains is then given to the load. The battery gets hot and wastes energy. We say that the battery has internal resistance.

The voltage drops when the battery is powering a device. The voltage may drop from 12 volts to, say, 10 volts. The greater the drop, the less efficient the battery.

A series circuit

A series circuit is a single loop linking the battery and the resistors.

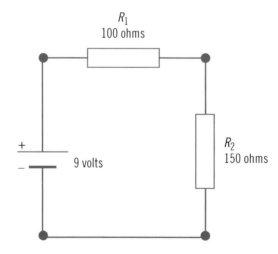

There are four basic rules or steps to use when working out electrical quantities in series circuits. They are given below.

Resistance

We start by finding the total resistance. Resistor values add up.

In this case we sum up the ohms of the two resistors to get what is called the total resistance of the circuit.

$$R_{total} = R_1 + R_2 = 100\,W + 150\,W = 250\,ohms\ or\ 250\,W$$

Current

Current (amps) is the same throughout the circuit.

Once we know the total resistance, the current coming out of the battery can be calculated. The same current passes through both resistors.

$$I = V \div R = 9\,V \div 250\,W = 0.036\,amp$$

So 0.036 amp leaves the battery, goes through the first resistor, then through the second resistor and back to the battery. No current is lost; whatever leaves the battery comes back to it. Note that current, as shown by an arrow, goes from positive to negative.

Voltage

What about the voltage in a series circuit?

Voltage is added up: $V = V_1 + V_2$.

The current through the 100 ohm resistor is 0.036 amp. This allows us to use Ohm's law to calculate the voltage:

For the $100\,\Omega$ resistor: $V = I \times R = 100 \times 0.036 = 3.6\,V$
For the $150\,\Omega$ resistor: $V = I \times R = 150 \times 0.036 = 5.4\,V$

You will notice that the resistors share the 9 V provided by the battery.

$$3.6\,V + 5.4\,V = 9.0\,V$$

This is called the potential divider principle. The voltage is divided between resistors. (Potential is another word for voltage.)

Power

Power, just like voltage, adds up.

To work out the power we multiply voltage by current.

The battery is 9 volts and the current through it is 0.036 amp. The power will be 0.324 watt. This is the total power input. $P = V \times I = 9\,V \times 0.036\,amp = 0.324\,watt$.

The power output for the two resistors will be:

P (for R_1) $= 3.6 \times 0.036 = 0.13\,watt$
P (for R_2) $= 5.4 \times 0.036 = 0.194\,watt$

Notice that 0.13 + 0.194 = 0.324, so that the power provided by the battery is shared by the resistors, but the total power output is the same as the power input. This is because of the 'conservation of energy' principle.

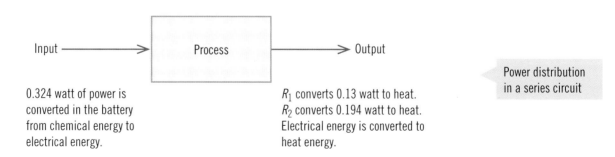

Input	Process	Output

0.324 watt of power is converted in the battery from chemical energy to electrical energy.

R_1 converts 0.13 watt to heat.
R_2 converts 0.194 watt to heat.
Electrical energy is converted to heat energy.

Power distribution in a series circuit

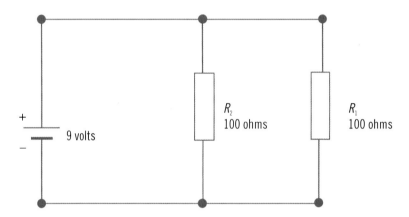

A variable resistor controls current, and hence the speed of a motor.

Variable resistor

+
9 volts
−

Motor

A parallel circuit

Similar to a series circuit, there are four rules or steps to remember for a parallel circuit. Applying the rules enables us to work out resistance, voltage, current and power for each component.

+
9 volts
−

R_2
100 ohms

R_1
100 ohms

Resistance

We start by finding the total resistance. The total resistance is given by using the following equation.

$$R_{\text{total}} = \frac{R_1 \times R_2}{R_1 + R_2}$$

The total resistance is halved from 100 ohms to 50 ohms – this is the case whenever the two resistors are identical. This means that a single 50 ohm resistor could replace the two 100 ohm resistors.

Voltage

Voltage is the same across components in parallel:

$$V = V_1 = V_2 = 9\ V$$

ISBN 9780170227452

Current

We can now use Ohm's law to work out the current through each resistor:

$$\text{Through } R_1, I_1 = V_1 \div R_1 = 9\,V \div 100\,\text{ohms} = 0.09\,\text{amp}$$
$$\text{Through } R_2, I_2 = V_2 \div R_2 = 9\,V \div 100\,\text{ohms} = 0.09\,\text{amp}$$

The current, as expected, should be the same as the resistors are the same. If the resistors are not identical, the currents will not be, but they will still add up.

Current from the battery splits and is shared between the resistors, but must add up as it leaves and re-enters the battery. No current is lost in a circuit.

The total current I from the battery is therefore

$$I = I_1 + I_2$$
$$= 0.09\,A + 0.09\,A$$
$$= 0.18\,A$$

Power

We can work out power as we now know the voltage and the current for each component.

The power output of the battery, the power output will be:

$$P = V \times I$$
$$= 9\,V \times 0.18\,A = 1.62\,W$$

For R_1 the power $P_1 = V_1 \times I_1 = 9\,V \times 0.09\,A = 0.81\,W$.
For R_2 the power $P_2 = V_2 \times I_2 = 9\,V \times 0.09\,A = 0.81\,W$, the same as for R_1.
Note that $0.81 + 0.81 = 1.62$.

Here again the conservation of energy applies. The two resistors share the power output from the battery, but the total power remains constant. No power is lost.

Alternating current electricity

Dissimilar to DC electricity, where the polarities (positive and negative) do not change, the polarities of alternating current (AC) power sources change from positive to negative and then back again. This means that the electric current in an AC circuit is continuously changing direction. A DC motor will not work if connected to an AC power source as the coil tries to spin one way and then the other way. Loudspeakers, however, rely on AC to make the cones move in and out. How fast a loudspeaker cone moves in and out depends on the frequency of the power source.

AC voltages and current can be measured using multimeters and an instrument called a cathode ray oscilloscope (CRO). The CRO will also display the waveform (see the illustration on page 160). The voltage values of AC electricity are changing all the time. Which value can we use? The answer is to quote the maximum or peak value or the RMS (root mean square) value.

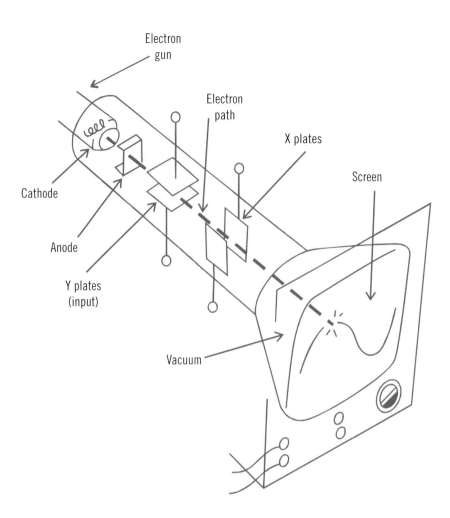

Electron gun

Electron path

X plates

Screen

Cathode

Anode

Y plates (input)

Vacuum

A CRO displaying an AC waveform

Peak value

The peak value of AC is the maximum value reached as the voltage rises and then falls.

RMS value

RMS stands for root mean square. A 12 volt RMS AC power source will provide the same power (in watts) as a 12 volt DC power source. A heater will produce the same amount of heat if connected to either power source. We can think of RMS as a DC equivalent. The RMS voltage of the AC power used in homes in Australia is 240 volts. The peak voltage is about 1.4 times higher.

The RMS value is about 70% of the maximum or peak value, and is some kind of average.

Frequency

Frequency is measured in hertz (Hz). The voltage goes through cycles as the changes are repeated. Mains electric power used in homes in Australia has a frequency of 50 hertz.

The frequency of AC is the number of cycles per second.

ISBN 9780170227452

Stepping up and stepping down AC voltages

One advantage of AC over DC is that it can be stepped up or down easily by using transformers. It can also be converted into DC by using diodes, capacitors and semiconductors (called regulators). The process of converting AC into DC is called rectification, and this is what happens in a laboratory power supply.

Rectification is the process of changing AC to DC.

Safety and electricity

Our body can conduct electricity. An electric current will pass through the body if we provide a path for it to do so. This will be the case if we touch a live mains power outlet while some part of our body is connected to earth. Electricity will flow through the body to earth. We can think of earth as a big object, or sink, always ready to accept electrons. Given half a chance, electrons will flow to earth.

The effect on the body will depend on the value of the electric current through it. Your heart will stop beating if the current is about 200 mA DC. Much smaller currents will cause pain and muscle contraction. Larger currents will result in severe burns.

The human body offers less resistance to AC electricity than to DC. This is because the body acts as a capacitor as well and capacitors allow AC current through, but will block DC currents. This is why exposure to even low values of AC can cause an electric shock.

Students are not permitted to work on electrical products or equipment that operate above 50 V AC or smoothed 120 V DC. Only people with an appropriate electrical licence are permitted to work on such products or equipment.

LEARNING ACTIVITY 5.8

1 List the four quantities we associate with electricity, give their symbols and state the unit of measurement for each of them.

2 If current is a measure of the flow of charge, what do each of the following measure?

  a Voltage

  b Resistance

  c Power

3 A simple circuit is made up of a battery of V volts connected to a single resistor of R ohms. The current in the circuit is I amps and the power is P watts. Copy and complete the table below, working out the missing quantities in each row.

R (Ω)	V (V)	I (A)	P (W)
12		4	
	6	2	
	12		36

4 What have you assumed about the battery when working out the quantities in Question **3**?

5 A 10 ohm resistor and a 5 ohm resistor are connected in series. A 30 volt battery supplies an electric current *I* to the resistors.

    a Draw the circuit diagram.

    a Calculate the value of the current *I*.

6 Calculate the power supplied by the battery and the power used by each resistor in the circuit in Question **5** and show that power or energy is conserved.

7 Calculate the total resistance of the following resistor combinations.

    a A 1K resistor in series with a 1.8K resistor

    b A 200 ohm resistor in series with 2.2K resistor

    c Two 18 ohm resistors in parallel

    d A 6 ohm resistor in parallel with a 3 ohm resistor

8 A 6 ohm resistor, a 3 ohm resistor and a 12 volt battery are all connected in parallel. Draw the circuit diagram and work out the following quantities.

    a Total resistance

    b Total current leaving the battery

    c Current through the 6 ohm resistor

    d Current through the 3 ohm resistor

    e Power delivered by the battery

    f Power used up by each resistor

9 Show that power is conserved in the circuit.

10 Explain the difference between AC and DC electricity.

11 What does RMS stand for? Explain the difference between peak and RMS values.

12 What can be used to step AC up or down?

13 What is the maximum AC voltage a student can work with?

Digital circuits

Logic gates, flip-flops, PICs, encoders and decoders are examples of digital circuits.

1 The outputs of these circuits are in digital form, either on or off, or high (1) or low (0).

2 A 'high' will represent the supply voltage, such as 5 volts, and a 'low' is zero volt.

3 The most common types of digital components are the transistor–transistor–logic (TTL) and the complementary metal oxide semiconductor (CMOS).

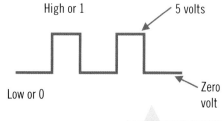

High or 1   5 volts

Low or 0   Zero volt

A digital signal

Logic gates and truth tables

There are many types of logic gates. Each gate has its own symbol and truth table. The truth table gives information about inputs and outputs. The most commonly used logic gates are described next.

NOT or INVERT gate

A NOT gate is the simplest and has just one input and one output. It is also called an inverter because it inverts the input, changing it from a low or 0 to a high or 1.

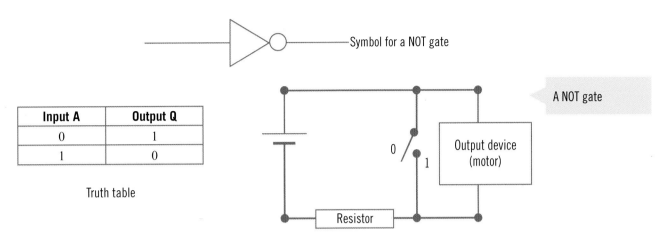

Symbol for a NOT gate

A NOT gate

Input A	Output Q
0	1
1	0

Truth table

The switch in the circuit acts as a NOT gate input. When it is OFF (0) the output device is ON (1) and vice versa.

The AND gate

The basic AND gate has two inputs and one output. More complex gates have several inputs. The output Q is high if both A and B inputs are high.

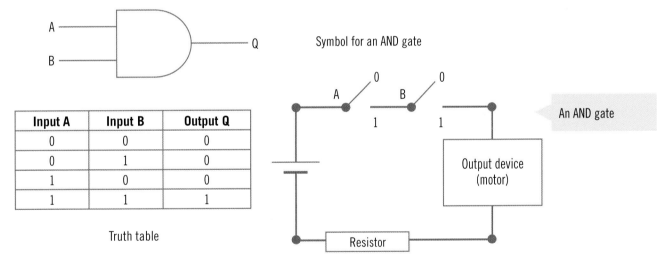

Symbol for an AND gate

An AND gate

Input A	Input B	Output Q
0	0	0
0	1	0
1	0	0
1	1	1

Truth table

Two switches in series with an output device act as the two inputs to an AND gate. Both switches must be ON (1) if the device is to be ON (1).

The NAND gate

The output of the NAND gate is the opposite of an AND gate. You just have to change (invert) the output of an AND gate to get the one for a NAND gate. The symbol is similar to the AND gate except for the small circle or bubble.

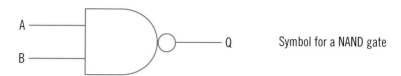

Symbol for a NAND gate

The NAND gate

Input A	Input B	Output Q
0	0	1
0	1	1
1	0	1
1	1	0

Truth table

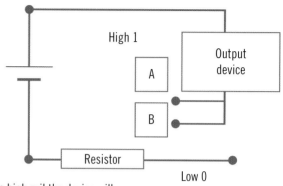

If both points A and B in the circuit are connected to the high rail the device will not turn on. This simulates the last row of the truth table.

The OR gate

The output of the OR gate will be high only if either input A OR input B (or both) are high.

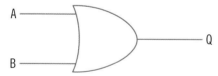

Symbol for an OR gate

The OR gate

Input A	Input B	Output Q
0	0	0
0	1	1
1	0	1
1	1	1

Truth table

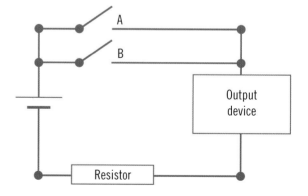

ISBN 9780170227452

The NOR gate

A NOR gate output is the opposite that of an OR gate. The symbol is similar except for the circle or bubble.

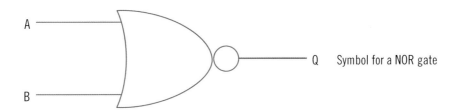

Symbol for a NOR gate

Input A	Input B	Output Q
0	0	1
0	1	0
1	0	0
1	1	0

Truth table

> The NOR gate

The XOR gate (or exclusive OR gate)

The XOR gate is similar to the OR gate except for the bottom row, for which the output is low. This only gives an output when the inputs are different, hence the name exclusive OR (that is, input A or input B).

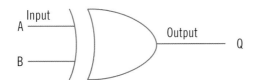

Symbol for an XOR gate

Input A	Input B	Output Q
0	0	0
0	1	1
1	0	1
1	1	0

Truth table

> The XOR gate

Uses of logic gates

Logic gates have many uses because they can combine two (at times more) inputs to give a single output. This means that they control the output. A typical 14-pin DIL (dual in-line) IC chip will contain four identical logic gates. Each gate will have three pins: two for inputs and one for output; therefore, 12 pins in all for the gates. The remaining two pins are used for the power source. Not all the gates in the chip have to be used.

The AND gate as used to control a machine is explained below. A safety system is designed such that a machine is turned off if the operator's face or hand gets too close to a dangerous part of the machinery. An alarm is also sounded.

1 As the face breaks the beam, the output of the sensor goes high (1). This and the output of the machine (1) form the inputs of the AND gate.

2 If they are both high (1), the output of the gate will be high, turning on the alarm and the relay.

3 The relay can then turn the machine off.

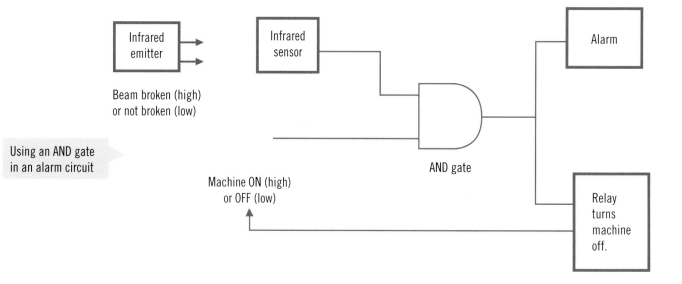

Using an AND gate in an alarm circuit

LEARNING ACTIVITY 5.9

1 Give four examples of digital circuits.

2 Explain the difference between an analogue and a digital signal.

3 What do the letters TTL, CMOS and DIL stand for?

4 List five types of logic gates and draw the symbol for each one.

5 Draw the truth table for a NAND gate.

6 A buzzer (output) needs to sound (high) when a driver leaves the headlights on (input A is high) and turns off the ignition (input B is low). The buzzer should not sound for any other combination of headlight and ignition states. A student suggests that a logic gate circuit using a NAND or a NOR gate will perform the required function. Has the student solved the problem? If not, why not and can you solve the problem? The table below will help you reach a conclusion.

A: Headlight	B: Ignition	Q: Buzzer
Off	Off	
Off	On	
On	Off	
On	On	

ISBN 9780170227452

Designing and modelling systems

There are a number of methods available for building electronic circuits. Three of these will be discussed: breadboards, vero boards and printed circuit boards. Each has its advantages and disadvantages.

Breadboards

Breadboards (also called protoboards) do not involve any soldering. Components are inserted in holes in the board and are easily removed. This technique is very good for testing a circuit as different components can be tried in order to investigate their effects on the performance of the circuit.

The protoboards come in different sizes, but the spacing between the holes is the same. These holes are arranged in a special layout with a set number of holes connected by a copper strip running underneath. It is important to know which holes connect to which and which holes are not connected. Breadboards are good for testing circuits before permanent construction as there is no soldering involved.

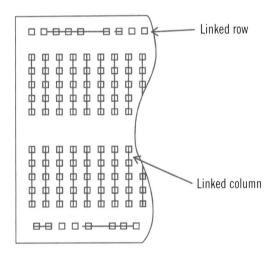

Linked row

Linked column

Part of a breadboard showing the copper strips

Vero (or strip) boards

Circuit boards are used to combine electronic components and connectors together to form a complete circuit. One type is the strip board. These boards are easy to use as no **etching** is involved. Rows of copper tracks are provided and the component leads are simply inserted in selected holes in the track and soldered into place. A track can be split in two by removing the copper around a hole.

- Vero or strip boards are good to use as no etching or milling is involved.

- This method is not suitable for mass production.

- The placement of components and the splitting of tracks need careful thought.

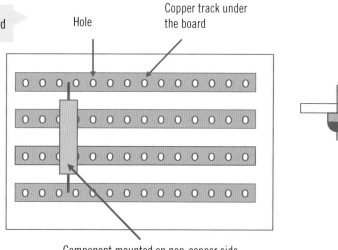

Hole

Copper track under the board

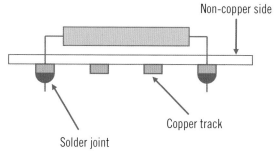

Non-copper side

Copper track

Solder joint

Component mounted on non-copper side

Care when using strip boards

1 Use pliers to bend component leads.

2 Bend the leads along the tracks. This reduces the risk of shorting tracks. The leads can be left at a 45° angle or pinched all the way down.

3 When soldering wires such as battery clip terminals, **tin** the ends before inserting into the holes. 'Tinning' means coating the strands with a small amount of solder. This process keeps the strands together, making it easy to solder onto the copper tracks and prevent shorts.

4 Use pliers as **heat sinks** when soldering to stop the components from overheating.

5 Use a multimeter to check whether tracks are shorting and do this every time you solder a joint rather than at the end. The sharp corner of a small screwdriver can be used to remove any small amount of solder that has joined two tracks.

6 Examine the soldering joints with a magnifying glass.

7 A track can be split into two or more tracks by removing the copper around a hole with a small drill (about 4 mm) turned by hand. Make sure this has been done where necessary. Count how many such disconnections are needed and check before the power is switched on.

Printed circuit boards

A printed circuit board (PCB) is made up of a laminate (an insulating material) that is about 1 mm thick with a very thin layer of copper foil bonded to it. In a single-sided PCB the copper is on one side only. There are also double-sided PCBs, and even multilayered ones made up of as many as 30 layers of copper.

PCBs are ideal if many circuits have to be made. Many components can also be fitted within a small area and the finished product looks good.

Preparing PCBs

PCBs can be prepared in a number of ways. Hand drawing, heat transferring or photo-etching the tracks are the main methods used. Methods using computers and special software are now gaining popularity as they have many advantages. The four steps for producing a board ready for component assembly are:

1 Clean the board with an abrasive cleaner. Wire wool can be used, though this tends to scratch the surface and may damage the copper. Dry the board. Avoid touching the copper to keep it grease-free.

2 Transfer the artwork – the tracks joining the components – to the board.

3 Remove the unwanted copper from the board by chemical etching or by using a milling machine for the computerised method.

4 Drill the holes for the components.

Drawing by hand

Tape the artwork to PCB with some carbon paper in between. Draw pattern with pen or pencil. This need not be very accurate. A copy of the artwork should appear on the copper. If there is no carbon paper, you could drill the holes after taping and draw the tracks with the etch-resist pen by linking the holes.

The advantage of this method is that it is cheap and does not need any expensive equipment.The disadvantage is that fine, thin tracks are difficult to draw and there is always a risk of the ink from the pen joining two tracks or pads (especially the pads needed for integrated circuits).

Heat transfer method

Heat is used to transfer the artwork from paper to the copper. The original artwork needs to be flipped to get a mirror image so that when it is pressed onto the copper and heated, we end up with the original. No etch-resist pen is needed. The process works best if the flipped image is on special paper called TTS paper. TTS stands for toner transfer system. Normal paper tends to burn easily, but TTS paper releases the ink more easily and does not burn readily.

There are many ways you can get a flipped image. You could use computer software to draw the artwork, flip the image and print it. Scanning instead of drawing the artwork is another possibility. Alternatively, some photocopiers will flip the image, or you can photocopy the image on clear acetate and flip it before photocopying it a second time.

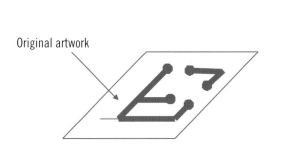

Original artwork

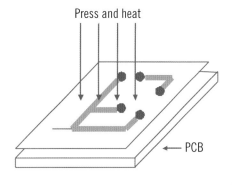

Press and heat

PCB

The heat transfer method

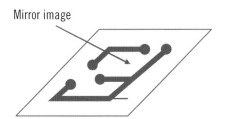

Mirror image

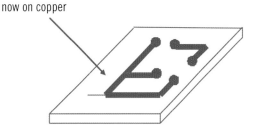

Original artwork now on copper

The flipped artwork needs to be pressed onto the copper and heated so that the ink is transferred to the metal. This can be done using a household iron, but the best results are obtained if the artwork is taped to the PCB and fed through a special heater called a TTS heater. The PCB together with the paper is then soaked in water. When the paper is peeled off slowly the artwork will be seen on the copper.

Advantages of using the head transfer method are:

1 This method produces good results if done properly. It is quick; no wet ink or chemicals are involved.

2 Thin tracks and pads can be transferred without problems. The final appearance is also much better than when using the hand-drawing system.

3 The success of this operation is greatly affected by the kind of printer, photocopier, paper and heating system used.

Photo-etching

In the photo-etching process, no dark ink is used in the transfer of the artwork to the PCB. A chemical replaces the ink. There are two types of photo-etching: positive and negative. In the positive process the original artwork is used; in the negative one, the artwork needs to be reversed so that the dark parts become transparent and vice versa. The chemical solutions used for each are different.

The positive process is simpler. First the artwork pattern is photocopied on a clear acetate sheet as used in overhead projectors. This pattern has to be transferred to the PCB. A special chemical (called positive photo-resist) is sprayed onto the copper side of the PCB and allowed to dry in darkness. The artwork is then placed on the PCB and the lot exposed to ultraviolet light for a set time. The PCB is then soaked in a solution called a developer. After a while the artwork will appear on the copper. Ultraviolet exposure time and developer concentration are given on the containers housing the chemicals.

Advantages of using photo-etching are:

1 Photo-etching is used extensively in industry for mass production of circuit boards.

2 Very fine tracks can be reproduced.

3 The artwork on acetate paper can be used more than once.

Using computer software

There are a number of software packages available that will produce the artwork needed for electronic circuits. The artwork can be printed out and used as described above, or a special milling machine linked to the computer can mill out the tracks. The advantage of this computerised method is that no chemical etching is needed. The tracks can, however, be very close together and care should be taken when soldering to avoid shorting the tracks. Many circuits can be prepared on one large board, which is then cut up.

Advantages of using computer software are:

1 No chemical is used in the preparation of boards, making the whole process very safe.

2 The initial cost of setting up a computerised system with a milling machine needs to be taken into account.

Etching the PCB

Once the artwork has been transferred to the PCB, the unwanted copper has to be removed from the board. This is done by leaving the board in a solution that dissolves copper, a process called etching. Ferric chloride or ammonium persulfate is commonly used. These chemicals need to be treated with care, and skin and eye protection should be used. Etching is not needed if a milling machine is used.

Corrosive chemicals are used in the etching process. The use and disposal of chemicals create safety issues.

Drilling the board

Holes through which the components leads go are drilled using a high-speed drill press fitted with a 0.8 mm or 1 mm drill bit. A few components may require a bigger bit. After drilling, the rim of the holes should be tidied up using a 2–3mm drill bit twisted by hand. This is called de-burring.

Mounting components on boards

The correct placing of components on a board improves the appearance of the final product. This also helps if the circuit does not work and needs to be tested. If you have to bend the leads of a component, you should use pliers to produce a neat 90° bend.

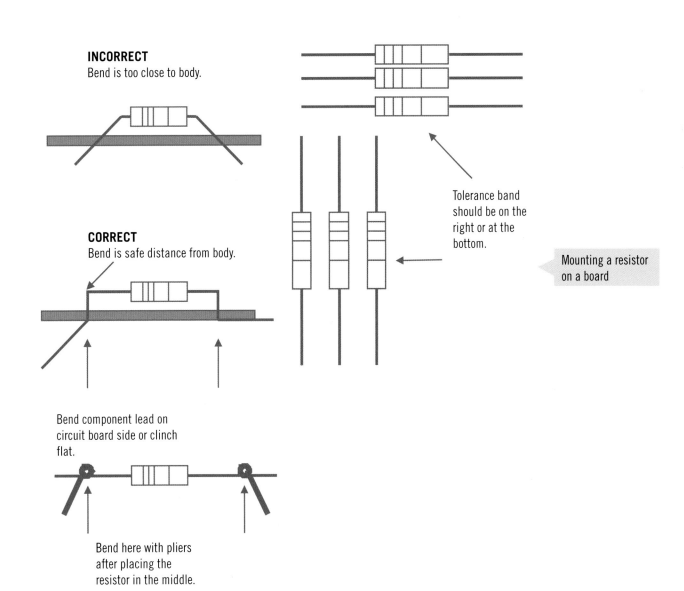

INCORRECT
Bend is too close to body.

CORRECT
Bend is safe distance from body.

Tolerance band should be on the right or at the bottom.

Mounting a resistor on a board

Bend component lead on circuit board side or clinch flat.

Bend here with pliers after placing the resistor in the middle.

Solder and soldering

Solder used in electronics is mainly a mixture of tin (60%) and lead (40%). Lead-free solder is also available. It melts at a higher temperature, but is safer to use. Solder conducts electricity well and melts easily compared with other metals. It is used to join component and terminal leads to copper on the circuit board. A soldering iron is used to melt the solder, which comes in the form of a thin wire.

Safety and care

1 When solder melts, a poisonous gas is released; you should avoid breathing these fumes. Solder in a space that is well ventilated. Do not eat or drink while soldering as the fumes will find an easy path to your lungs.

2 Wash your hands after handling solder wire as it contains lead, which is poisonous. Lead-free solder is available, but is more expensive.

3 The tip of the soldering iron is very hot at about 330°C. Always place the iron in a holder after soldering.

4 Use safety glasses when soldering.

5 Never flick solder from the tip of the iron and do not play around with molten solder.

6 Do not touch the tip to find out if it is hot. You should try to melt some solder. If the solder melts, the iron is hot.

7 Wipe the tip of the iron on a wet sponge to clean it. If the tip (or bit) of the iron is clean, solder does not form into balls but flows freely. The bit should look clean and shiny.

8 Do not use hard abrasives or files to clean the tip.

9 Before putting the iron away, melt a bit of solder onto the tip. This protects the bit and keeps it shiny. Do not clean the tip.

Getting ready for soldering

1 Make sure the copper surface and lead to be joined are clean.

2 Heat the iron. Set the temperature to 330°C if you are using a temperature-controlled one. A higher temperature setting will reduce the life of the bit.

3 Clean the tip by wiping it gently and slowly on a damp sponge.

4 Test for cleanliness by melting some solder. If the solder forms into a ball, repeat the cleaning process until the solder flows well.

Soldering components

1 Place the tip of the iron firmly against the component lead and the copper base.

2 Place a tiny amount of solder at the very tip of the iron to form what is called a heat bridge. The component lead and the copper will heat up more quickly if you do this.

3 Place the end of the solder wire on the copper just where the component lead is. The solder should melt. If it does not, try again. Do not move the iron. When the solder stars melting, apply more around the joint. Do not move the iron.

4 When enough solder has been melted, remove the solder wire and, at the same time, lift the iron tip straight up. Clean the bit if it is dirty and place the iron in the holder.

5 Let the solder joint cool; do not blow on it.

ISBN 9780170227452

Inspecting a solder joint

1 The surface should be clean, smooth and shiny.

2 There should be enough solder around the joint. Too much solder will join up the copper tracks.

3 The joint should not be ball-shaped. Too much solder, a dirty copper surface, a dirty iron tip and inadequate heating will result in a badly soldered joint.

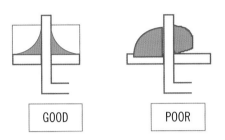

GOOD   POOR

Solder joints

LEARNING ACTIVITY 5.10

1 What are the three methods of preparing PCBs?

2 Draw up a table that outlines the advantages and disadvantages of each method of preparing PCBs.

3 List the four steps required to prepare a PCB ready for the assembly of components.

4 What are the four methods of transferring artwork tracks to a PCB?

5 What is de-burring?

6 Solder is a mixture of which two metals?

7 Write down four safety precautions necessary when soldering.

8 Write down two procedures for keeping a soldering iron in good condition.

9 What is a heat bridge?

10 List the causes of a low-grade soldered joint.

1 List the colours of the following four-band resistors of 5% tolerance.
   a   1.2K
   b   56K
   c   3.3M
   d   12R

2 A student is given two 120 ohm resistors of 5% tolerance. What are the colours of the resistor?

3 What is the total resistance if the two resistors of Question 2 are connected in series?

4 What is the total resistance if the two resistors of Question 2 are connected in parallel?

5 Write down the values for the resistors with the first three colours below.
   a   Yellow white red
   b   Brown green orange

6 Write down the value and tolerance of the capacitors with the following markings.
   a   102J
   b   472K

7 Calculate the total capacitance of the following electrolytic capacitors.
   a   Two 33 μF capacitors in parallel
   b   Two 100 μF capacitors in series

8 Which type of semiconductor makes a good temperature sensor and why?

9 Use words and diagrams to explain the difference between a forward-biased diode and a reverse-biased one.

10 Explain how you would identify the negative terminal of the following components.
   a   An LED
   b   A diode
   c   A polarised capacitor

11 Draw the symbols for a PNP and an NPN transistor.

12 Explain the conditions for a transistor to act as:
   a   an off switch
   b   an on switch.

13 State the input and the output of a transistor that is used as an amplifier.

14 Draw the pin layout for a 14-pin integrated circuit. Indicate all the pin numbers.

15 Explain the input, output and process of the following transducers.
   a   Loudspeaker
   b   Electric motor
   c   Microphone

16 What type of sensor would you select in the following situations?
   a   An alarm sounds when a burglar opens a door
   b   A buzzer sounds when an appliance tips over
   c   A buzzer sounds when a car engine overheats

17 Using words and diagrams, explain how a relay switch works.

18 Outline one application of a relay switch.

19 Draw a circuit diagram to show how a DPDT switch can be used to reverse the rotation of a motor.

20 Work out the voltage available if three 1.5 volt batteries are connected:
   a   in series
   b   in parallel.
21 What is the main advantage of connecting batteries in parallel?
22 A lithium ion battery used in a video camera has a 1.5 amp-hour capacity. How long can the camera operate before the battery goes completely flat?
23 Use Ohm's law to work out the current in a circuit in which a 12 ohm resistor is connected to a 24 volt battery.
24 Calculate the power supplied by the battery in Question **23**.
25 Calculate the total resistance and the current in a circuit in which two 5 ohm resistors are connected in series to a power supply of 10 volts.
   a   What will be the voltage across each resistor?
   b   Calculate the power delivered by the battery and that used by each resistor.
26 a   What would be the total resistance and the current from the power supply if the resistors in Question **25** were connected in parallel to the same battery?
   b   Calculate the power delivered by the battery and that used by each resistor.
27 Draw the symbol and the truth table for the following logic gates.
   a   OR gate
   b   AND gate
   c   NOR gate
   d   XOR gate
28 You have two push-button switches, A and B, and a red LED. Draw a system using a logic gate where the LED will light up if either A or B is pressed, but not both at the same time.
29 What will happen if a NOT gate is placed just before the LED in your answer to Question **28**?
30 List all the safety precautions and care needed when soldering components.
31 List the correct sequence required when soldering.

6

INTEGRATED AND DIGITAL MANUFACTURING

In this chapter you will learn about digital manufacturing and the processes used to achieve it. Terminology such as computer numerical control, computer-aided manufacture, computer-aided design will also be discussed and explained. Common industrial machines such as numerically controlled lathe, mill/router, laser cutter and 3D printer will play a key part in this chapter and provide students with the underpinning knowledge required to understand key concepts.

Early manufacturing

For as long as humans have been on Earth, they have been on a quest to improve the manufacturing process. Archaeological discoveries about early humans give credence to this claim; for example, crude tools and implements made from earthly raw materials were ingenious solutions to basic problems. Humans were soon using simple machines to erect stone monuments. However, it wasn't until the Industrial Revolution in the 1800s that this manufacturing quest grew exponentially: they were now able to use machinery such as lathes and mills to manufacture parts and products from refined and processed materials.

This mechanised method of manufacturing continued into the 1900s. Although the manufacturing processes and equipment became refined over time, it was evident that the effort to produce many of these products required repetitious human input that was susceptible to human error and inconsistencies. During the 1950s a new method of manufacturing was conceived and eventually led to the birth of the digital manufacturing process.

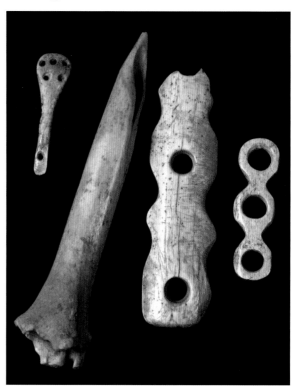

Corbis/Nathan Benn/Ottochrome

ISBN 9780170227452

1 Use the Internet to research the Industrial Revolution.

2 Write a one-paragraph summary that outlines the key points of your findings.

Digital manufacturing

Digital manufacturing, or computer-aided manufacturing (CAM) as it is known in industry, is the making of parts and products using a computer process. Many of the early CAM machines were just ordinary machines connected to a computer and driven by servo motors. Today's modern computer numerical control (CNC) machines are a far cry from their predecessors. These are now purpose-built machines that use movement produced from stepper motors to perform specific tasks such as high-end turning and milling operations.

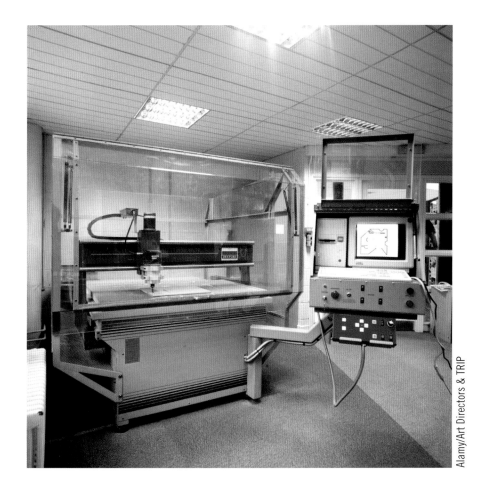

A flatbed CNC 3-axis router

Alamy/Art Directors & TRIP

A multicam router is a CNC machine that is capable of accommodating a full-size 2400 mm × 1200 mm timber sheet on its work table. Tiny holes on its table allow for a vacuum to secure the sheet while machining. The three-phase electric motor attached to the cutting head has an impressive 3 kW of power. These and similar CNC machines are now being used in some Victorian schools. However, the majority are commissioned to cut out flat pack kitchens in cabinet-making businesses across Australia.

LEARNING ACTIVITY 6.2

CNC machines have made a considerable impact on the Australian manufacturing sector. Write a brief statement that argues the pros and cons of the use of these machines within our industry sectors.

CNC machines

CNC machines work by having a computer connected to a control box, which is then connected to the axes' **stepper motors**. The computer sends coded information to the control box where it is processed and converted. The control box sends this converted information as an output voltage to the stepper motors on the **axes**, which facilitates movement in the X, Y or Z planes.

CNC block diagram

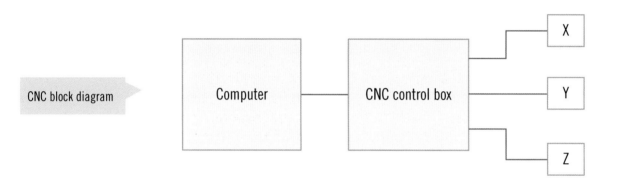

CNC machines operate through machine language known as 'G' and 'M' codes. The G codes instruct the cutting tool where to move, how fast to move and along what path to move. M codes operate machine functions, such as instructing the spindle motor to turn clockwise or anticlockwise or to turn the coolant pump off or on. Using this machine language an operator can write his or her own program by entering the specific G and M codes directly into the machine. The codes are compiled and the machine cycle is started.

Manual programming like this requires a complex level of machine language understanding and can be an arduous task. Commonly today most machining programs are generated by CAM software packages that can output the file directly to the CNC machine. This is known as **post-processing**.

The CNC machine works by means of travelling axes that are driven by stepper motors. Stepper motors differ from conventional electric motors: they move their output shaft in any direction, at variable speeds, with small or large increments. Most CNC machines have a separate stepper motor attached to each moving axis.

For example, the CNC lathe diagram below shows two axes of numerical control. The 'X' axis moves the cutting tool at right angles to the chuck, which determines the depth of cut. The 'Z' axis moves the cutting tool parallel to the chuck and this determines the length of cut.

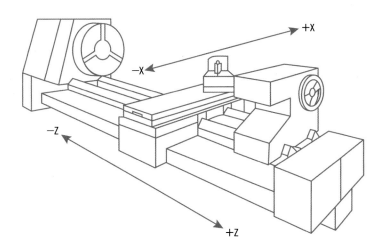

CNC lathe

The CNC mill diagram differs from that of a lathe. This machine has a minimum of three axes of numerical control. The 'X' axis controls the cutter in the left and right horizontal plane, the 'Y' axis controls the cutter in the forward and back horizontal plane and the 'Z' axis controls the cutter in the vertical plane. Simply put, the computer software uses the G and M codes to plot points on the machine's bed similar to plotting X and Y points on a graph. These codes direct the cutting tool to move in the direction required to produce the desired part.

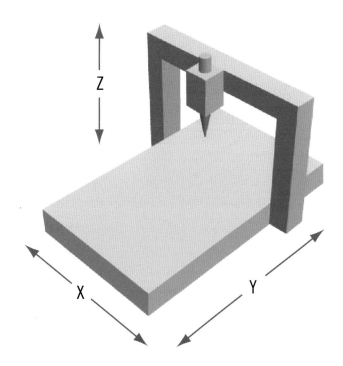

A CNC mill illustration showing axes direction

LEARNING ACTIVITY 6.3

Copy the IPO diagram below into your student workbook. Complete it by stating the input, process and output of a CNC machine.

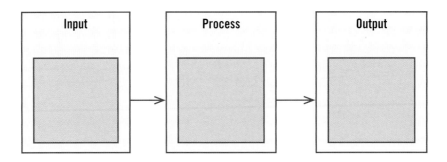

CNC language

As mentioned, CNC machines rely on machine language known as G and M codes to operate. On the next page is a sample code that was written by CAM software and post-processed. The program was used on a CNC router to cut out a small square piece of MDF material. The bed of the machine is shown in grid form that is 55 mm × 55 mm, and the part is shown as a simple square located within the grid with a material size of 50 mm × 50 mm × 3 mm. The cutting tool has a diameter of 3 mm and will cut outside of the line. Notice that the code is in bold text and the explanation is in italics.

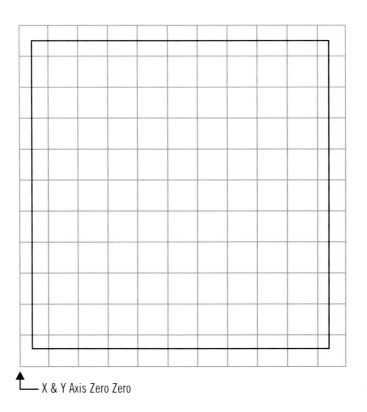

X & Y Axis Zero Zero

Sample NC program

```
G97 (constant spindle speed)
T1 (Tool 1)
G0 Z20.0000 (rapid position z-axis 20 mm above material)
G0 X0.0000 Y0.0000 S10000 M03 (rapid position x- and y-axis to zero-
zero, spindle 10000 rpm clockwise rotation)
G0 X1.0000 Y2.5000 Z6.0000 (rapid position x-axis 1 mm and y-axis 2.5 mm
in, move z-axis 6 mm above material)
G1 Z-3.0000 F100.0 (linear movement z-axis to 3 mm below material at 100 mm/s
feed rate)
G3 X2.5000 Y1.0000 I2.5000 J2.5000 F500.0 (interpolation counterclockwise
movement)
G1 X52.5000 (linear movement of x-axis to 52.5 mm)
G3 X54.0000 Y2.5000 I52.5000 J2.5000 (interpolation counterclockwise
movement)
G1 Y52.5000 (linear movement of the y-axis to 52.5 mm)
G3 X52.5000 Y54.0000 I52.5000 J52.5000 (interpolation counterclockwise
movement)
G1 X2.5000 (linear movement of the x-axis to 2.5 mm)
G3 X1.0000 Y52.5000 I2.5000 J52.5000 (interpolation counterclockwise movement)
G1 Y2.5000 (linear movement of y-axis to 2.5 mm)
G0 Z6.0000 (rapid position of z-axis to 6 mm above material)
G0 Z20.0000 (rapid position of z-axis to 20 mm above material)
G0 X0.0000 Y0.0000 (rapid position of x- and y-axes to the zero-zero
position)
M30 (end of program return to program top)
```

LEARNING ACTIVITY 6.4

1 Use the Internet to search for the following codes 'G50', 'G28' and 'M30'.

2 Write a sentence on each code that explains what it means.

Why CNC machines are used

The threaded tapered shaft shown is a good example of why you could or should use a CNC process. The shaft itself is not that complex as it consists of two parallel turned sections: one tapered turned section and a threaded end. If you had to make only one of these, you would probably do it manually on the lathe. Working from the engineering drawing, the required material would be selected and secured in the lathe's chuck. With the correct speed and feed rates the operator would face, counter-sink and secure the end by the **tail stock** with a **live centre**. The material would be roughed down to size on both parallel sections and finished to the required outside diameters. The compound slide would be offset to the correct angle and the taper would be machined. Finally, the thread could be cut with **threading die** or with a thread tool on the lathe and the shaft cut to the correct length.

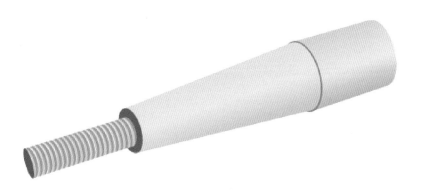

Threaded tapered shaft

The above description sounds relatively easy, but this simple part is not that simple to produce. Making this as a one-off item would take a competent machinist approximately 30 minutes on the lathe. Furthermore, chances are the finished part would not be 100% accurate as this is solely dependent on the skill level of the operator. If the same machinist machined 1000 of these parts manually, the probability of success would be low and the error rate would be high.

The advantage of digital manufacturing is that each part you machine is identical to the one before it. Once programmed, a CNC machine does not necessarily require a qualified machinist to operate it and such a machine can be operated by a trained worker. CNC machines are commonly used in high-end machining processes where multiple products are required. Another advantage of CNC machines is that they are similar to robots. That is, they do not get tired, sick or lose their concentration, nor do they require meal or restroom breaks.

Types of CNC machines

CNC laser

A CNC laser is a versatile machine that can be used to engrave text and images or cut out complex shapes and parts. A CNC laser is a 'non-contact' type of machine as it has no physical contact with the material that it is cutting or engraving. It does this by creating an infra-red laser beam within a CO_2 tube. This tube emits an infra-red light beam which is then focused through a **parabolic lens**. This lens concentrates the beam, allowing it to penetrate most things it is focused on. The power output of the beam determines whether it cuts through the material or engraves onto the surface that it is focused on. For example, a small hand-held laser pointer has an operating power of approximately 300 mW. In contrast, the laser machine used to cut out the blue 3 mm acrylic robot parts below operates at between 30 W and 60 W power.

A CNC laser machine

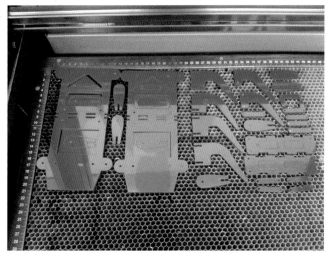

CNC laser-cut robot parts

CNC 3D printer

A 3D printer can produce three-dimensional solid models from a computer file. These types of CNC machines are used extensively for rapid prototyping on a small scale and are not usually used for large production runs. Three-dimensional printing machines usually work by an additive process. That is, material is constantly added to a surface at the exact coordinates to build the model up slowly over time (with multiple passes).

There are many different types of 3D printers on the market. Some of these work by laying down a special powder and adding an adhesive at the specific time. Others work by extruding melted plastic out of a nozzle like a hot glue gun. A common 3D printer used in many secondary schools is the small UP! Printer. It can make 3D parts or models to any size within a 140 mm sided cube.

D UP! printer

3D UP! printer in action

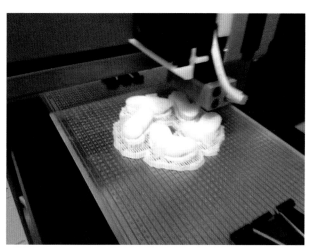

CNC lathe

Just like a conventional lathe, a CNC lathe is used to make precision-machined items. CNC lathes are used extensively in industry for the machining of parts that require a high degree of accuracy or mass quantities. A lathe differs from other machines because it turns the product, and the stationary cutting tool is moved to obtain the desired shape. In a basic two-axis CNC lathe, one stepper motor is attached to the longitudinal feed to control the 'Z' axis and another stepper motor is attached to the cross feed, which controls the 'X' axis. The CNC program determines the single or combined use of the axes to obtain the desired shape of the product. CNC lathes are used to produce many items, such as radio control hobby parts, automotive accessories and even military munitions.

HAAS CNC lathe

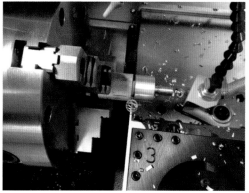

HAAS CNC lathe in action

CNC mill and router

CNC milling and routing machines are almost similar in nature, as they both have a minimum of three numerical axes of control in the X, Y and Z planes. By nature, a CNC router usually has a larger working area (bed size) than that of a CNC mill. However, both are capable of two- and three-dimensional milling. Therefore this process of CNC manufacturing has its advantages over laser and plasma cutting as it allows for the creation of three-dimensional products. In contrast to 3D printing, a CNC mill operates via a **subtractive process**. That is, it removes the material from a solid piece until the desired outcome is achieved. Some CNC milling machines like the Roland MDX540 have a provision for a revolving fourth axis. This 'A' axis allows the mill to make round and intricate objects like those made on a CNC lathe.

A CNC milling machine

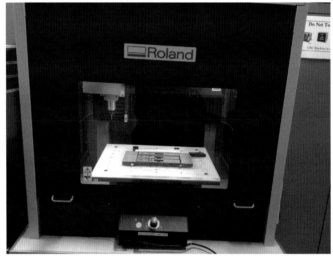

CNC plasma machine

CNC plasma cutter

A CNC plasma cutter is similar to a CNC router. However, most only have numerical control in the X and Y axes. Plasma cutters are predominantly used for cutting sheet metals of various thicknesses. They can cut mild steel, stainless steel, brass and even aluminium. Some machines have a dedicated plasma head attached or use an externally mounted plasma torch.

The plasma cutting process is simple. An electric arc is initiated by the torch within an inert gas. The arc is hot enough to heat the material red hot. A high-pressure blast of compressed air is focused on the heated area, causing it to melt and be blown away.

ISBN 9780170227452

Shutterstock.com/xtrekx

CNC plasma
cutting in action

Computer-aided design

Computer-aided design (CAD) allows the drafting of drawings via a computer, an idea that was originally conceived during the 1960s. Before the invention of CAD, all technical drawings were laboriously drawn by hand using pencil and ink. Any pencil or ink mistakes made by the draftsperson had to be rubbed out with an eraser or skilfully scratched off the paper with a scalpel blade. In contrast, any mistakes or amendments required to the CAD drawing can be simply selected with the mouse, and then altered or deleted.

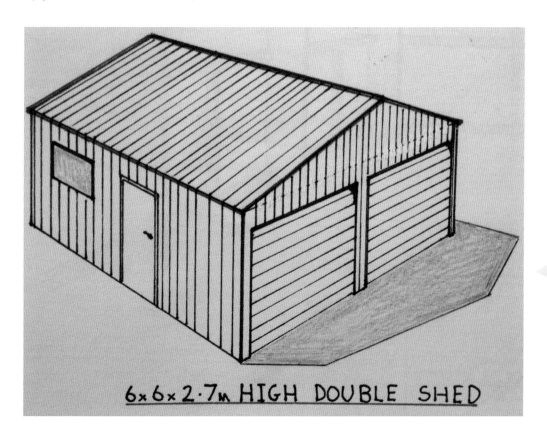

Hand-drawn
perspective drawing

A key advantage of CAD over traditional hand drawings are its ability to save, scale, and print or plot the final design. As the CAD file is saved to the computer's hard drive in digital format, it can be reproduced over and over without distortion or loss of clarity.

Another advantage is its capacity to create and produce the item via a rapid prototyping process from the drawing file. These files can be exported in **DXF** or **STL** format. DXF stands for drawing exchange format and is used to exchange (share) drawings files across different CAD–CAM systems. STL stands for stereolithography; these types of files are more commonly used to create three-dimensional shapes in the 3D milling or 3D modelling production process. Although not entirely correct, it is easy to associate the use of DXF files with producing 2D shapes and STL file use with the production of 3D shapes.

Types of CAD

There are many different types and brands of CAD programs on offer in the marketplace. Some programs offer 3D (solid modelling) capabilities, whereas others still adhere to the traditional 2D drawing format. Either way, these programs offer powerful solutions to rapid prototyping and provide the end user with the unique ability to manufacture using CAD–CAM.

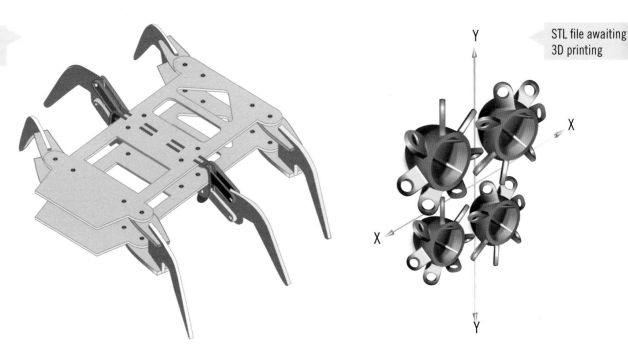

3D CAD view of a hexapod

STL file awaiting 3D printing

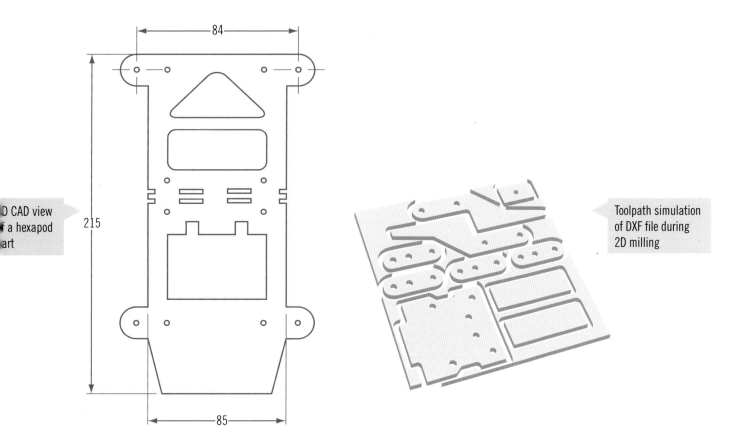

D CAD view
 a hexapod
 art

Toolpath simulation
of DXF file during
2D milling

CAD for electronics

Another typical example of CAD drawing, especially within the subject area of systems,
is that of designing and producing your own electronic printed circuit boards. The idea of
using CAD in the creation of electronic circuits is rather special as it allows the user to
design, simulate and produce a functioning printed circuit board (PCB). This idea of
manufacturing in CAD supports the principles of '**lean manufacturing**'. That is, it
minimises lost time, effort, waste and errors as the design can be thoroughly tested
before the product is made. The examples on the next page highlight one student's ability to
produce a PCB from schematic design, to the artwork and computerised milling of her
circuit board.

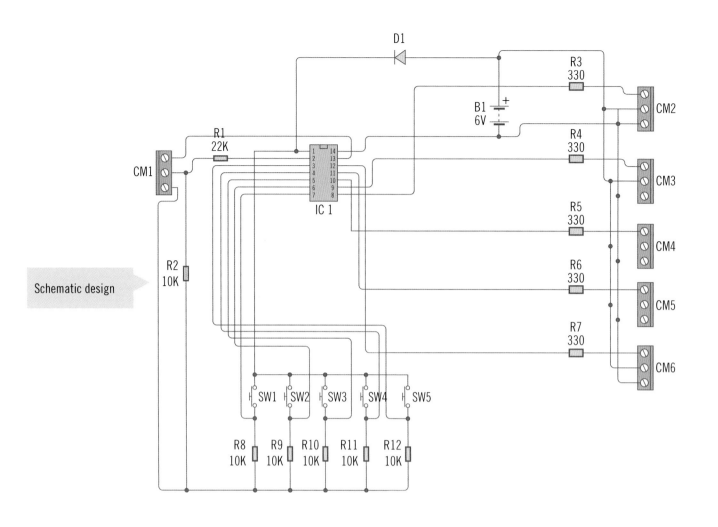

Schematic design

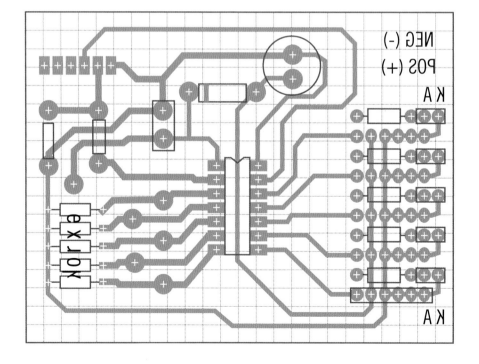

PCB artwork

ISBN 9780170227452

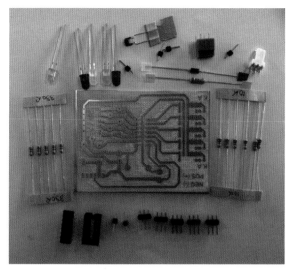

CNC milled circuit board

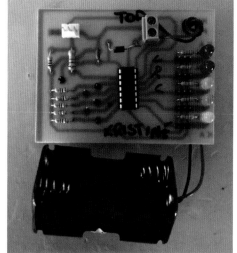

Finished PCB

Electronics design with CAD

The process of designing your own PCB with CAD is relatively easy. The first step is to research your design and to ascertain what electronics parts you will require. It is also very important to check the data sheet of your electronic components to ensure they are used within their correct parameters.

The steps below highlight the design process of a small continuity tester.

1   Import your electronic components one at a time into the design screen. When all of your parts have been imported, join the components as required. Although you can design in elementary form, it is strongly recommended that you use schematic symbols as this is industry standard.

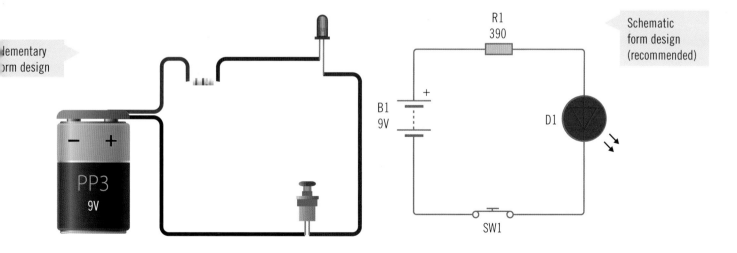

Elementary form design

Schematic form design (recommended)

2 Simulate your design to ensure your components are connected correctly and that you have selected the correct values for your circuit design. In the design below you can see that the simulation has blown the LED. This was caused by excessive current due to the selection of the incorrect resistor value.

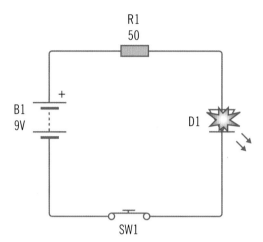

3 Most electronic CAD packages, such as Circuit Wizard, will provide auto-routing and nesting of your components. This feature creates your PCB and helps with the alignment of all components. This layout is not final as components can be moved manually if required.

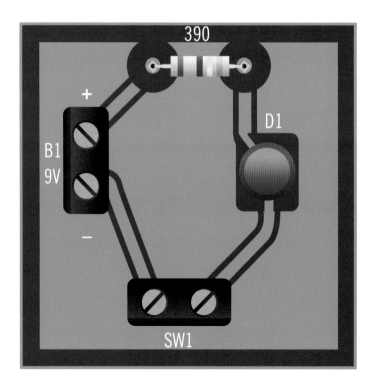

4 After the PCB is created it is possible to obtain the artwork. The artwork is required to create your printed circuit board. This can be done either via a traditional chemical etching method, or by exporting the CAD–CAM data and engraving your board by means of a subtractive process on a CNC mill.

PCB artwork circuit simulation

The Roland CNC mill will machine your PCB.

Weblinks

Educational CNC machines: www.intellecta.com.au

Roland CNC machines: www.rolanddg.com.au

CNC user forum: www.cnczone.com

HAAS Automation: www.haascnc.com

END-OF-CHAPTER ACTIVITIES

1 What do each of the following acronyms and abbreviations mean?

   a   CAD

   b   CAM

   c   CNC

   d   NC

   e   PCB

2 List three different advantages of using a CNC process over a manual machining process.

3 Draw a block diagram that depicts a CNC milling machine equipped with a fourth axis.

4 Compare and contrast the differences between G codes and M codes.

5 Using your own words, explain each of the following components and briefly describe their purpose.

   a   Personal computer

   b   Computer numerical control box

   c   Stepper motors

   d   Travelling axes

6 Describe the DXF and STL file types and explain where they would most likely be used.

7 Define the subtractive and additive production methods and provide an example of each.

8 Compare and contrast the differences between laser cutting and plasma cutting.

9 What are some of the advantages of designing with CAD?

10 What are the key differences between a CNC mill and a CNC lathe?

11 In your own words, explain the rapid prototyping process.

12 In regard to PCB design, explain the differences between elementary and schematic design.

13 State the advantages and disadvantages of 3D printing.

7

INTEGRATED CONTROL SYSTEMS

This chapter will outline control systems and their application within contemporary society. By reading this chapter you will learn about the different types of control systems and how each is specific to a particular application. A key focus of this chapter is logic controllers and radio control apparatuses. The chapter will further investigate microcontrollers and provide some practical examples of their use within systems projects.

Control

Since the advent of mechanisation, humans have continually sought out and invented different methods of controlling their creations. Control systems, as they are now known, are devices or sets of devices that can directly affect the behaviour of the system. That is, they manage or manipulate an output through direct, predetermined or programmed instruction.

Nowadays, control technologies are a 'quantum leap' ahead of the early generations of control in the late 19th and 20th centuries. Nikola Tesla was one of those early pioneers; in the 1890s, he invented a method of remote controlling a small model boat by sending a signal across the radio waves. This crude method of control is one of the earliest forms of radio control and remained a passion of Tesla's up until the First World War.

Since these early and humble beginnings, control systems have continued to propagate and are now widespread among the community and across the globe. Controlling a system remotely or autonomously can be achieved by numerous methods, such as radio control, infra-red control and/or logic control. Control systems are used extensively in military, industry, home entertainment, recreational and hobby applications.

Military

Today's modern military has an insatiable appetite for control systems within their diverse arsenal range. Control systems allow the military to operate specialised equipment in high risk environments without placing defence force personnel at risk. Some of this specialised equipment includes bomb disposal robots and unmanned aerial vehicles which are controlled by radio and logic control systems.

The Heron unmanned aerial vehicle (UAV) was designed and produced by Israel Aerospace Industries and is predominantly used for surveillance over land and sea. The Heron is capable of being armed, but is usually used for its modular radar, sensors and electronic intelligence packages. The Heron currently provides air support to Australian troops deployed in Afghanistan.

The Heron unmanned aviation vehicle (UAV)

The Echidna MK1 is an Australian-made 280 kg explosive ordinance demolition robot (EODR). Originally built in 1989, these robots have seen service with the Australian Defence Force and the Victorian Police. Dubbed 'Eric' by the Victorian police service, their robot was capable of being armed with a shotgun and once successfully disarmed an armed gunman without exposing the police officers to risk. Eric is now on display at the Victorian Police Museum.

The Echidna MK1 (EODR)

Industry

Automated control systems are used throughout industry. Commonly referred to as PLCs (programmable logic controllers), they allow for semi- or full automatic control of equipment, machinery, production lines and amusement park rides. The PLCs are responsible for monitoring the process and feedback of the system and have a vast array of input and output arrangements. Coupled to a personal computer, they provide a superior method of automated control that provides trouble-free operation to the system they are controlling.

Dreamworld's Wipeout amusement park ride was built by Netherlands' ride manufacturer Verkoma and was first commissioned in 1993. The Wipeout uses a PLC to control the huge arms that are responsible for spinning and flipping the 40-seat gondola through various pre-programmed routines. The PLC controls everything from the seat and lap bar harnesses, speed and direction of the electric motors, to the operation of the hydraulic harnesses and walkways. Some safety features of the PLC program ensure that the cycle will not start until all harnesses are in the closed position and the walkways are fully retracted.

Wipeout amusement ride

Getty Images

Home entertainment

The home entertainment scene largely comprises televisions, DVD and video players, stereo systems and portable media devices. These are all predominantly controlled by an infra-red remote controller. These small inexpensive devices offer a wide range of control of volume, channel change and other operational adjustments by sending from the transmitter an infra-red light signal, which is received by the infra-red receiver on the device.

The in-car iPod dock provides a simple solution for people who wish to listen to music from their iPod in a vehicle that does not offer iPod connectivity. A small digital transmitter connects to the iPod, and the cigarette socket adapter offers a continual power supply to the device. The iPod's music is transmitted over the FM band wave and is received on a normal car radio on a preset channel.

In-car iPod dock with infra-red remote control

Recreation and hobbies

Commercially available radio control systems have been available since the early 1950s. Although these early controllers were crude and bulky they offered a method of control by the operator to at least one axis on the model. Today, most radio control units offer four to 14 channels of control. For example, a radio controlled helicopter requires a minimum of five channels of operation: throttle, collective pitch, elevator, aileron and rudder.

Today's radio control market offers an extensive range of models and products that are available to the hobbyist or consumers alike. Radio controlled helicopters are a niche market and have evolved immensely over the years. The Align range of electric helicopters is an example of this; they offer a huge power-to-weight ratio thanks to the advancement in lithium–polymer battery and brushless motor technologies.

ISBN 9780170227452

Development

Control systems owe their development to the evolution of electronic components and advancement in computing power. Australia's first computer was built in 1947 by CSIRO under contract from the Commonwealth Government. Named CSIRAC, this goliath mainframe computer weighed 2500 kg and was only the fourth computer in the world. Its massive size took up an entire floor and consumed 30 000 W of power. CSIRAC used 2000 thermionic valves (vacuum tubes) and had a processing speed of 500–1000 Hz. In contrast, today's modern computers have a processing speed of 2000 million Hz, weigh only 2 kg and have a microchip that is equivalent to tens of millions of valves.

The images below highlight the evolution of the valve. A valve is a form of electronic switch. In most cases, thermionic valves have been replaced by solid state devices, such as transistors and other semiconductor devices like the microchip.

From left to right: Shutterstock.com/ Arturo Limon; Shutterstock.com/Stu49; Shutterstock.com/Garsya

Thermionic valve, transistor and microchip

1 Look around your classroom and workshop and identify the apparatuses that use a control system to operate or function. List these in your workbook and explain the type of control they use.

2 Research Nikola Tesla and write a paragraph that defines the man and outlines some of his main achievements in his working life.

3 The Heron UAV is a complex integrated system. Identify and list as many systems and subsystems you can in this unmanned aerial vehicle.

4 Use the Internet to research infra-red signal. Write a brief paragraph that explains this.

5 a Working in small groups, discuss the control systems required to operate a bomb disposal robot and write these into your notebook.

b Have a brief peer discussion, and choose one system from your list and complete an IPO diagram to explain it. Ensure you include the feedback loop.

Logic control

A logic controller is a computer (digital apparatus) used to monitor the inputs and control the outputs of an integrated system. The two most common types of logic controllers are PLCs and microcontrollers.

Programmable logic controllers

Programmable logic controllers (PLCs) are used extensively in industry applications for automating the control of electromechanical processes such as production lines, assembly lines, amusement rides and buildings. In simple terms, a PLC is a specialised computer that uses non-volatile memory, and is resistant to heat, vibrations and noise. A normal desktop computer connects to the PLC, which allows the operator to write, simulate, run and save his or her desired program. The PLC unit has numerous input and output connections capable of handling digital and analogue signals. The PLC inputs accept a wide range of sensors such as thermocouples and pressure and flow meters that allow for monitoring of the system. The PLC outputs control the operation of output devices, such as relays, electric motors, hydraulic or pneumatic devices.

A programmable logic controller

iStockphoto/Gianni Furlan

Microcontrollers

Microcontrollers, or PICs (programmable interface controllers) as they are commonly known, are small digital integrated circuit chips that are used by industry and hobbyists alike. A microcontroller is a computer on a chip, and is capable of storing and processing data in its memory. Microcontrollers have input and output connections and can be programmed to carry out a vast range of tasks, from flashing LEDs to operating autonomous robots. Outside of hobby and educational applications, microcontrollers are used in everyday items, like microwave ovens and automotive engine control systems.

Many different brands of microcontrollers are on the market. Some of the common types of microcontrollers used for educational purposes within Australian schools are discussed briefly below.

PICAXE® is a low-cost and easy-to-program microcontroller. Originally designed in the United Kingdom for educational purposes, these 'micros' are designed to be the brain of your electronic or integrated system project. Hundreds of thousands of PICAXE micros have been sold and many are widely used by electronics enthusiasts around the world. PICAXE microcontrollers come in variety of sizes: 8, 14, 18, 20, 28 and 40 pin micros.

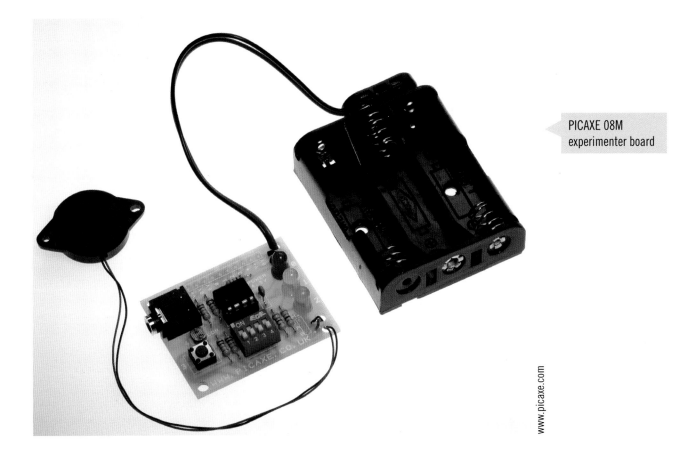

PICAXE 08M
experimenter board

www.picaxe.com

GENIE® is another low-cost microcontroller designed exclusively for educational purposes by New Wave Concepts. The flagship of New Wave Concepts is their circuit design and simulation software called 'Circuit Wizard'. The GENIE microcontroller was designed exclusively for Circuit Wizard and the software is capable of designing, simulating and programming GENIE microcontrollers.

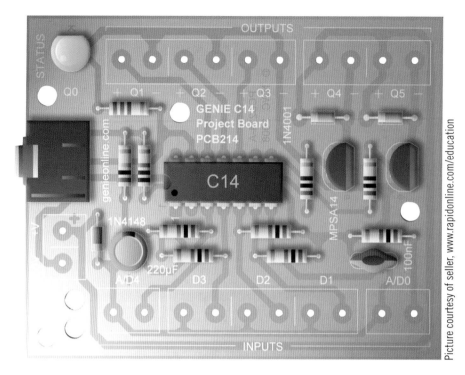

GENIE C14 board

Parallax® is a private company situated in the United States that designs, manufactures and sells BASIC stamp microcontrollers. Parallax offers user-friendly and high-quality kits to hobbyists and educational institutions. Many schools in the United States use these microcontrollers to deliver STEM (science, technology, engineering and mathematics) across the curriculum. Parallax offers a wide range of accessories such as ultrasonic sensors that can be used to expand the capabilities of its microcontroller. Many of these are also compatible with other microcontrollers on the market.

Parallax propeller demonstration board

ISBN 9780170227452

Arduino® is an open-source electronics prototyping platform based on flexible, easy-to-use hardware and software. It's intended for artists, designers, hobbyists and anyone interested in creating interactive objects or environments.

Photo courtesy of © Circuits@Home 2006–2012

Arduino UNO board

Atmel® microcontrollers are high-end, industry-standard chips. Commonly used in the automotive and appliance sectors, these 8–32 bit microcontrollers deliver a unique combination of power, performance and design flexibility. Atmel microcontrollers are extensively used in the TAFE and university institutions to teach microcontroller programming within certificate and degree programs.

PIC application and use

Example 1: flash LED

A schematic diagram of the PICAXE-08M experimenter board is presented below. Notice that pin 7 is output '0' (red LED), pin 6 is output '1' (yellow LED) and pin 5 is output '2' (green LED and piezo speaker).

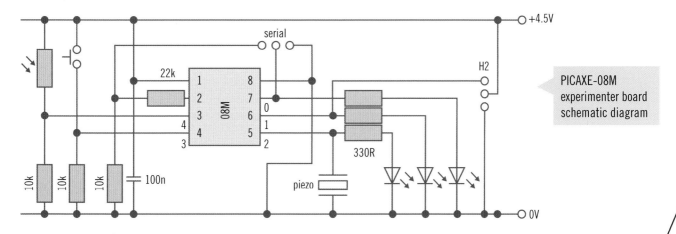

PICAXE-08M experimenter board schematic diagram

There are two methods of programming the chip via the PICAXE programming editor: 'basic' and 'flow chart'. When programming it is important to remember that a 'high' command represents 'on' and that a 'low' command represents 'off'. The pause command tells the microchip to halt in milliseconds. For example, 1000 milliseconds are equal to 1 second.

This program instructs output 2 to go high and low every 500 milliseconds (half a second), causing the LED to flash on and off. Because the LED shares the same circuit as the piezo speaker, a ticking sound will also be emitted.

PICAXE programming editor

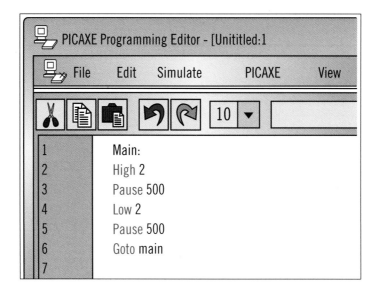

Example 2: turn LED on via an LDR input

The program on the right has been written in flow chart form. Many students find the flow chart method of programming easier as very little prior programming knowledge is required. Furthermore, the information is depicted graphically rather than in text form.

The PICAXE program editor is capable of converting the flow chart program into basic. However, it is not possible to go from basic to flow chart.

If you focus your attention to the schematic diagram on page 201, you will notice that a light-dependent resistor is connected to input 4, which is pin 3.

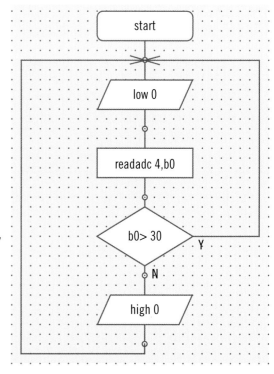

This program instructs the red LED to remain off while the light valve of the analogue LDR sensor on input 4 is greater than a value of 30. If the light drops below this valve the red LED will be instructed to turn on.

Example 3: hexapod

The hexapod robot shown below is a six-legged walker that is capable of forward, reverse and turning motions. Leg movement is facilitated via the application of three radio control servo motors. The left legs on the front and rear are controlled by the left servo motor; the right legs on the front and rear are controlled by the right servo motor; and both centre legs are operated by the centre servo motor.

Hexapod robot

Radio controlled servo motor

Alamy/© David J. Green – technology

The movement is similar to that of a soldier crawling along the ground. The centre leg lifts one side of the body up, allowing the raised side legs to swing forwards, but at the same time the opposite legs drag the body forwards or back.

The PICAXE 08M UniBoard™ microcontroller was selected to operate and control the integrated system due to its low cost, ease of construction and simple programming. Although similar in appearance to the experimenter board, the UniBoard™ has the added feature of being able to switch 6V DC, which can drive a motor directly. The 8-pin 08M chip is the smallest in the PICAXE series; with 256 bytes of memory, it is capable of 80 lines of code. This PIC has a total of five I/O (input–output) pins.

PICAXE-08M
uniboard

The PICAXE footprint highlights the 8-pin chip and alphanumerically depicts where each pin is connected. This will be explained below; however, keep in mind that the schematic diagram needs to be used in conjunction with this if you are designing and building your own circuit as electronic components such as resistors and diodes are also required.

```
+V        1        8    0 V
Serial in 2        7    Out0 / Serial out
In4 / Out4 / ADC4 3  6  In1 / Out1 / ADC1
In3 / Infrain 4    5    In2 / Out2 / ADC2
```

PICAXE 08M chip footprint

- Pin 1: connected to positive battery voltage

- Pin 2: programming lead input

- Pin 3: (input 4) micro switch

- Pin 4: (input 3) infra-red receiver for remote control

- Pin 5: (output 2) connected to right servo legs

- Pin 6: (output 1) connected to left servo legs

- Pin 7: (output 0) connected to centre servo legs

- Pin 8: connected to negative battery voltage

Two programming examples of the PICAXE-08M chip have been provided below. The text variety is known as 'basic' and the other is called 'flow chart'. The chip is capable of controlling radio controlled servo motors as it can output a pulse from 0.75 to 2.25 milliseconds. The RC servo has three wires attached to it: red, brown and orange. The red wire attaches to positive 6 V DC, the brown wire connects to negative 6 V DC and the orange wire is the signal wire that connects to outputs 0, 1 or 2. A low-millisecond pulse sends the servo horn anticlockwise and a high-millisecond pulse sends the servo clockwise.

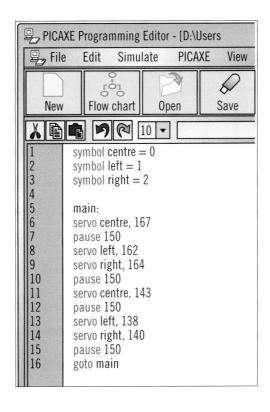

```
PICAXE Programming Editor - [D:\Users

  File    Edit    Simulate    PICAXE    View

  New    Flow chart    Open    Save

  ✂ 📋 📋 ↩ ↪ 10 ▼

1    symbol centre = 0
2    symbol left = 1
3    symbol right = 2
4
5    main:
6    servo centre, 167
7    pause 150
8    servo left, 162
9    servo right, 164
10   pause 150
11   servo centre, 143
12   pause 150
13   servo left, 138
14   servo right, 140
15   pause 150
16   goto main
```

'Basic' PICAXE program controlling the 3 servo motor on the hexapod

'Flow chart' PICAXE program

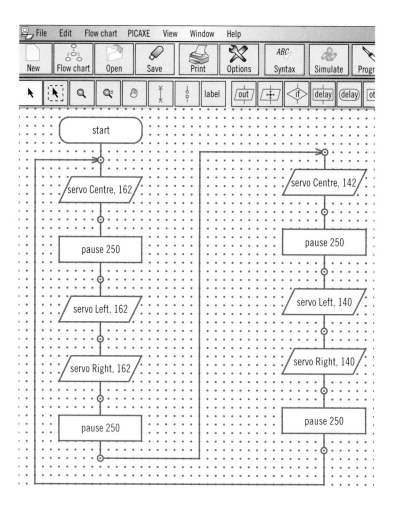

The basic and flow chart programs are examples that instruct the robot to walk forwards only.

LEARNING ACTIVITY 7.2

1 Outline the two types of logic controllers and explain each in your own words.

2 Provide five examples of where PLCs are commonly used.

3 Microcontrollers are regularly used by school students and hobbyists alike. Provide three other examples where microcontrollers are used in everyday apparatuses.

4 A local brick company requires automation control of their machines at a new plant. What type of logic controller would best suit? Explain your answer.

5 Refer to example 2 of the 'PIC application and use' section. Provide a practical example of where such a program could or would be used in everyday life.

ISBN 9780170227452

Radio control

History

Radio control, or RC as it is also known, is a method whereby an apparatus is used to control a device by sending pulse signals through the radio waves. It is used in industrial applications and also by hobby enthusiasts. This part of the chapter will focus on radio control systems that are used within the hobby sector, such as RC cars, boats, planes and helicopters.

RC systems have had significant evolutionary changes since their early conception. The first generation of radio controllers were capable only of providing control to a single channel output. These primitive systems operated using valves and required heavy batteries. The next generation of control was the 'carrier wave' system. This system used signals to operate a clocklike mechanism that had to be pre-wound before use. The carrier wave system was soon superseded by the 'tone' system. The tone system used musical notes (tones) sent across the air waves; these were decoded by the receiver and sent to the control surface mechanism.

Proportional and digital control

Proportional and digital proportional radio controllers did not come onto the market until the 1960s and 1970s. These types of RC systems use crystals that are preset to a specific radio frequency (RF). The radio transmitter sends out steady streams of tone pulses from the transmitter (TX) to the receiver (RX). Altering the relationship between the duration of the 'on' and 'off' pulse periods is how the control is achieved. That is, the receiver processes this information and sends it to the DC servo motors to facilitate movement. The block diagram provided below outlays the basis of a RC system. In this system the human operator is the feedback loop.

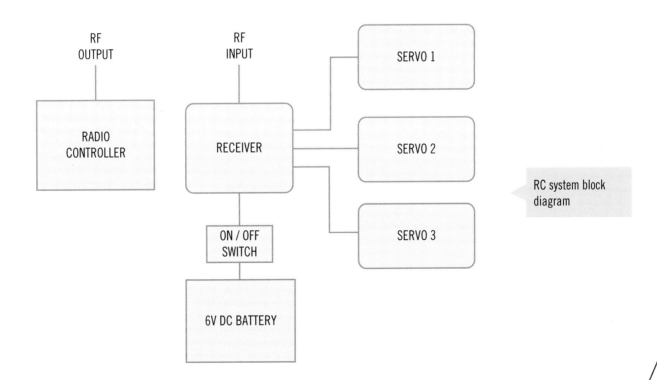

RC system block diagram

Futaba 14MZ high-end radio control system

Trex 550 radio controlled helicopter

Frequency

RC models operated in Australia must comply with subsection 132(1) and section 135 of the *Radiocommunications Act 1992*. This Act specifies that only specific frequencies can be used for RC models. These specified frequencies must be within the 29 MHz and 36 MHz frequency range and must not cause inference with other radio-communication devices.

Recently in Australia a new breed of RC systems have come on the market. These new systems, such as the Futaba 14 MZ shown above, transmit on the 2.4 GHz frequency range. This new technology offers a safer system less prone to interference and offers a 100% impenetrable link. This is because the signal continuously hops from one to another.

ISBN 9780170227452

END-OF-CHAPTER ACTIVITIES

1 Write the meaning of the following acronyms and abbreviations.

   a TX

   b RX

   c RF

   d MHz

   e GHz

2 What do 'high' and 'low' commands mean?

3 How many seconds are in 1000 milliseconds?

4 Draw the following flow chart symbols in your workbook.

   a start

   b input

   c output decision

   d end

5 Bluetooth technology was not discussed in this chapter. Research Bluetooth and provide a description of its operation and three examples of its use.

6 The CSIRO claim the discovery and/or invention of 'wi-fi' technology. Look into this claim and explain what CSIRO had to do to claim its title and any royalties owed to it.

7 In regard to radio control, explain what the term 'frequency hopping' means.

8 Draw an IPO diagram of a radio controlled car.

9 **a** Microcontrollers come in different sizes. What is the difference between the sizes?

   b Why would you chose one size over another?

10 Research task: visit **http://museumvictoria.com.au/csirac/index.aspx** and click on 'Programming'. Locate the hand drawn flow chart diagram on the right of the screen and click to enlarge. Elaborate on how similar or dissimilar this 1960s flow chart is to the flow chart programmer used in the PICAXE program editor.

Weblinks

PICAXE microcontrollers: www.picaxe.com

Circuit Wizard simulation software:www.new-wave-concepts.com

GENIE microcontrollers: www.new-wave-concepts.com/ed/circuit.html www.genieonline.com/

Parallax microcontrollers: www.parallax.com
Arduino microcontrollers: www.arduino.cc

Atmel microcontrollers: www.atmel.com

Allen Bradley PLC: ab.rockwellautomation.com

Seimens PLC: www.automation.siemens.com

CSIRAC: museumvictoria.com.au/csirac/index.aspx

ERIC, the police bomb robot: www.police.vic.gov.au/content.asp?Document_ID=12562

Heron UAV: www.iai.co.il/18900-en/BusinessAreas_UnmannedAirSystems_HeronFamily.aspx

Futaba Radio Control Systems: www.futaba-rc.com

Align RC Helicopters: www.wattsuprc.com.au

PICAXE system projects: www.youtube.com/user/DCTTeacher1

CASE STUDY 4

Remote control systems

This case study was written by Dr Christopher Anderson from the Defence Science & Technology Organisation (DSTO). Chris completed his VCE at Whittlesea College before completing a bachelor degree and PhD in Mechanical Engineering at Victoria University. Chris joined the DSTO in 2002 and has worked on various scientific research programs relating to the protection of vehicle occupants for defence and National Security government agencies.

The case study explains how a remote controlled system was conceived and developed for operational use.

The author follows logical thinking and problem-solving processes, similar to the systems engineering process followed in this book.

Problem identified

In late 2010 a problem presented itself. This, in itself, was not unusual since the very nature of the work we do in applied research is problem based. What made this problem unique in my mind was that the ultimate solution was not the immediate obvious choice.

In order to explain the problem, I need to first set the scene. Australian troops were deployed in Afghanistan. The operational tempo was providing a strong energetic push to conduct applied research in the area of vehicle protection. My team and I were working towards improving the survivability of deployed vehicles against improvised explosive devices (IEDs). As research scientists it is our job to conduct various research activities to understand, predict and demonstrate mitigation measures. Within the scope of this case study, a mitigation measure is additional armour that could be applied to a vehicle to make it stronger. To this end, we were conducting numerical simulations to predict vehicle performance against IEDs and were working towards a series of full scale live fire vehicle tests. These experiments involved detonating an explosive device against real vehicles.

A surrogate IED event against some protected vehicles. The mannequins in the foreground were positioned at 6, 8 and 10 m (although the 6 m mannequin is completely engulfed at the time of the picture). The vehicles being tested here are also completely engulfed by the detonation products or fire ball. The image resolution here is reduced as it has been taken off high speed video footage which runs at 8000 frames per second and has a 680 × 480 image size.

ISBN 9780170227452

Our ability to numerically predict the explosive event had recently advanced greatly. Therefore the need to obtain accurate and detailed experimental results to validate the predictions was greater than it had ever been previously. Consequently we needed to also advance our experimental data capture capabilities. One particular aspect was the need to accurately capture the motion of the vehicle during the blast. The size of the explosive charges being used was great enough to lift vehicles into the air and even completely flip some smaller vehicles.

We were in the process of deploying a 3D stereoscopy system to capture this vehicle motion. It worked by placing two cameras at different positions and then synchronising them to capture frames at the same time. Commercial software was then able to track the motion of particles or objects, such as the vehicle, during the event. It works much like the cameras that filmed the AVATAR movie, but much more accurately. This technique had worked brilliantly for us on some earlier events and had proven to be a very valuable tool.

Unfortunately, the technique required that both cameras maintained a complete view of the object to be tracked for the entire duration of the event. Sometimes, the debris and fire ball from the blast are large enough to completely obscure the vehicle from the cameras and hence the system no longer works. Herein lies the problem. We needed to be able to place our cameras in a position that gave them clear views of the vehicle for up to 3 seconds. This time may not seem like much but in our world time is measured in microseconds. Three seconds is long enough for the vehicle to be thrown into the air and then return to the ground and come to rest.

At first glance the problem seemed relatively simple. We needed to put the cameras somewhere that they could see the vehicle, not get obscured by the blast, and not get destroyed. Based on my experience conducting many of these sorts of events I knew that the best position for viewing was basically above the vehicle and slightly off to the opposite side to the blast. By looking down on the vehicle then the bulk of the blast output is absorbed by the vehicle and the cameras would be in a pocket of air that was relatively clear and calm.

Analysis, research and development

The brainstorming and thought processes led us to explore the following suggestions:

1 scaffold
2 cherry picker
3 pile of dirt
4 shipping containers
5 satellite
6 helicopter.

First, the scaffold idea seemed to be a good one. However, a couple of issues arose regarding the OH&S legislation that would require suitably qualified trades people to erect and dismantle the scaffold. This presented a problem for us since some of the work we do is of a sensitive nature and we would have difficulty granting access to tradespeople that do not have the appropriate clearances. Furthermore, the possibility of the scaffold being damaged during the blast was very real and hence the scaffold would potentially be unsafe afterwards, so was not to be.

Second, we explored the idea of using a cherry picker. This seemed to meet our entire criteria. The only problem was that we couldn't find anybody who was willing to put their very expensive truck next to an explosion, since it would void the warranties and the truck would no longer have been certified as safe. This made it a very expensive option so it was not feasible.

Options three and four – making a pile of dirt or stack of shipping containers large enough to get a reasonable angle looking down – was briefly considered. Some quick trigonometry ruled out both these options since the height required to get enough down angle was not practical.

The fifth idea to task a satellite to record the event for us was explored. This is not as farfetched as it seems but unfortunately introduces a timing difficulty. The firing of the event would need to be timed with pinpoint accuracy to have the correct camera angle and field of view. This would be a difficult thing to achieve since our experiments have so many sophisticated measuring devices which can be time consuming to set up. Furthermore, if the day of the event was heavily overcast with bad weather then we would not be able to see anything from the satellite.

The sixth option was to get a helicopter to fly over the range at the time of the event. This would be far more easily timed than the satellite since it could be waiting on the ground nearby and only get airborne when we were ready to detonate. Unfortunately, the use of manned aircraft on the range is forbidden. However, this still became our solution, in a way. If manned aircraft are forbidden, for obvious safety reasons, then what about unmanned aircraft?

A final option had presented itself as a natural evolution when all other options had proven to be impossible or impractical. Now that we had our proposed solution we needed to make it happen.

The first sensible step was to explore if the capability to put a remote controlled aircraft above our vehicle during an event existed as a commercial venture. It would have been far easier for us to simply pay a contractor to come and film our event for us. We managed to find a courageous contractor that was prepared to expose his helicopter to the blast and organised a test run. The first attempt was successful in capturing video during the event, and from that perspective it was a successful demonstration of the capability. However, the platform used was designed primarily to be flown in calm conditions and didn't have the size or power to be stable in the windy conditions on the range that day, so the footage captured was unstable. This led us to develop the capability further ourselves. Luckily one of our team members (me) was a remote control aircraft pilot in his private time.

We proceeded to map out the various components required to make a remote control helicopter perform our desired role. We needed it to be able to:

1 Carry the cameras.
2 Fly to the desired height and position and then stay there, as still as possible.
3 Have telemetry video back to the base station so that the pilot and camera operator could see what the helicopter cameras could see.
4 Be capable of holding itself in position for 3 seconds.
5 Be capable of flying in high winds.

Note that surviving the event is not listed here. Right from the beginning I made it clear to everybody that the helicopter does not need to survive the blast. It only needs to survive the first 3 seconds. After 3 seconds, the event is over and the video has been captured so if the helicopter crashes we would still be able to retrieve the solid state memory cards from the wreckage.

The problem now became one of integrating various commercial off-the-shelf products onto a typical remote control platform. The classic system of systems approach was in play. My background in sports and hobby flying gave me the experience to choose an Align brand Trex 700 Electric. I was familiar with these platforms and knew that they could carry the payload and were still extremely stable in high winds.

ISBN 9780170227452

The helicopter platform chosen was an Align brand Trex 700 Electric. Nitro versions of this platform also exist and have superior flight time but the smoke from the exhaust can obscure the video so electric is the preferred option.

Solution, testing and evaluating

I chose the best flight control system commercially available for non-military applications that would provide the desired stability control. The control system uses multiple redundant sensors to provide superior position stabilisation. The helicopter became so incredibly stable with the control system that there was no need for a stabilised camera mount. A normal helicopter control system uses three gyroscopes to sense the relative movement of the fuselage. The control system uses actual positional awareness via optical and infra-red sensors which look at the ground and work similar to the way an optical 'laser' mouse works on a computer. In addition, the control system has inertia, GPS and pressure sensors to improve its positional awareness. All these sensors combine to give minute flight control inputs to the blades. The end result is a 'fly-by-wire' feel where pilot input commands are interpreted by the control system in accordance with the sensors' information and then the blades are adjusted accordingly.

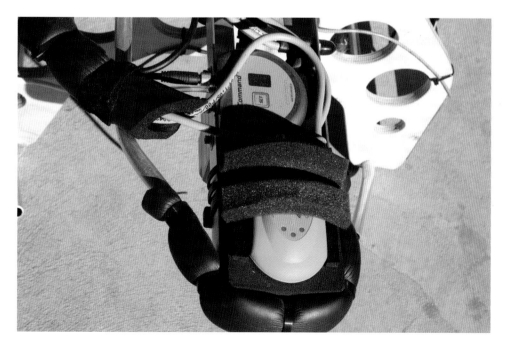

The flight control system and GPS unit

The next system added was remote first person video (FPV). This is an onboard video camera that transmits its signal back to the pilot so the pilot can see what the helicopter sees. This has the advantage that by adding a second FPV system, then the pilot and co-pilot can both see what is going on. The pilot needs to see positional information, and hence needs the camera to be aimed at the horizon. Whereas the co-pilot needs to see the test vehicle and ensure that the high speed instrumentation cameras are correctly tracking the target prior to the event. The challenge with integrating the FPV systems was to ensure that the frequencies of transmission did not interfere with the avionics and flight control systems, since that would lead to a crash or at the very least a fuzzy camera image. Finally, the FPV system gave us the ability to maintain visual contact with the helicopter while safely inside a bunker. Normal flying requires the pilot to stand out in the open, but this would not be safe during explosive events.

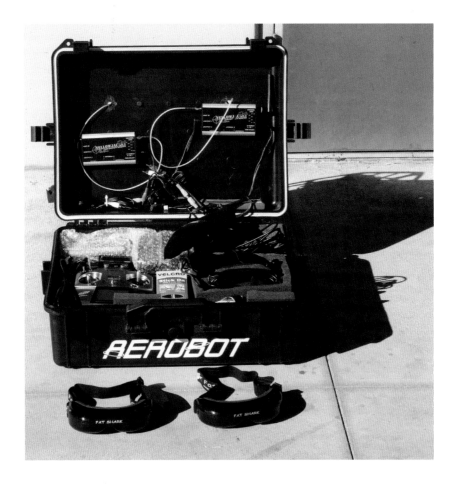

First person video (FPV) goggles and receiver base station. LCD monitors and a video recording system will be added to improve the functionality.

A protection system presented another challenge. How could we add armour to the helicopter to protect the most critical components when the entire payload was being used up to carry the instrumentation cameras? In the end, protection was achieved by selective placement of key components rather than by the addition of armour plates. By using the sacrificial components to shield the critical ones, we were able to achieve a risk reduction/mitigation that would effectively protect the vital components. At the top of the priority list were the flash cards within the instrumentation cameras.

ISBN 9780170227452

For the 3D tracking software to work accurately then the position of the two cameras relative to each other needs to be kept constant. Furthermore, the cameras need to be as far apart as possible in order to give an oblique view of the vehicle. This means that the cameras need to be mounted on booms out either side of the helicopter, but still need to be steerable by the co-pilot. Luckily this is all able to be achieved using existing RC hobby components such as servos to control the motion. The steerable camera mount shown here will have the booms connected out each side to achieve this.

The camera mount can remotely rotate the camera platform in three axes.

The final part of the system, and arguably the most important, is the production of a safe operating procedure. Detailed risk assessments and job safety analysis (JSA) documents need to be produced to ensure that the final operating procedure is robust and will not expose staff to any risk of personal injury. Furthermore, there are a number of regulations associated with the safe and legal operation of such equipment and these rules must be catered for within the operating procedure. This part of the system is not to be discounted since it is not uncommon for this part of the process to be more involved, complex and time consuming than all of the engineering components put together.

8

TESTING ENGINEERING SYSTEMS

In this chapter you will learn about the need to maintain, repair and test engineering systems. When you design and produce systems projects you need to test throughout the production stages and on completion of the task, often using a wide range of test apparatus. This chapter assists you with this and explains how you can develop strategies for planning and performing reliable diagnostic testing procedures to achieve accurate results.

When we work with technical systems an important task that we frequently perform is to test systems, subsystems and component parts. Systems often need to be tested to measure their effectiveness, or to find out why they are not working. This is what we do when performing diagnostic tests. Tests can be carried out at the prototype stage, during assembly, on completion, and throughout the life of a system.

A well-built technological system requires reliable parts and subsystems. It also needs to be safe to operate. We should therefore test to see if components and systems meet acceptable Australian Standards for design specifications, reliability and safety. Accurate testing, both during and after production, will detect failure in parts or components. This provides information regarding the performance and effectiveness of the system. These tests may also lead to modifications in the design of a working system. The best manufacturers of electronic equipment expose their products to operational conditions for hundreds of hours to simulate one full year of normal use. This is called **burn-in**. They also perform environmental stress screen tests in which the products are placed in ovens, then freezers and also subjected to vibration and shaking. For instance, car manufacturers carry out a large number of tests on vehicles to ensure the vehicles are reliable and that they are safe to drive. You may not have the facilities to carry out such tests, but there are a number of similar tests that you can plan to ensure that the system you build is reliable, safe and performs well.

Shutterstock.com/Tyler Olson

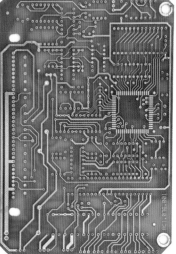

Car testing using a magnifier and PCB

Shutterstock.com/Ingvar Bjork Shutterstock.com/Laborant

ISBN 9780170227452

Read through case study 5, 'Testing flight data systems', on pages 233–242 in this book. The material discusses why and how tests are performed on modern aircraft. This should help you understand many of the concepts and issues raised throughout this chapter.

Why we test systems

We test systems for a number of reasons.

1 To find out why they are not working, or to find a fault

2 To find out why they are not performing effectively

3 To establish how well they work and satisfy their specified requirements

4 To assist with routine checks to monitor and ensure acceptable operational performances throughout their lifetime

5 To assist with maintaining, modifying and repairing procedures

6 To understand how they work

7 To assess their effectiveness under different conditions and environments

There are two main methods of testing. The first involves observation by using our senses. The second requires the use of test instruments to gather data, which is then analysed and a conclusion reached.

Identifying causes and effects of faults

We can generally tell if a system is working correctly by observing it in operation. We can also identify faults with a system when we look at it, listen to it, smell or touch it to find that something is not right. For instance, with incorrect car engine timing, we can hear the engine running too fast or too slow when the car is stationary.

Parts or components have to be the right ones, especially in electronic circuits. You should check that resistors, capacitors, transistors, diodes and so on have the correct codes and have been placed properly. In mechanical systems, you should observe the system working and check for smooth operation, with parts aligning properly. You should also listen carefully as parts could be hitting or rubbing against each other when they should not be doing so. Your sense of smell should detect whether any components or parts are overheating and burning. Electronic components, leads, gears, pulleys, cams, pistons and so on should be checked to see if they fit together and are not loose or disconnected.

Other examples of faults that can be identified in this way are:

1 a car engine overheating due to a lack of lubrication, an ineffective cooling system or damage such as a cracked cylinder head

2 an engine cooling system overheating because of insufficient coolant, air locks, blockage, leaks or thermostat problems

3 poor car braking due to worn brake shoes and pads or low levels of brake fluid in the system causing a reduction in brake pressure

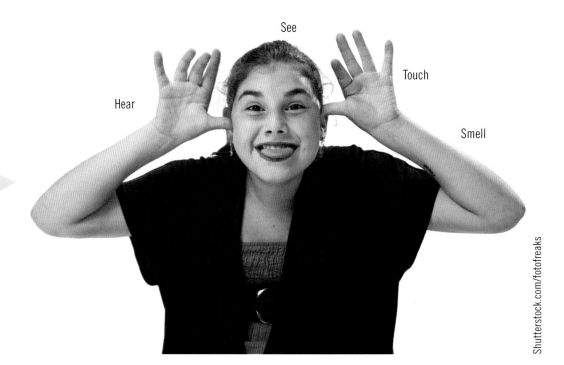

See

Touch

Smell

Hear

Human senses

Shutterstock.com/fotofreaks

4 a drilling machine output spindle not rotating when the machine is switched on, as a result of loose pulleys or worn and broken belts

5 a battery-powered vehicle failing to move at its expected speed due to low power, incorrect motor selection, motor wear or spindle damage, inaccurate motor and gear alignment, or high vehicle load

6 an electronic circuit failing to provide an output as a result of broken or damaged tracks, incorrectly positioned components, poor soldering, damaged components or incorrect circuit design.

LEARNING ACTIVITY 8.1

1 Describe a fault that occurred in a system you have worked with.

2 State how you identified the fault and how the fault affected the system.

3 Suggest observations that could be made in order to detect faults in:

a a car engine

b an electric motor

c a speaker

d a printed circuit board

e assembly of resistors, capacitors, diodes and transistors on a PCB.

As you can see, probably all of the above effects and their related faults, or causes, can be identified easily by observation. Faults are usually brought to our attention, because we hear or see that something is wrong, but we don't always look for them.

ISBN 9780170227452

To understand how faults occur and to gain an accurate assessment of the causes and effects of faults, we normally take readings or measurements using specialised testing equipment. We also do this to assess the effectiveness of operational systems, for the reasons outlined earlier. A wide range of tools and equipment is available to us when we need to test and measure particular systems.

Shutterstock.com/kreatorex

Shutterstock.com/Ljupco Smokovski

Alamy/David J. Green – studio

Testing equipment: digital multimeter, torque wrench and digital tachometer

Selecting test equipment

When we test systems we carry out some form of measurement. Test equipment should therefore be selected and used appropriately. Each device has been designed for a particular purpose and is often based on scientific or technological principles. For instance, we use multimeters to measure concepts such as resistance, current and voltage in electronic circuits, concepts that are based on Ohm's law. We use mechanical measuring devices such as compression testers to check and measure compression in engine cylinders. The compression tester is based on the **principle of forces**.

There are many other instruments such as Vernier callipers, micrometers, dial test indicators, continuity testers, engine analysers, transistor testers, light meters, decibel sound meters, electronic counters and logic probes that are used for testing electrical, electronic and mechanical systems.

A light meter

Alamy/Hugh Threlfall

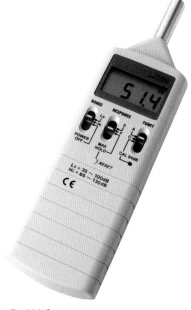
A decibel sound meter

Alamy/David J. Green

Computers are increasingly being used for diagnostic testing. Sensors such as thermistors, light-dependent resistors, photodiodes, and microswitches are used in conjunction with special circuits and programs to sense and record information on the condition of operational systems. The table below shows the main principles associated with selected test instruments and the unit quantities measured by them.

Test instrument	Technological principles associated with instrument	Unit measured
Analogue multimeter	Torque on a coil Ohm's law: voltage = current × resistance	Resistance Current Voltage Transistor gain
Digital multimeter	Analogue to digital conversion	As for analogue multimeter
Cathode ray oscilloscope (CRO)	Electron beam deflection	Voltage Frequency Phase difference
Torque wrench	Torque = force × distance	Torque
Analogue tachometer	Torque on a coil	Revolutions per minute (rpm)
Liquid thermometer	Expansion of liquid	Temperature
Digital thermometer	Analogue to digital conversion	Temperature
Spring balance, scales	Expansion or compression of springs: Hooke's law	Mass Weight
Compression tester	Pressure = force ÷ area	Pressure

Other test and measuring equipment

A mechanical tachometer (rev counter) can be used when testing rotational speed. By attaching the tachometer to the rotating wheel or shaft, a reading can be obtained. If the tachometer does not have a timer, a stopwatch can be used to calculate revolutions per minute (rpm).

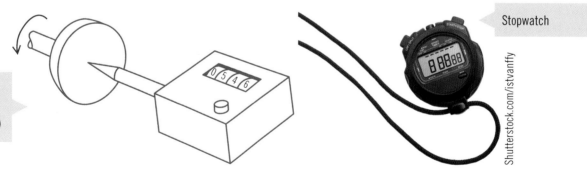

Mechanical tachometer (revolution counter)

Stopwatch

Shutterstock.com/istvanffy

ISBN 9780170227452

Stroboscopes and photocells can also be used for this kind of test. Computer-interfaced light, rotation and angle sensors are increasingly used for control technology project work.

A microswitch and counter can be used to test rotational speed. The microswitch can be set to contact gear teeth on a rotating wheel. The number of teeth a gear has needs to be known in order to calculate the number of revolutions made.

Stroboscope

iStockphoto

Touch sensors, microcounters and switches can measure cam rotation. Oscillations and cycles of different followers can be counted each time the follower makes contact with the sensing device.

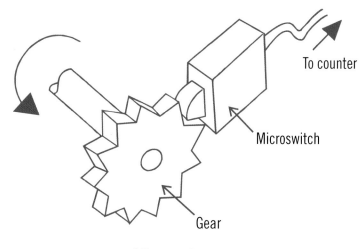

To counter

Microswitch

Gear

Microcounter

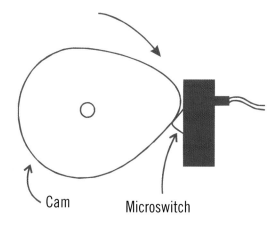

Cam

Microswitch

Measuring equipment

1 Micrometers are tools for making measurement that are accurate to 0.01 mm. They are made in sizes that go up in steps of 25 mm, such as 0–25 mm, 25–50 mm and so on. Where a more accurate measurement is required, a Vernier micrometer would be used. It has an accuracy of 0.002 mm. An inside micrometer can be used to measure the diameter of holes, such as the diameter of a cylinder in an internal combustion engine.

2 Vernier callipers can measure both inside and outside measurements and are often used in situations where micrometers will not reach. Vernier callipers are accurate but not as accurate as micrometers.

3 Dial test indicators are used to accurately measure small distances. A common type measures from 0 to 5 mm. The dial is graduated in 0.01 mm markings.

4 Multimeters are used to measure voltage, current and resistance in electrical circuits. The instrument may have an analogue (dial) or digital readout. To measure current, the circuit must be broken to allow the ammeter to be connected in series. Ammeters must have a low resistance. To measure potential difference (voltage), the circuit is not changed; the voltmeter is connected in parallel. Voltmeters must have a high resistance. To measure resistance, the component must be removed from the circuit altogether. Ohmmeters work by passing a current through the component being tested.

5 Pressure gauges are used to measure the pressure in tyres, car lubrication systems, air compressors and the cylinders of an internal compression engine. There are simple types such as the sliding-scale pen-sized gauges used on car tyres and analogue and digital readout types on larger systems. A gauge is used to measure the very small pressure on the stylus on old vinyl-record players.

6 Thermometers are often used to check the operating temperature of a system, such as the cooling system in a car, or the environment in which a system is operating. The most common thermometers have an analogue or digital display.

Micrometer and Vernier calliper

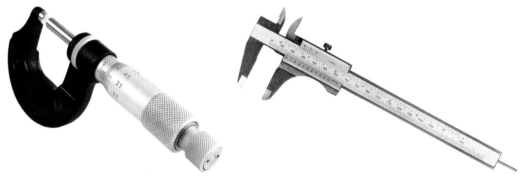

Shutterstock.com/Ari N

Shutterstock.com/Winai Tepsuttinun

ISBN 9780170227452

Before you begin

When designing and planning systems projects, you should develop performance criteria or specifications for the system. Here, you specify exactly what the system should do when it is operating. For example, specify the efficiency, voltage, output speed and the distance a model vehicle should move. You can even set simple tests for individual components or devices, before and during assembly, to help you to model and predict the overall performance of the system.

Getting accurate results

Testing similar devices

Motors, for example, should be tested to see if their output speeds are correct. This is important, otherwise we are assuming that the manufacturer's specifications are correct. This is essential after long periods of use as components become less efficient due to friction and wear.

Comparisons should be made when using two or more motors on projects in which the input speeds should be the same. Boom gates or automatic door-opening devices require their motors to rotate simultaneously.

Testing efficiency

Checking the efficiency of a system is another important test procedure. This is performed to see if the theoretical outputs are achievable and match the specification for the system. For instance, a motor and gear transmission can be calculated to achieve a certain output speed. However, under accurate test conditions, the system may not achieve the intended output speed. This would indicate some of the following problems and the need for further tests and maintenance:

1 Input energy is insufficient.

2 Motor specifications do not meet the requirements of the system.

3 Motor is inefficient due to friction and wear.

4 Shafts and gears are poorly fitted or worn.

Comparative tests

The actual testing and measuring equipment (sensors, switches, meters, counters and so on) should be checked for accuracy. Sometimes these devices are inaccurate and need to be calibrated, or reset each time they are used. A comparative test is often made to check the accuracy of test equipment. To do this, you simply take a measurement or reading with two similar testing devices, and then compare the two sets of readings.

LEARNING ACTIVITY 8.2

1 Suggest how diagnostic tests relate to planned performance criteria or specifications for a system.

2 Give reasons why some rotary systems do not achieve their expected output speed under accurate test conditions.

3 What is the purpose of a comparative test?

Measurable quantities

There are a number of basic quantities that can be measured for both mechanical and electrical systems. Examples for mechanical systems are distance, time, force, pressure, linear speed, rotational speed and torque. In electrical systems we can measure resistance, voltage, current and frequency. The measurement of these basic quantities and the application of scientific and technological principles allow us to work out other quantities such as velocity ratio, mechanical advantage, energy consumption, power input, power output and efficiency.

Measuring input and output

Many school projects use a battery to power a mechanical system in which the output is motion energy, such as a model car. The input power (electrical) and the useful output energy (mechanical) can be calculated after taking some basic measurements as shown below.

Input electrical power, in watts, is calculated after measuring the voltage of the battery and the current it provides.

$$\text{Input} = \text{voltage} \times \text{current}$$
$$(P = V \times I)$$

The mechanical output energy is motion energy (kinetic energy). Two quantities are needed to work out the mass, m: kinetic energy of the car (in kilograms) and its speed, v (in metres per second).

$$\text{Mechanical energy output} = \tfrac{1}{2} \times \text{mass} \times \text{speed}^2$$
$$(E = \tfrac{1}{2}\,mv^2)$$

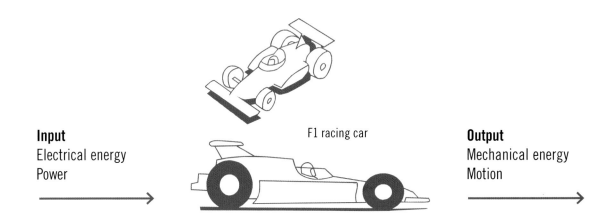

F1 racing car

Input
Electrical energy
Power

Output
Mechanical energy
Motion

Torque or force transfer is what occurs during the process stage in many mechanical systems such as gearboxes, lathes and vehicle jacks. The type, size and arrangement of gears determine the relationship between input and output. Measuring quantities such as the rotational speed (revolutions per minute) of motor shafts, gears and wheels allow us to compare actual performances with those predicted.

ISBN 9780170227452

Calculating speed and distance

Measuring devices can also be used to find speed and distance. When testing projects such as bicycles, go-karts, remote control vehicles and scooters, you can calculate how fast they move. You will need to know the wheel circumference as this is the distance the wheel moves with each rotation.

For example, a cyclist decided to measure how fast he could move on his bicycle. He attached a rev counter to his bicycle and found that after 10 minutes the wheels had turned 2310 revolutions. He then measured the wheel circumference at 2 m. Multiplying 2310 revolutions by 2 m, he found that he had travelled 4620 m in 10 minutes. He therefore calculated his speed to be 27.72 km per hour.

Shutterstock.com/Dick Stada

Example: calculating speed

If a gear has 48 teeth, then each multiple of 48 on the counter equals 1 revolution. This can be timed for 1 minute, or for a shorter period like 10 seconds, and then multiplied by 6, the number of 10-second periods in 1 minute, to get the total revolutions per minute (rpm) of the gearwheel.

Calculate the speed of a rotating gear using a counter and microswitch given the following information:

- counter reading = 3657
- gear size = 48 teeth
- time = 1 minute
- speed = 3657 ÷ 48 × 1 = 76.2.
  The approximate gear speed is 76.2 rpm.

If the input speed was increased and a counter reading of 8464 (the total number of teeth counted) was taken after 10 seconds, we simply multiply 8464 by 6 to estimate the number of teeth counted in 1 minute as 50 784. We divide this by 48 to obtain a speed of 1058 rpm.

Testing circuits

A circuit needs to be tested if it is not working properly or if measurements regarding its performance are needed. Such measurements could relate to the input, the process or the output. If a circuit does not work, there could be a number of reasons. Some of these are listed below.

Components

Are the components the correct ones? Have they been mounted the correct way? Are any missing? Are they faulty? Check the following.

- **Colour code on the resistors:**
  - Are they the correct resistors?
  - Capacitors, diodes and transistors
  - Are they the right ones and have they been mounted in the correct way?

- **Integrated circuits:**
  - Are the pins where they should be?
  - Are they damaged? Have they been inserted fully, if an adaptor has been used?

- **Switches and batteries:**
  - Have the right connections been used on the switches?
  - Are the switches working?
  - Is the battery flat?

Soldering circuit boards

Where there are poorly soldered joints or loose component leads, or solder has joined two tracks or pads, check for short circuits using a multimeter.

It is always a good idea to check components before they are mounted. A multimeter can be used to check resistors, capacitors, diodes, switches and transistors. Once these components are soldered to complete a circuit, testing is more difficult as other components may affect the readings and make any decision unreliable.

Testing the input

The power source (batteries, solar cells, generators, power packs and so on) is the major input device for an electronic circuit. Sensors and transducers (LDRs, thermistors, photodiodes, microphones and so forth) can also relate to the input section of a system. When testing inputs you should find data that are of some use if the circuit needs to be modified or calibrated. Manufacturers of electrical equipment measure the power consumption of some household equipment such as refrigerators and washing machines, and these are allocated star ratings as a result. A four-star machine consumes much less power than a two-star one and is cheaper to run.

ISBN 9780170227452

Input power in watts

To find out how much power is needed to operate a circuit, you will need to measure two quantities: voltage and current. Then you just multiply them to get the power in watts. An example is shown.

Voltage $= 9$ V

Current $= 200$ mA $= 0.2$ A

Power $=$ voltage $\times$ current ($P = V \times I$)

$= 9 \times 0.2$

$= 1.8$ W

Convert mA into A before multiplying.

Measuring voltage

This is not difficult to measure voltage as all you have to do is to connect a multimeter (set to measure DC volts) across the battery or power source.

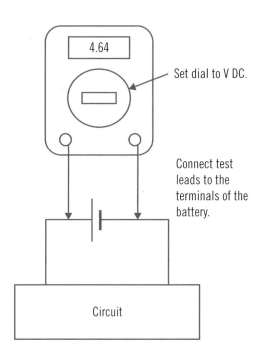

4.64

Set dial to V DC.

Connect test leads to the terminals of the battery.

Circuit

Measuring voltage

Measuring current

Measuring current is a little harder than measuring voltage and, if not done correctly, may damage the multimeter. In most cases a fuse inside the meter will blow. The power source needs to be disconnected and the multimeter (set to measure DC amps) connected between (in series with) the battery and the circuit. If you measure amps without disconnecting the battery you will damage the test instrument.

Measuring current

Disconnect battery at one end. Make the electricity go through the meter and back to the circuit.

Set dial to DC amps, or select highest range, and then reduce the range.

08

Circuit

Testing the process

The input needs to be converted to an output. Components such as resistors, capacitors, diodes, transistors, regulators and integrated circuits perform this process. The operation of a circuit made up of only a few components can be easy to explain and test. Complex circuits will require a thorough knowledge of component behaviour and circuit theory. Testing the process also helps us diagnose faults in the circuit or get indications of how the circuit can be improved.

Resistor operation

Resistors are used to set voltage values or protect other components in the circuit. Variable resistors allow control of these voltages. You can measure the voltage across the resistors with a multimeter and check whether the resistors are doing what they are supposed to do. Voltage values are often quoted in some electronic circuit diagrams or they can be obtained using special software packages.

Transistor operation

A transistor is used as a switch or an amplifier. You can measure the voltage between the base and the emitter. As a switch, the transistor is fully 'on' if this voltage is greater than 1.4 V and fully 'off' if it is less than 0.6 V. As an amplifier, the voltage should be between these two values.

Capacitor operation

A capacitor will charge and then discharge. As it does so the voltage across it increases and decreases. This can be measured with a good analogue multimeter if it is charging and discharging slowly. An analogue multimeter is better than a digital one for measuring slow voltage changes. A cathode ray oscilloscope (CRO) is needed if the process is rapid.

Integrated circuit operation

Integrated circuits such as the 555 timer have at least two of their pins connected to the power source. The voltage across these pins should be the same as that of the battery. The voltages at the input and output pins can also be monitored by a multimeter, a CRO or a logic probe, depending on the function of the IC in the circuit.

ISBN 9780170227452

Testing the output

Components and devices such as light-emitting diodes, relays, solenoids, motors and buzzers make up the output of an electronic system. You can measure the voltage across and the current through the device and work out the useful electrical power output. This is done in a similar way to measuring the input power.

If input power and useful output power are known, the efficiency of the process can be worked out. This should be less than 100% because resistors and transistors heat up and waste power. You could investigate and experiment with ways of improving the efficiency of the system.

Modifying circuits

Components that relate to the input, process and output can be changed to make the circuit perform differently. If the output is a buzzer, some other output device such as a relay or a small motor can at times replace the buzzer. An LED can be made brighter by replacing the protective resistor with one of a lesser value. If you decide to change components, try values that do not differ greatly, otherwise the complete circuit may not work.

Planning and performing tests

To plan and perform diagnostic tests on systems, you should follow these sequential and logical steps:

1 Prepare a test sequence.

2 Give reasons or purpose for the test.

3 Specify expected test results.

4 Plan test procedures.

5 Perform the actual test and record results.

6 Analyse actual versus intended results.

Advice for planning and testing systems

Notes, diagrams and sketches are used to explain the purpose of any planned test. You need to plan the test procedures and which test instruments, tools and equipment are required. Safety precautions to prevent injury and any precautions needed so as not to cause instrument damage should be listed.

Sources of error or mistakes in taking measurements and actions to reduce these errors should also be considered. The actual testing and measuring equipment (sensors, switches, counters and so on) should be checked for accuracy. Sometimes these devices are inaccurate and need to be calibrated, or reset each time they are used. You should always take several readings as a checking procedure. Ensure that measuring devices are set at zero when required.

A comparative test can be done to check the accuracy of test equipment. A measurement or reading is taken using two similar testing devices. The two readings are compared to see if they are the same.

You also need to ensure that you read instruments correctly. When using digital instruments, check that the range is set correctly or your reading could be out by one or more decimal places. The same precaution is needed with analogue equipment; you need to ensure that you are reading the correct scale. With analogue equipment, parallax error is common. This occurs when the needle position is not viewed from front dead centre. For instance, if you view the needle from right of centre, you see it aligning with a value that is actually to the left of the correct value on the scale. You should try this for yourself by looking at the minute hand of a clock from both left and right of centre.

Parallax error occurs when a needle is not viewed from front dead centre.

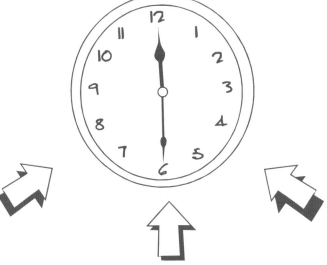

Expected test results should be clearly stated if they are known. If they are not, you should indicate in general terms the expected outcome of the test. For instance, input power is expected to be greater than the useful output power as a system is not expected to be 100% efficient.

Perform the actual test safely and accurately according to the test plan. Record test results and any changes made to the test procedures.

An analysis of the actual versus the intended results should be made. This could be a simple comparison of intended and actual results backed by test data, or a detailed analysis that includes tables, calculations and graphs. A discussion of the difficulties and the sources of errors encountered when measuring should also be included; for example, difficulty in obtaining accurate results due to the meter needle not being steady. There should be clear statements as to whether the system being tested is satisfactory; if not, an explanation should be given.

LEARNING ACTIVITY 8.3

1 Briefly describe each stage involved in planning and testing a system.

2 Name a system you have worked with and prepare a brief plan for testing.

3 a Describe two types of error that can occur when reading test instruments.

  b Suggest how these could be prevented.

Maintenance procedures

Once a product has been built, maintenance procedures are needed. If a product is well maintained, it should be reliable with little or no need for major repairs or replacements. Unexpected use or abuse can damage systems of any kind. Manufacturers publish manuals that give instructions to consumers about the procedures required to maintain their products and keep them performing as efficiently as possible. Maintenance is mainly about repair, upkeep and periodical replacement of parts to prolong the operational life of a system and ensure optimal performance.

Regular service and maintenance checks save a lot of maintenance and expense in the long term.

Electrical and electronic devices may not need a lot of maintenance, but this does not mean that they will last forever if basic maintenance is not done. An electrical or electronic system will only operate properly if the power source is within specified voltages. If, for instance, the battery is weak, the voltage supplied may not be enough to power the circuit. If the battery rating (in amp-hours) is known, the designer can recommend the appropriate time when a new battery needs to be fitted. The **density** or specific gravity of the electrolyte (acid) in a car battery needs to be checked regularly to ensure that the battery stays in good condition.

Most electronic components require some maintenance; some, which include mechanical contacts (such as relays and switches), have a recommended limit regarding the number of times they are designed to operate without failing. You can find such data in suppliers' catalogues and listed in handbook specifications. DC electric motors and alternators have carbon brushes that have to be inspected and replaced if worn.

Mechanical systems made up of gears, bearings, pulleys and linkages are likely to suffer wear and tear after long periods of use due to friction. Bearings, bushes and pulley belts are common components that need more frequent attention and replacement. Spark plugs, leads and ignition points require attention at determined intervals. Maintenance also involves lubrication of moving parts and measuring the oil level in machines and engines.

Weblinks

www.technologystudent.com
www.viengineering.com
www.dataweek.co

END-OF-CHAPTER ACTIVITIES

1 Give four reasons for testing systems.
2 Describe two typical faults and their effects on their respective systems.
3 Describe three methods of detecting a fault in a system.
4 Name four testing devices (two electrical and two mechanical) and explain the scientific principles on which each is based.
5 What are the advantages of using test equipment?
6 Name an electromechanical system that you have worked with and list the maintenance procedures required to ensure reliability and high performance.
7 Explain the consequences if maintenance procedures are not carried out on the system identified in Question **6**.
8 Name an electrical or electronic system and list the maintenance procedures required to ensure reliability and high performance.
9 Explain the consequences if maintenance procedures are not carried out on the system identified in Question **8**.
10 What is parallax error?
11 Describe a diagnostic test that you have performed and how you planned the test.
12 For the above system describe the inputs, processes and outputs, including any known and obtained numerical values.

ISBN 9780170227452

CASE STUDY 5

Testing flight data systems

This case study by Darren Privitera examines the design, development and function of aircraft flight data systems. Darren expands on a number of the themes discussed throughout the testing chapter in this book. He explains why testing and servicing tasks are necessary to ensure accuracy and reliability. Darren is the Director of Flight Data Systems, Melbourne (**www.flightdata.com.au**).

Flight data systems

The black box flight recorder is an Australian invention. The device was invented in 1958 by Dr David Warren at the Aeronautical Research Laboratories in Melbourne. While the early black boxes were quite sophisticated for their day (incorporating electrical and mechanical technology), they are now a complex electronics system that interfaces to all parts of an aircraft and is capable of surviving tremendously severe aircraft accidents.

The black box flight recorder is a device which operates on an aircraft, and is designed to help determine the cause of an aircraft accident. It can be comprised of two separate recorders, one known as a flight data recorder and the other known as a cockpit voice recorder.

Flight data recorder

Corbis/Evan Schnieder/epa

The 'black box flight recorder' is actually a bright orange box with reflective stripes on its sides, and raised lettering indicating 'FLIGHT RECORDER DO NOT OPEN' on its outer case. These physical characteristics help to aid recovery of the black box at an aircraft crash site. In addition to its bright orange appearance, the black box also has attached to it a sonar beacon which is known as an 'underwater locator beacon' to aid recovery of the black box at sea.

How flight data recorders work

The flight data recorder collects and records measured aircraft data to help crash investigators determine how an accident happened. The types of aircraft data or 'parameters' collected by the flight data recorder include information such as altitude, air speed, magnetic heading, engine information, aircraft attitude and information such as pitch and roll. The number of measured parameters recorded by a flight data recorder varies, depending on the size, type and age of an aircraft, but can range from six parameters to as many as 2500 parameters.

The flight data recorder records aircraft parameters for at least 25 hours. Once the memory is full, the new data then start recording over the oldest information, therefore retaining the last 25 hours of aircraft information before the recorder ceased to operate.

The cockpit voice recorder collects pilot voice and cockpit area noises to help crash investigators determine 'why' an accident happened. The audio collected includes pilots' voices from each microphone, air traffic control messages, general cockpit noises such as switch activations, audible warning indications, and background noises such as wind, airframe and engine noises.

The cockpit voice recorder records cockpit audio for a minimum of 30 minutes. The newest cockpit voice recorders are now required to record 2 hours of audio. As with the flight data recorder, the cockpit voice recorder also records over the oldest information after 2 hours.

The flight recorder system incorporates three main subsystems:

1 aircraft sensors
2 the flight data acquisition unit
3 the flight data recorder, which houses the 'crash-protected memory module'.

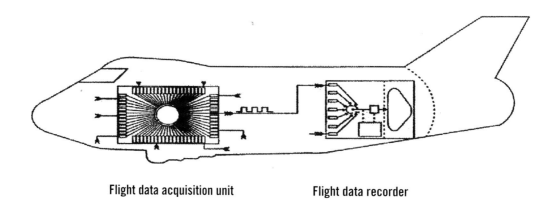

Flight data acquisition unit   **Flight data recorder**

The type of aircraft sensors used can vary widely, depending on the particular measurement required to be recorded on the flight recorder. Generally, in a flight recorder system there are devices which convert a physical movement of an object into an electrical signal. An example of such a device is a sensor called a potentiometer. The potentiometer connects to a moving section of the aircraft (rudder, flap and so on) via a retractable wire cable. The distance the cable moves is directly proportional to the voltage output of the device.

ISBN 9780170227452

Other types of sensors convert aircraft motion into acceleration, or the altitude and air pressure into electrical signal outputs. All of these converted signals, which are now electrical in nature, are collected by a system called a flight data acquisition unit.

The flight data acquisition unit (FDAU) is a device that collects all of the electrical outputs of the aircraft sensors; in some aircraft this can be as many as 2500 signals. The FDAU systematically takes a sample of each of the many sensor voltages at its input, and organises and converts these voltages into a single digital data stream for input into the flight data recorder.

The main function of a flight data recorder is to accept the digital data stream from the FDAU, and store this information in its internal crash-protected memory module in order to protect the aircraft information from being destroyed in case of an aircraft accident.

Changing technology improving design

The evolution of technology over the years has influenced the design of the black box flight recorder in many ways. Black box flight recorders have constantly evolved, taking advantage of advances in materials technology to enable the black box to survive high temperatures for longer and to survive much higher impact and shock, as well as compression experienced from deep sea emersion. Advances in electronics technology enable the black box to cope with the ever-growing demand to record many more aircraft parameters at much higher rates.

Evolution of the flight data recorder

The earliest black boxes (1960s) used reels of metal tape 150 mm wide and many metres long as the recording medium. The method of recording the flight data was to use six scribers, some diamond tipped, which scribed etchings longitudinally on the metal tape as it passed by. In this type of black box, the metal tape itself was the 'crash protection' of the

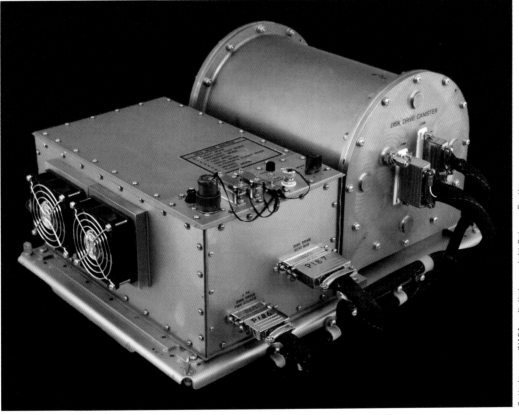

Scriber type black box (1960s)

Magnetic tape type black box (1980s)

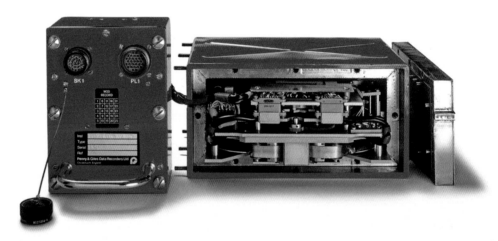

Current new generation solid state type black box

data. Metal tape was used because of its high resistance to damage from fire and impact. The distance between an edge track scribed on the tape (zero reference) and the scribe mark for each parameter is directly related to the value of the parameter. For example, as the altitude signal increased, the scribe mark would move further away from the zero reference line.

This type of recorder had its limitations. Some of the disadvantages were the limited number of parameters that could be recorded due to the number of scribers that could reasonably fit into a recorder, but more importantly the protection of the data relied solely on the metal tape surviving an accident.

ISBN 9780170227452

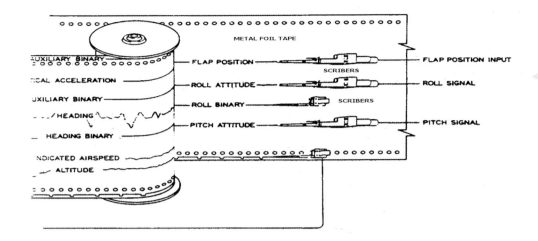

METAL FOIL TAPE

AUXILIARY BINARY

:CAL ACCELERATION

:UXILIARY BINARY

- - - / HEADING

_ HEADING BINARY

NDICATED AIRSPEED

_ / ALTITUDE

FLAP POSITION ———————————————— FLAP POSITION INPUT

SCRIBERS

ROLL ATTITUDE ———————————————— ROLL SIGNAL

ROLL BINARY ———————— SCRIBERS

PITCH ATTITUDE ———————————————— PITCH SIGNAL

Typical mechanism for recording data on a metal tape recorder

With the rapid growth in digital electronics technology in the 1980s, it was then possible to record data electronically, with more parameters, on magnetic tape. In the magnetic tape recorders, data was recorded onto the magnetic tape using magnetic read and write heads, much like the common reel-to-reel audio tape recorders used in recording studios. Unlike the metal foil recorders, the magnetic tape was easily destroyed by fire, impact and salt water, so the tape itself needed to be protected. Crash-protected modules made of metal and using fire insulators were used to protect the magnetic tape.

New generation (current technology) black boxes have advanced in the area of memory medium used to store the aircraft parameters. Solid state memory is used by black box manufacturers and mandated by aviation authorities. Solid state memory as a storage medium provides many advantages over older tape technology. It allows error-free data recording, has high reliability and requires very little maintenance. The rapid growth in memory size of solid state technology and the corresponding cost reduction make solid state technology an extremely economical option. Solid state technology is also able to provide the very high data rates now demanded on new generation aircraft, recording large numbers of aircraft parameters.

In comparison, magnetic tape recorders were less reliable, required higher maintenance and generally had poor recording quality. These characteristics result from the mechanical wear of tape transport components and the abrasive effects of magnetic tape on record and replay heads.

How the black box survives an aircraft accident

Over the years, black boxes may have failed to protect the stored aircraft parameters through weaknesses in their design. This has resulted in the issuing of new specifications which increase the crash-worthiness of the black box to ensure the data are protected. Also, to aid its survival, the black box is normally installed as far back as possible in the tail section of the aircraft. This is because the tail section is the section most likely to incur the least damage in an accident.

Black boxes are designed to protect the memory medium from destruction, by using crash-protected memory modules which house the memory medium. These devices protect the memory against various possible conditions experienced during a crash sequence of an aircraft. Memory modules are designed to withstand:

1 the impact of an aircraft
2 the piercing of the module by aircraft components such as metal rods
3 high-temperature fuel fires
4 lower temperature but long-duration fires
5 the crushing of the module
6 the corrosive effects of immersion in sea water
7 the enormous pressure experienced during deep sea immersion, which can crush solid state memory.

Typical specifications required

	Metal foil	Magnetic tape	Solid state
Impact	100 g	1000 g	3400 g
Pierce	227 kg	227 kg	227 kg
Fire	1100°C for 30 min	1100°C for 30 min	1100°C for 60 min 260°C for 10 h
Crush		2272 kg for 5 min	2272 kg for 5 min 22.25 kN
Sea water	36 hours	36 hours	3 m for 30 days
Deep sea pressure			6000 m

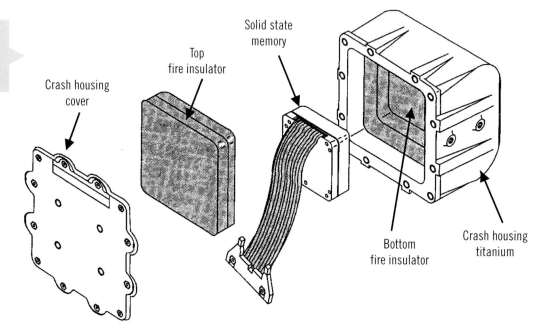

Typical components of a black box crash-protected memory module

Crash housing cover

Top fire insulator

Solid state memory

Bottom fire insulator

Crash housing titanium

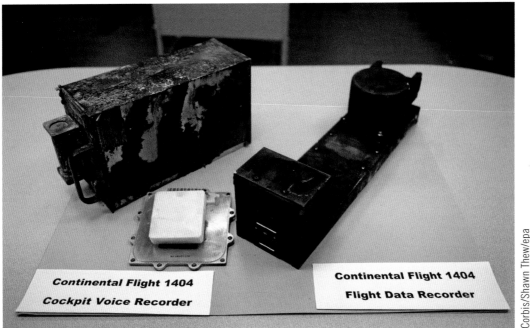

Fire-damaged module

Continental Flight 1404
Cockpit Voice Recorder

Continental Flight 1404
Flight Data Recorder

Corbis/Shawn Thew/epa

Checking and testing systems

All aircraft systems are required to be routinely tested to ensure they are correctly working or 'serviceable'. This is important to ensure the safety of the aircraft and it includes all areas of an aircraft (engines, airframe, hydraulics and avionics systems). While the black box is not critical to the aircraft's ability to fly, it is considered a mandatory item and must be fitted and proven to be serviceable in order for the aircraft to be allowed to operate.

The black box collects signals from all areas of the aircraft. To test that the black box itself is working and correctly recording, it is therefore necessary to have a test system that replicates or simulates the aircraft signals.

Test conditions

Tests are performed using test equipment located in an approved avionics workshop and operated by skilled avionics technicians. The workshop test equipment is usually an aircraft simulator that supplies the black box with the necessary aircraft parameters (airspeed signal, altitude signal and various other types of signals) so that the black box can be verified to be recording the information correctly.

Test equipment is also regularly tested to ensure that the information it is simulating is accurate, and that measurements taken from the flight recorder are accurate. For example, when the test equipment supplies the black box with a simulated 5000 metre altitude signal, we must be sure that the signal from the test equipment is providing accurate data.

Other tests

In addition to the black box itself requiring testing in a workshop, the aircraft system, which incorporates the sensors that provide the data parameters to the black box, needs to be verified as being serviceable. This involves doing regular flight data copying or 'downloads' from the black box when it is installed in the aircraft, then replaying the flight data to ensure that:

- all of the data parameters were received and stored in the crash-protected memory module
- each parameter recorded looks reasonable and is functioning correctly. From this we can confirm that the sensor or system supplying the information is serviceable.

A maintenance readout report which details each parameter and its serviceability is then produced.

System being tested and repaired

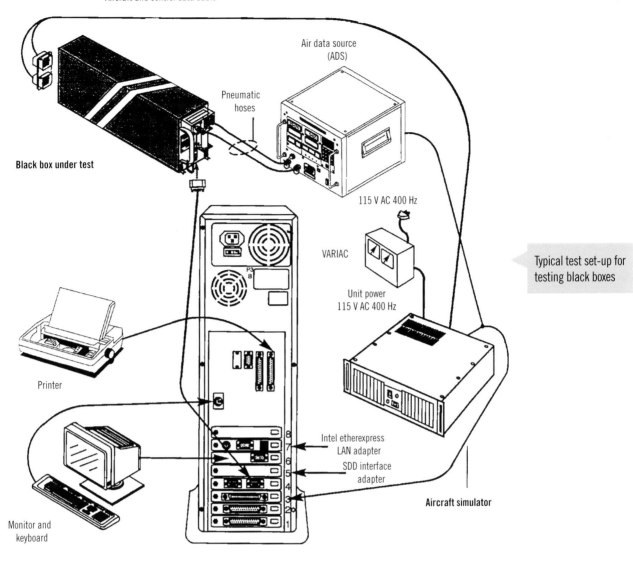

Aircraft and control data cable

Air data source
(ADS)

Pneumatic
hoses

Black box under test

115 V AC 400 Hz

VARIAC

Typical test set-up for
testing black boxes

Unit power
115 V AC 400 Hz

Printer

Intel etherexpress
LAN adapter

SDD interface
adapter

Aircraft simulator

Monitor and
keyboard

Using the recorded information

The primary use of the black box is to aid crash investigators in determining the cause of an
aircraft incident or accident, and to help prevent further accidents occurring. Because the
black box records aircraft parameter information from all areas of the aircraft, there are other
uses for these data if they are made available to other specialist areas:

1 Engineering departments use the data for monitoring engine condition.
2 Flight operations departments use the data to monitor how the aircraft is being flown, to
  help avoid incidents occurring, and to help train pilots.
3 Flight safety departments use the data to investigate incidents that may have occurred.
4 Crash investigators use the data to determine the cause of a serious incident or
  accident.

Once the information recorded on the black box is downloaded, the data are processed using sophisticated replay software. The software is capable of producing engineering unit listings of the recorded information to present the data in formats that are easily recognisable, such as metres, knots and degrees. The software also provides graphical outputs and realistic animations of the flight.

Simulated flight path

9

THE SYSTEMS ENGINEERING PROCESS

In this chapter you will learn about the systems engineering process and the stages involved in identifying, researching, designing, planning, making, testing and evaluating engineering systems. You will develop an understanding of the process and how to apply it to your design and production tasks. Worked examples and actual student folio samples are used throughout to illustrate a number of the stages and procedures involved. The chapter text refers you to various sections of the book for further detailed work and related procedures. Student folio samples and a usable design folio template have been provided to assist you with your project work. You can view these on the website **www.cengage.com.au/syseng** to gain ideas for presentation and development, and use and modify the template to suit your own particular needs and presentation style.

About design

Design plays a very important part in all of our lives. Every created object that we use or see around us has been designed by someone to satisfy our needs in some way. We would find it difficult to cope in a world without systems such as computers, fridges, televisions, engines, aeroplanes and electricity. Most of the systems that we use are of benefit to us; however, many also have disadvantages in the form of undesirable outputs. Some of these include motor vehicle emissions, industrial waste and heat losses from poorly insulated buildings, all requiring expensive maintenance or upgrading. Designing is basically a process that helps us to consider needs or problems and to develop appropriate solutions. Designers therefore have the responsibility to design suitable solutions that have little or no negative effects upon people or the environment.

Designers are employed in many areas including product design, mechanical design, electronic design, automotive design, building design, interior design and fashion design. Although designers from each of these areas are specialists and require different types of knowledge and skill, they all perform similar design processes.

You too are a designer! As you go through each day, you make decisions and plan the things that you have to do. What you need to wear to suit different weather conditions and how you get to where you need to go are typical situations that you consider and for which you devise suitable solutions.

If you are keeping a diary or project planner to structure your task throughout the weeks or months ahead, you do not simply enter details into each page without first giving some thought to what, how and when you do things. You often think about those factors that can influence your outcomes and make decisions before entering the necessary information. By giving some thought to each situation or problem, you consider possible options and make decisions about what should be the best solution.

Why we design

Products are designed or redesigned for a number of reasons, including:

1 the changing needs of society – rising costs, environmental concerns, trends, specific needs, and so on

2 the invention or development of new technologies

3 the need for manufacturers to modify existing products to ensure a high and continuous turnover so they can survive and compete in the marketplace.

Changing needs of society

Our need for products and systems changes for various reasons. When we perform different activities, change our lifestyles or attempt to cope with social and environmental influences, we develop new requirements or different needs. An example of this is our change in lifestyle over recent years in terms of the time we spend using computers. Our sitting position or posture is often not suited to spending long periods of time at a computer. It can lead to muscle tension and back pain, and the need for better, ergonomically designed furniture.

Development of new technology

Designers develop new ideas and modify existing designs all the time. Frequently, this is a result of research and testing prototypes and systems. When a designer creates a new concept it is often used to improve an existing product or system. The development of integrated circuits and miniaturisation, for example, has resulted in smaller, more effective computers and multifunctional mobile phones, and in major advances in the control of existing systems such as washing machines, ovens, cameras and motor vehicles.

Design and modify

Manufacturers need to survive in a competitive marketplace. Besides developing improved technologies and satisfying demand, manufacturers often modify existing products so that they continue to appeal to potential customers. If you examine some of the latest computers, mobile phones or household appliances you will see that little has changed in terms of its function since the previous model. What you will often see are a few minor technical improvements combined with modifications to the style and presentation of the product.

This ensures a continuous turnover and product output, which keeps the producer in business. The latest 'model' (or 'version') is a term that is used to describe these products. If you think about it, you will probably conclude that people often purchase products based on aesthetic appeal, trends and good marketing techniques.

What in fact does happen is a combination (to some degree) of all three. Manufacturers develop and improve existing technologies while taking user needs into account. To continue in business, they produce updated versions that appeal to users and help to maintain a profitable output. A continuous cycle of design, production and redesign is common practice for manufacturers.

Planned obsolescence

Linked to all of this is the fact that many of the products developed today have in-built obsolescence. That is, they are designed to be thrown away after use, rather than reused.

Many products are virtually impossible to mend if broken and have been designed this way to ensure that we replace them frequently. In some cases this is because the cost of producing and buying a replacement is less than repair costs. The result is a great deal of waste and a high turnover of products, which in turn increases the amount of design that is needed. A more essential reason for this, however, is the need to guarantee safety and reliability of product use.

The 'Manufacturing and technology' case study in this book helps us look at the concepts and issues discussed in this section. You should read through the relevant sections of the case study. It discusses the above material in some depth and should give you some useful background knowledge to help you work through this chapter.

Designing integrated systems

When we design and produce systems, the process generally involves devising and planning the configuration, assembly, modification or integration of systems, subsystems and components to produce a useful working device. As you become more experienced in this process, you begin to realise the importance of designing as a means of generating good solutions. You learn to place greater emphasis on planning, testing and evaluating your work as your production tasks become more complex, integrated and controlled.

This chapter should help you to understand the design process for planning, testing and evaluating production work. Designers from various backgrounds interpret and apply the process differently. They modify their approach to suit the type of work they are involved in and the types of products they are designing. They do, however, follow a common path in arriving at final solutions to their tasks. In doing so, they are flexible in their approach as projects vary and sometimes greater (or less) emphasis is required at certain stages of the process. You may also experience this each time you design and plan different types of projects, while following the same basic stages.

A simplified version of a design and production loop is shown below. This gives some indication of the common steps followed by different designers as they work from a design brief and research or investigate the problem and solutions. From this a designer can develop ideas and actual solutions. The product is manufactured, tested and evaluated to see if it satisfies the needs of the design brief. If the product can be improved, the design loop or relevant stages of the loop are revisited so that the next version is more successful.

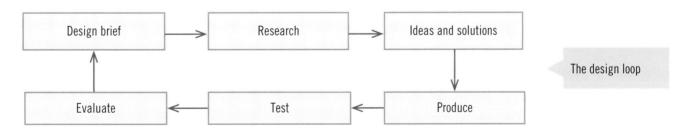

The design loop

As you will see, when designing systems we follow a similar design and production process; however, the stages are broken down further and involve a number of detailed and challenging activities due to the nature and complexity of technical systems. We call this process the systems engineering process. Doing this also ensures that all the essential technical details are examined and that planning for production and testing is adequate. This is essentially good project management.

The systems engineering process

The diagram on page 247 is an overview of the systems engineering process. You should attempt to follow this process, its stages and the tasks involved when designing, making, testing and evaluating your project work.

At first glance the diagram may seem to suggest a linear sequence of stages through the process. (*Note*: The stages are shown in a linear form for presentation only.) As we rarely experience a linear sequence, the process has been structured with reiteration (links shown with arrows) to enable and encourage you to move back and forth through the stages to reflect, reassess, modify, reselect or evaluate as you progress towards the completion of a quality, effective working system.

For instance, you may find a prototype is flawed; you therefore go back to select another option for testing and further prototyping. Or you find that some specification points or parameters are irrelevant, so you decide to amend these before further development work proceeds.

You should familiarise yourself with the diagram below to get a better understanding of the process. Following the diagram is a detailed written description of the activities involved in the process. The stages have been broken down for a clearer explanation. You will find this a useful guide and checklist to your design and production tasks.

- Identify and outline the situation or background, and then develop a design brief that gives some account of what is needed.

- Research or investigate relevant background information and consider factors that may influence the project task, such as cost, time line, environment, skills, component or parts availability, safety, legislation and standards. These can be 'limitations and possibilities' and more specific 'design parameters' to assist with developing ideas and solutions.

- Develop a detailed description of the proposed system. Describing systems involves identifying the purpose and function of systems and their input, process, control and output devices. Descriptions can be in written and diagrammatic form.

- Decide the specifications for the system (what it should do) and the criteria for evaluating the completed task. Specifications are important as they describe the features that are fixed and those that should remain flexible and open to change when developing solutions. These are 'parameters' within which the system must be developed and completed. Specifications can be used at the testing and evaluating stages as the basis for developing criteria for evaluating the system.

- Design ideas, options or possible solutions that satisfy the brief and specification requirements. These can be in the form of drawings, computer-aided design (CAD) development work, prototypes, subsystem modelling, miniature or scaled system, flow diagrams, and so on.

- Select the best option and justify its selection based on the specification requirements.

- Develop the selected option to a fully detailed stage.

- List the required resources, including equipment, parts, components and materials.

- Plan for production by working out the sequence or stages of production and indicating what is involved at each stage. Consider production options and constraints. Identify any safety concerns or risks and find solutions to these.

ISBN 9780170227452

- Production work: make the product.

- Test the system and its operational characteristics. Testing is an important part of product manufacture. We test completed systems to see how effective they are while in operation and to establish whether or not they satisfy the recommended specifications and parameters set out in the project requirements. We also test where failure or unsatisfactory performances occur so that suitable modifications can be recommended and implemented.

- Evaluate the plan, the production activities and the effectiveness of the system. Evaluating is concerned with the whole process of designing, planning, making and testing a complete and operational system. We need to reflect upon all the activities involved in the task and identify successes, difficulties and changes made to the planned processes and product. Any further improvements that can be made to the system should be identified and stated.

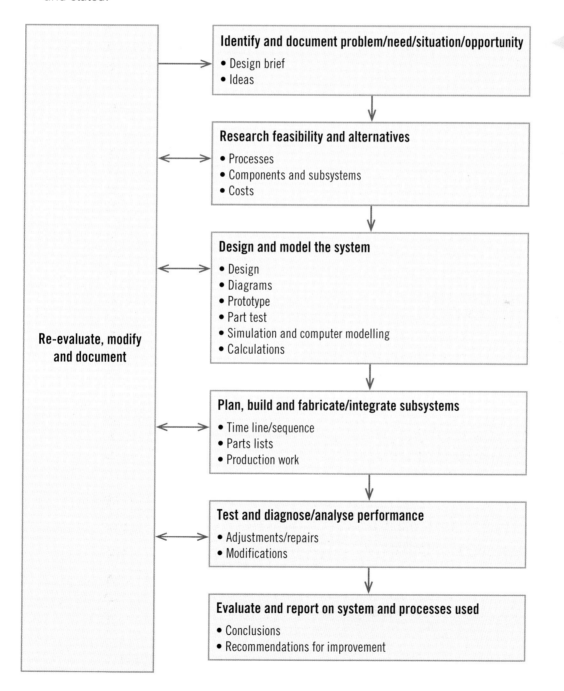

The systems engineering process

Re-evaluate, modify and document

Identify and document problem/need/situation/opportunity
- Design brief
- Ideas

Research feasibility and alternatives
- Processes
- Components and subsystems
- Costs

Design and model the system
- Design
- Diagrams
- Prototype
- Part test
- Simulation and computer modelling
- Calculations

Plan, build and fabricate/integrate subsystems
- Time line/sequence
- Parts lists
- Production work

Test and diagnose/analyse performance
- Adjustments/repairs
- Modifications

Evaluate and report on system and processes used
- Conclusions
- Recommendations for improvement

Remember: the list on page 246 is a description of what is involved in the process – not a linear sequence, but one where you reiterate as necessary to reach the best possible outcome.

Designers keep logbooks or journals as records of progress for their project work. You should do this to record any changes you make while you go along. You can also use the logbook to note the things you need to do, to plan and organise, just as you would use a diary or planner. Logbook material can take the form of written notes, sketches, diagrams, photographs, videos, blogs or any other means of recording information. When you evaluate your work, the logbook becomes an important point of reference or source of information.

The remainder of this chapter takes you through stages of systems engineering process to explain in detail and guides you with each task. Some worked examples and several systems engineering student folio works are used as reference material.

Before you begin: approaches to generating project ideas and proposals

Before you begin the process of designing and planning for production you should consider the approach you may wish to use. Finding ideas for projects is sometimes a difficult task.

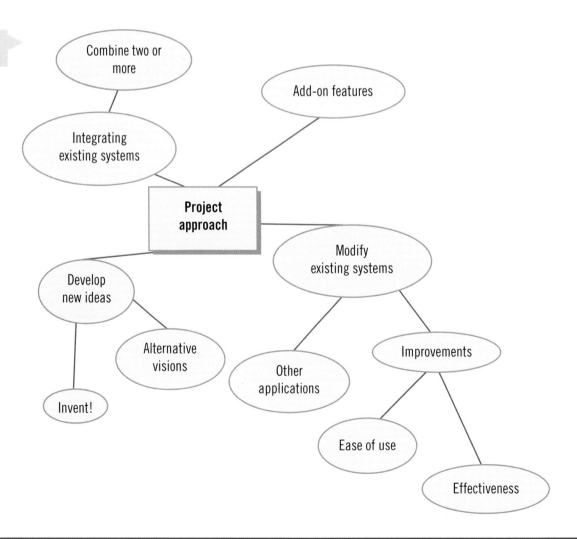

 ISBN 9780170227452

You may already have some project possibilities that you want to explore; however, you should consider all options. The type of project that you undertake will vary and the activities involved may require you to do things differently. Some possible approaches to project work are listed.

- Consider several of your own project options, then develop suitable ideas and solutions. This requires some creativity, as you are basically developing a new product and manufacturing the complete system using raw materials and individual components. For instance, you could design and make a model motorised vehicle by producing the chassis, body, gear assembly, steering device and electronic circuit for sensing and switching. You are manufacturing the complete system from start to finish.

- Devise some means of integrating a number of existing systems to form a new product. For instance, you could design the assembly of an audio and speaker system, and then integrate a motorised rotating light to form a sound and light system. Another possibility is to consider using the mechanised vehicle assembly described above, and add lights and sound to create an electronic toy, robot or game with a moulded body. You can add features such as touch sensors and remote control as your knowledge and skills increase.

- Plan the modification of existing systems. This could involve rearranging the motors and drive mechanisms on a robot arm, lifting device or solar sun-tracker to increase effectiveness. You can also develop some means of increasing transmission and fuel system efficiency, or use compound gear systems on a robot arm. You can extend these projects by adding speed, distance or movement indicators.

The systems engineering process

Describe the situation

To begin the process you need to describe the situation that created the need in the first place. The actual difficulties brought about by the problem and the improvements that can be made by developing a solution should also be defined. By doing this, you develop a clearer understanding of the problem and you can use this knowledge as a guide when formulating the design brief.

Design brief

The design brief is a clear statement that describes what has to be done to solve a particular problem or need. The brief should be clearly written to direct the designer, while being open-ended enough to allow for creativity. Sometimes design briefs are quite detailed with specific requirements. Including some specific details in a design brief can be useful as they tell more about what is needed – for example, 'design and make a piece of home gym apparatus for upper body and arm exercise; the device should be portable, possibly folding and free-standing'.

1 For the home gym apparatus brief, describe a possible situation that created a need for the device.

2 Explain the purpose of the 'design brief'.

3 Research and analyse a situation facing motor vehicle owners and issues related to security of their cars.

4 Write a design brief for a situation where theft from motor vehicles is becoming a concern.

Research and investigate

This stage involves finding out more about the problem and researching background information that could be useful when developing ideas as design options.

If we take the 'gym apparatus' design brief as an example and work through the design process, we need to proceed by considering certain design factors. These include function, safety, materials, aesthetics, technical features, production processes, availability of component and parts, assembly methods, ergonomics, tools and equipment cost.

We need to know exactly what the operator is physically capable of doing and what limitations are imposed. Looking at other similar devices can be useful to see whether or not they are suitable or capable of being modified. The design brief required 'gym apparatus'. This is often a purely mechanical device, which may prove difficult for some people to operate. Consideration should therefore be given to the possibility of introducing adjustments, or a simple way of varying loads on the device. Investigate these technical options (electronic and mechanical systems) by researching technical data, textbooks, websites and commercially produced software as workable solutions can be usually found here. Modelling or constructing prototypes of different mechanical devices can also be developed at this stage. Go to a local gym or sports shop to see what kinds of devices already exist. Further prototype work may be needed later when developing and testing ideas.

When the necessary research has been completed and important questions have been answered, the task should be much clearer. Now decisions can be made about what kind of solutions could be worked towards. For example, if we consider technical factors, a conclusion could be: 'A pulley system or levers can be employed'.

The process of consideration and conclusion should be repeated for each factor. Doing so enables a set of specifications to be produced for the system.

Describing systems

Based upon decisions made at the research stage, you should now be able to make a detailed description of a proposed system. You are at an early stage of the design process, so the system you describe is your initial idea. This needs to be refined later when you have developed your final idea or solution.

Chapter 1 of this book takes you through the methods for describing systems; a number of detailed descriptions are given in other chapters. Chapter 4, for instance, gives a detailed description of a bench-mounted drilling machine. Use the example as a guide when doing your own project work descriptions.

You should use block diagrams to show the configuration of the inputs, processes, outputs and any control devices used. Written descriptions are useful, as they give more detail and clearly explain how the system functions.

What you need to do when describing a system

1 Give a written description of the system that includes:
   - the purpose and function of the system
   - the purpose and function of the input, process, control and output devices.

2 Construct block diagrams that detail each of the above and any subsystem. Include numerical values such as input and output speed, force, voltage, and so on.

LEARNING ACTIVITY 9.2

From the project brief, research the considerations and conclusions reached for the gym equipment. Use a flow block diagram (similar to the diagram below) to describe what you think could be the main features of such a device.

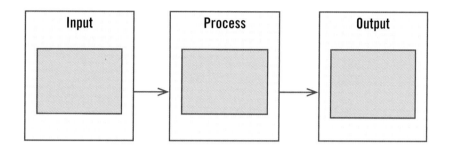

A detailed example using flow block diagrams to describe the system and subsystems of an electromechanical lifting device is given in the diagrams below and on page 252.

Radio control

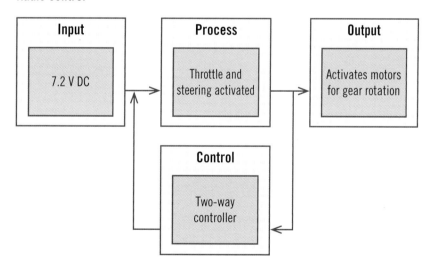

Simple gearbox attached to cable motor

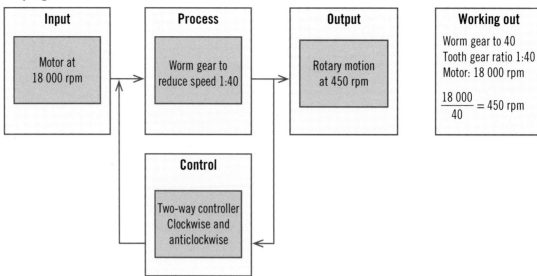

Input	Process	Output	Working out
Motor at 18 000 rpm	Worm gear to reduce speed 1:40	Rotary motion at 450 rpm	Worm gear to 40 Tooth gear ratio 1:40 Motor: 18 000 rpm $\dfrac{18\ 000}{40} = 450$ rpm

Control

Two-way controller
Clockwise and anticlockwise

Rotation of top section

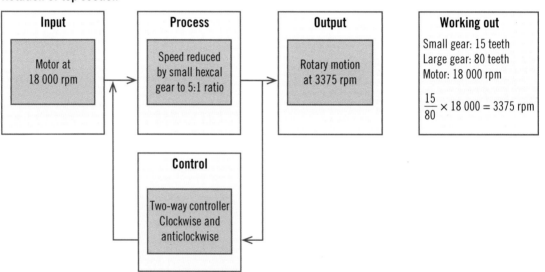

Input	Process	Output	Working out
Motor at 18 000 rpm	Speed reduced by small hexcal gear to 5:1 ratio	Rotary motion at 3375 rpm	Small gear: 15 teeth Large gear: 80 teeth Motor: 18 000 rpm $\dfrac{15}{80} \times 18\ 000 = 3375$ rpm

Control

Two-way controller
Clockwise and anticlockwise

ISBN 9780170227452

A more detailed example, using a table to segment and describe the system and subsystems of a remote control vehicle, is given below.

		Inputs	Processes	Outputs
Subsystem 1 Transmitter stages	Remote control transmitter	12V direct current 8AA 1.5V rechargeable NiCad batteries.	Current through transmitter circuit allows the remote to function.	Response to transmitter actuator sticks.
	Transmitter PWCM (pulse width code modulation) subsystem	Input of physical movement of the transmitter actuator.	Alteration in circuit current. Modification to the transmitted pulse width signal. Encoding of the pulse width signal.	Amplification and transmittance of the encoded PWS frequency to the receiver.
Subsystem 2 Receiver stage	Receiver unit	6V direct current 4AA 1.5V DC recharge NiCad batteries.	Current through the receiver allows receiver to function.	Response to radio waves and encoded PWCM.
	Receiver unit PWCM subsystem	Signal is received and interpreted by the receiver unit and sent to the decoder chip.	Decoder chip changes the PWCM into PCS.	The PCS is then sent to the corresponding servo that then changes the position of the servo.
	Receiver to servo communication subsystem	PCS signal to corresponding servo and interpreted by the internal servo electronics module.	Servo emulates the received PCS from the receiver. The internal electronic unit and rotation sensor detects the position of the servo axle.	The combination of the servo rotation sensor and electronic unit monitors the position of the servo axle and matches this position with that required by the PWC.
Subsystem 3 Engine cycle	Induction	Inlet valve opens; exhaust closes.	Fuel and air mixture is drawn into the cylinder.	Inlet valve closes by moving piston.
	Compression	Inlet and exhaust valves close.	Fuel and air mix is compressed.	Compressed mixture is hot, causing the petrol to vaporise.
	Power	Both valves close.	Compressed fuel and air is ignited by spark. Gases expand.	Piston forced down; exhaust valve opens.
	Exhaust	Inlet valve closes; exhaust opens.	Piston rises.	Burnt gases expelled.

Schematic diagrams can be useful alternatives to tables and block diagrams as they show the actual layout and configuration of a system, as shown in this example.

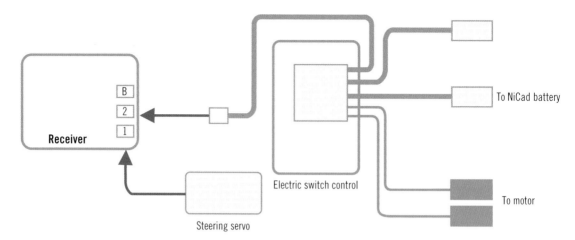

To NiCad battery

To motor

Receiver

Electric switch control

Steering servo

1: steering; 2: throttle; B: battery

Specifications

The design specifications are important as they describe the features that are fixed and those that should remain flexible and open to change when developing solutions. The specifications can be used later (at the testing and evaluating stages) as a set of criteria for evaluating the system.

How to arrive at specifications and design parameters

Look again at the design brief 'Design and make a shoulder and arm exercise device for a home gymnasium'. Some conclusions were that 'the device should be lightweight and portable'.

Based on these conclusions, a specification point could simply say 'folding and made from aluminium'. These are more specific points as the material has been identified and the construction method established.

Specification points should be established for each conclusion and any decision made. Sometimes this can be quite a long list! If some conclusions were not reached, the specification can allow for options, for example 'pulleys or levers can be employed', or it can be very open-ended and say 'the device should operate mechanically'.

Example 1: basic specifications for gym apparatus

Design and make a piece of home gym apparatus for upper body and arm exercise.

- The device should be portable and free standing (maximum 1.5 m × 1 m × 0.5 m).

- It should be lightweight (maximum 40 kg), so the frame should be made from aluminium.

- Pulleys and levers should be used.

- It should have some means of adjusting loads or tension for different user strengths.

- An electronic counter should be attached to count movements.

- It should be easy to maintain and repair.

Example 2: detailed technical specifications for a guitar project

Sound output	20–18000 Hz
Body dimensions	600 mm × 500 mm × 45 mm
Floyd rose	Pivot 60° left and right, increase or decrease each note by three tones
Pickups	70 mm × 40 mm 20–18000 Hz
Preamp unit	Adjust between distorted and clean sounds
Tone control unit	Variable range Adjust between treble and bass sounds Master volume
Fret board	24 frets 400 mm radius
Distorted frequency	Variable range
Tone control	Variable range Adjusts individual pickup's tone Functions independently
Volume control	20–18000 Hz Variable range Adjusts pickup's volume

Ideas and solutions

This is the stage in the design process where you become openly creative and begin to put your ideas down on paper. Based upon your research and specifications you should have some clear thoughts about the kind of ideas you hope to develop. Some of your ideas could be laid out in diagrams or systems that you have sourced from books, manuals or relevant software that you intend to use as part of your system. You can also modify these to suit your exact requirements.

Sketches and drawings enable you to put ideas on paper so you can refer to these when seeking advice and consulting with others. Sketches can be modified as ideas start to develop and you begin to assess their viability. Notes are also important and should be added to your sketches and drawings to record your thoughts as you go along. You can construct basic models – computer-designed (CAD) and computer-simulated systems, three-dimensional prototypes and so on – of your initial ideas to see if they are worth developing further. Each time you do this you should refer back to the specifications as criteria or guidelines by which to judge each proposal.

Each design option should attempt to satisfy the specifications; keep this in mind as you work. If an idea doesn't fulfil the needs of the specifications, it should be modified or improved until you are satisfied that it does, or that it goes some way towards doing so.

What you should do

1 Complete a range of sketches and drawings (freehand and computer generated) of your ideas.

2 Use sourced drawings and diagrams and circuit diagrams from books, magazines, technical software, websites and so on.

3 Use notes to explain your ideas in detail.

4 Model and prototype (three-dimensional scaled models, computer simulations, subsystem trials, microprocessor techniques and so on) to test if the ideas are workable.

5 Compare each of your ideas to one another and to the specifications.

6 Decide which of the ideas are worth developing further.

Selecting and developing design options

You may choose to select one or several ideas as possible solutions. By developing your ideas you are in fact attempting to make improvements and trying to clarify how effective the proposal is before actually making it. You should develop what you regard as the best option. If this proves to be successful you can select it for production; if problems occur, you can make further modifications or select another option. You can do further tests to each proposal in turn by building prototypes or models of the whole system or parts of it. For instance, you can model electronic circuits on breadboard or simulate these and mechanical systems using appropriate computer software. Mechanical systems can be prototyped using kit components or simply by sketching and performing relevant calculations.

Working drawings that show different views of the system are useful as they display the shape and profile of the system. Orthogonal drawings that show the front, end and plan views should give enough detail of the parts and the complete system. You need to fully dimension these drawings to include sizes such as length, width, diameter and thread size.

Selecting and justifying preferred options

Whenever you select an option (for further development or as a result of developmental work) that you plan to carry through to the production stage, you could put together a checklist for each specification point, then compare and score the selected option to the list. This could also be incorporated into testing and evaluating tasks.

If you have several options, compare each one by giving a score for each specification point, for instance a 1–5 score; a 'yes' or 'no'; high, medium and low criteria; tick boxes (☑); or any combination of these. You could use a PMI (plus, minus, interesting) table (see below) to list the positive, negative and interesting features of each proposal. The following examples should give you some ideas.

Comparing design options

	Option 1	Option 2
Plus		
Minus		
Interesting		

Example 1: justifying design options – gym equipment

Design and make a piece of home gym apparatus for upper body and arm exercise.

☑ The device should be portable and free-standing.

☑ It should be lightweight, so the frame should be made from aluminium.

☑ Pulleys and levers should be used.

ISBN 9780170227452

☑ It should have adjusting loads or tension for different user strengths.

☑ An electronic counter should be attached to count movements.

☑ It should be easy to maintain and repair.

Example 2: justifying design options – gym equipment

Design and make a piece of home gym apparatus for upper body and arm exercise: selected design option checklist

Specifications	Score	Comment
The device should be portable and free-standing.	High	Folding with wheels on base; most compact and lightest prototype.
It should be lightweight, so the frame should be made from aluminium.	Yes	
Pulleys and levers should be used.	Yes	
It should have adjusting loads or tension for different user strengths.	Medium	Yes, bolt type and locking pins; secure but time consuming when adjusting.
An electronic counter should be attached to count movements.	Yes	
It should be easy to maintain and repair.	Medium	Mechanical parts require attention.

Careful consideration must be given to choosing the best option. Checklists and data tables (such as in the previous two examples) based on specifications are an accurate way of assisting with this task. You also need to justify your selection by giving a written account with good and clear reasons 'why' and 'how' you think this satisfies the design brief and specifications for the system. For instance, a number of folding methods may have been tested for the gym apparatus frame and one particular option was found to fold more easily and to be more compact in size. This 'evidence' needs to be established and documented when justifying choices.

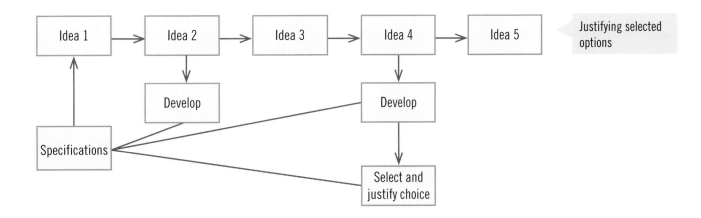

Planning for production

Before production work can begin you need to carry out a number of important planning tasks. Good planning or project management makes the task easier and enables you to think through any potential problems.

Production planning involves the following tasks:

1 compiling component and materials lists

2 listing the tools and equipment required

3 developing a plan and time line for production work

4 developing risk-assessment plans for production.

Components and materials

Ensure that you have all the necessary components and materials needed to manufacture the complete project. This saves time during production as parts often have to be ordered and purchased and there could be delays with delivery. You also have to think about alternative resources if you are unable to find the parts you require.

You should list all of the components and parts needed, stating how many are required and any values related to these. Material type and sizes should also be listed as materials have to be purchased and prepared.

A typical materials and parts list for the gym equipment project could be:

- aluminium square section – 2 m × 40 mm

- aluminium rod – 1 m × 20 mm

- aluminium angle/L section – 1 m × 25 mm

- M8 × 50 nuts, bolts and washers – 10

- pulley wheels 80 mm – 3

- pulley cable – 2 m

- handle sleeve/grips – 2

- electronic counter circuit (list all components and the total required).

Equipment and tools

Having the necessary tools and equipment available for production work is essential. This means that planned production processes can be done without having to make changes to the design or having to find alternative parts. This factor should have been considered at the research stage, as you need to ensure that production work can be done with available resources and equipment.

Tools and equipment can be listed in the same way as the materials and components; for instance:

- drilling machine
- metalwork lathe
- welder
- etch tank
- soldering iron

- spanners, 8 mm
- screwdriver set
- 5 and 8 mm drill bits
- hammer
- centre punch

ISBN 9780170227452

- scriber
- files
- cable clips and crimpers
- countersink bit, 12 mm
- metal saws
- pliers.

Production sequence

Organising production work is an important task that requires considerable knowledge of the processes involved in manufacturing. With a sound knowledge of your designed system and the processes involved in making it, you should plan the sequence of production to ensure that progress is smooth and there are no unnecessary delays.

Sequence plans can be written as lists (similar to the components and equipment list described earlier) with each of the stages numbered. Flow charts or block diagrams can also be very effective; they are graphic representations and the stages are easily identified at a glance. You should also develop a time line for production work. Doing so helps you to maintain and monitor your progress and prepare for unexpected problems. Weekly time lines are adequate for most production tasks.

You could create a basic sequence list to describe your production plan. A counter circuit sequence plan might be like this

1 Clean the printed circuit board (PCB), then attach a template for the hole locations.

2 Drill 1 mm holes or larger where required.

3 Remove template, clean surface with steel wool and draw tracks on PCB.

4 Etch PCB in etch tank, checking at intervals until ready.

5 Remove, rinse and clean off remaining surface ink.

6 Check quality of tracks for continuity – visually and with a multimeter at resistance settings.

A gym equipment sequence plan might be like this.

1 Mark out and cut materials for frame body.

2 Shape parts to profile and sizes.

3 Mark out and drill holes.

4 Weld frame.

5 Assemble mechanical parts.

6 Fit and secure pulley cable.

7 Attach handles.

8 Mark out and drill printed circuit board.

9 Mark out circuit tracks.

10 Etch PCB.

11 Assemble components to PCB.

12 Test circuit.

13 Manufacture housing for circuit.

14 Connect circuit to pulley spindle.

15 Complete assembly and final test.

Alternatively, you could show production stages with materials and components and the required tools and equipment in a table.

Stage detail	Materials/component	Equipment
1 Mark out sizes and profiles, then cut material for frame body.	Aluminium square section – 2 m × 40 mm Aluminium rod – 1 m × 20 mm Aluminium angle/L section – 1 m × 25 mm	Scriber Steel rule Metalwork square Bench vice
2 Shape parts to profile and sizes.		Bench vice Metal saws Metal files
3 Mark out and drill holes.		Scriber Steel rule Metalwork square Centre punch Hammer Drill machine Machine vice 5 and 8 mm drill bits Countersink, etc.
And so on …		

A Gantt chart could also be included to show production stages, time line and actual progress.

Remote controlled aircraft: production planning Gantt chart

Description/week	Week 1	Week 2	Week 3	Week 4	Week 5	Week 6	Week 7	Week 8	Week 9	Week 10
Organise	Est.									
	Act.									
Purchase materials	Est.									
	Act.									
Construction on fuselage	Est.	Est.	Est.							
	Act.	Act.	Act.	Act.						
Construction on wing				Est.	Est.					
					Act.	Act.				
Construction on fuselage					Est.					
							Act.			
Construction on rudder						Est.				
							Act.			
Construction on tail plane						Est.				
							Act.	Act.		
Construction on wing							Est.			
								Act.		
Construction on control arms							Est.	Est.		
								Act.		
Mount engine								Est.		
									Act.	
Testing and evaluating									Est.	Est.
										Act.

ISBN 9780170227452

Risk assessment and risk management

Risk assessment is basically a process of analysing all the possible risks related to the design, production, testing, operation and maintenance of a system throughout its lifetime. What you are in fact doing is 'managing risk'.

Risk assessment helps you to consider and show that you have established the following criteria:

- You have the skills to perform any planned tasks.

- The equipment and planned production methods are hazard free.

- Planned testing and maintenance procedures are risk free.

- The system or product is designed for safety and ease of use.

Depending on the time available, you may decide to make risk assessments for the major production and testing tasks, and for obvious risk situations only.

Risk assessment is explained further in Chapter 10, 'Production: equipment, safety and materials'. You should read the section on risk assessment to see how the procedure is carried out, before proceeding with this chapter.

LEARNING ACTIVITY 9.3

1 Search the Internet for information on risk assessment that you can use in project planning.

2 Use the completed risk-assessment plan below as a guide to producing a plan for a practical task required in your production work.

Partial risk-assessment plans

Example 1: gym equipment counter circuit – PCB etching process: use of tools, equipment and processing (including chemicals) with a degree of danger

Identification of risks, hazards and safety issues	Assessment	Eliminate or control risk
Chemical usage hazard: ammonium persulfate – inhalation, skin contact and absorption possible	Chemical hazard if contact with skin, eyes, etc; can cause injury – from minor to serious irritation and damage to skin and eyes	Follow the manufacturer's materials data sheet advice. 'Teacher only' to use this equipment. Etch tank should be located in a suitable chemical or fume extraction unit. Wear suitable hand and eye safety protection. PCB should be placed in tank basket or tray and slowly immersed into tank.
Fume or vapour inhalation possible	Low to medium level	Cover tank, close unit door. Switch on heater, pump and extractor.
PCB artwork to be complete and accurate for operational use	Possibility of over/under-etching tracks or boards	Check condition of boards during process. Switch off heater, pump and extractor when process is completed. Remove basket or tray and flush etched boards. Quality check or test.

Example 2: remote controlled aircraft

Hazard	Risk	Risk control	Personal protective equipment
Hand tools Shutterstock.com/Albo0003	Sharp Pinch Crush Lacerations Abrasions	Should be used safely and appropriately. Use correct tool for correct job. See user instructions before use.	Glasses Ear muffs Footwear
CNC laser printer	Fumes are toxic. Laser beam Electricity Cutting material	Dust extractor must be used at all times to prevent toxic fumes. Lid must be shut while in use. Only use correct material. Never use PVC plastic. Electricity is dangerous. Never have water or fluid nearby. Ensure tested and tagged.	Glasses Ear muffs Footwear
Environment (CNC – computer numerical controlled – room)	Cluttered Crowding Limited space	The room needs to be managed safely and appropriately. One person at a time on each machine.	Glasses Safety clothing Footwear Hair net
Battery drill iStockphoto/© manley099	Penetration Sharp Pointed	Should be used safely and appropriately. Observe at all times to prevent accidents. Ensure tested and tagged.	Footwear

View student folio samples and a usable design folio template on the website
www.cengage.com.au/syseng.

Example 3: vehicle

Hazard	Assessment level of risk (low/mid/high)	Action necessary to avoid hazard
Contact with filings of PVC chassis from drilling, cutting, filing and other methods of refinement. Filings of plastic may come into contact with the user's eyes. Filings may also enter the throat or penetrate the skin.	The filings may be able to blind, choke and even cut the user. The filings may cause infection in the eyes or skin due to bad bacteria entering the body. Level of risk: low to mid	Wear safety goggles and gloves. Be in an adequate working environment that is not enclosed. Brush away filings or any other by-products constantly when refining the PVC board.

ISBN 9780170227452

Hazard	Assessment level of risk (low/mid/high)	Action necessary to avoid hazard
Heating from soldering electronic components	The heat from the tip of the iron has the ability to damage the components to be soldered onto the circuit board, e.g. transistors. Level of risk: mid to high	Use pliers to grip onto the wire of the component close to where it is soldered. This will enable most of the heat to be absorbed in the pliers rather than the component itself. Use a heat sink to assist.
Hot glue from glue gun coming into contact with skin of user	The heat from the glue is able to burn the user. Level of risk: mid	Wear protective gloves. Whenever using glue, ensure the trigger is disengaged completely when the glue gun is not in use. Apply only small amounts of glue at a time.
Inappropriate positioning or size of materials when cutting it using the scroll saw	The user may accidentally sever fingers when attempting to cut material if it is too small. If too large the material will bend and twist the blade of the saw, which will eventually break. Level of risk: mid to high	Ensure that the material used is suitably sized for the scroll saw to cut. Allow hands to be a safe distance away from the scroll saw. When cutting curved shapes ensure that the material is moved slowly around the blade.

Testing systems

Testing is an important part of product manufacture. We test completed systems to see how effective they are while in operation and to establish if they satisfy the recommended specifications. We also test in the event of failure or unsatisfactory performances, so that appropriate modifications can be recommended and implemented.

Subsystems and major components can also be tested before and during production and assembly stages. This enables us to identify problems or inefficiencies that can be dealt with before assembly and final testing. For instance, an electric motor may not achieve the expected output speed, so a decision can be made at an early stage to repair or replace it with a better one. Inputs, processes, monitoring devices, control devices and outputs should always be measured to see if they are accurate and as intended.

Chapter 8, 'Testing engineering systems', looks at methods and procedures for testing systems. You should refer to the chapter when planning and performing your own tests. The case study, 'Testing, flight data systems', also deals with this topic. Read the case study on pages 233–242, if you have not done so.

Planning tests

To plan and perform tests on systems there are a number of stages that you should follow. Planning in a logical sequence means that your work is structured and you know exactly what you are setting out to achieve and how to do this. For each test you should do the following.

- Give the reason or purpose for the test – for example, to measure vehicle speed under different running and technical conditions.

- Specify the expected test results. These would be expected values such as output speeds, volume, input and output voltage, compression, temperature range and timing.

- Plan test procedures. Plan each step of the test and list the test equipment to be used.

- Perform the actual test and record the results.

- Analyse the actual results and compare them to the intended outcome.

- Discuss both sets of data. They may be acceptable. If they are different, you need to make recommendations. This could be to modify the system or replace parts. When you do this, repeat the test to check if the intended results are achieved.

LEARNING ACTIVITY 9.4

1 Read the diagnostic test report that follows. Note how the student covers all of the stages and main points in discussing the project being tested.

2 Suggest if and how the report can be improved.

View student folio samples and a usable design folio template on the website **www.cengage.com.au/syseng**.

Student sample: diagnostic test

Purpose

This test is designed to evaluate the effectiveness of the engine and drive train system on a model racing car. The drive train consists of a four-wheel drive through belts driven by the motor. The aim is to extract the maximum amount of acceleration possible without sacrificing cornering speed or straight-line stability.

Test sequence

1 Find a place where the road surface is flat with consistent grip levels and dry weather conditions.

2 Start the engine and make sure the fuel tank is filled with the exact amount of fuel. Any difference in this may yield inconsistent results.

3 Mark a 15 m distance for the start and end of the test track.

4 Prepare time facility or ideally perform test at a dedicated remote control track with a computer timing system.

5 Place the vehicle at the beginning of the track and accelerate using maximum carburettor aperture.

6 When the 15 m distance has been passed, apply the brakes and come to a rest.

7 Repeat steps using different car set-ups or conditions to find which situation best suits maximum acceleration.

8 Enter results and compare to find the optimum set-up or condition to accommodate maximum acceleration.

Perform three tests

1 The first set-up without body and standard tyres

2 The second using a body with standard tyres

3 The third test using a body and sponge tyres.

Equipment needed

- Vehicle, tyres and body
- Fuel
- Test track
- Starter
- Tool kit
- Timer/clock

Testing and recording results

Test	Result 1 (s)	Result 2 (s)	Result 3 (s)
Expected rating	4.0	4.0	4.0
Actual rating	3.8	3.5	2.7

Analysis

The first two results differed only slightly from the expected ratings. The final test far exceeded the expectations. Different tyre compounds certainly affect grip and speed. The body weight had little effect on the output speed. This car is fast due to its light weight coupled with the powerful and hard revving motor. The use of a different nitro percentage will give modified results. This should be the next test performed. Colder air plays a part as it is denser and creates greater down force, and may increase the air–fuel mixture. The result is a faster car, as it will produce more power as well as better grip. Overall, the test conditions were kept fairly static during the testing period, so the results should be accurate in this respect.

View student folio samples and a usable design folio template on the website **www.cengage.com.au/syseng**.

Here is a good method of planning and recording data and text results.

Student sample: remote controlled aircraft diagnostic test plan

A complete test plan, recorded data and analysis. One of four tests performed on the project.

Diagnostic test aim

The aim of this diagnostic test is to ascertain how much static thrust the OS Max 25 LA engine is able to achieve while turning a 9 × 6 propeller.

An OS Max 25 LA engine parts

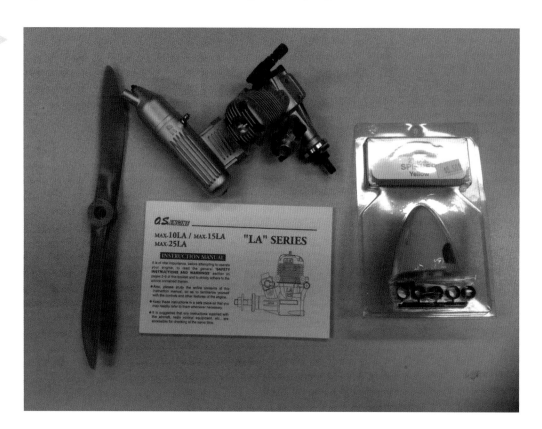

Expected results

I am unsure on how much static thrust this little motor will develop. I have looked at the specifications of this engine and it states that it capable of delivering 0.6 horsepower @ 15 000 rpm. As the horsepower isn't an SI unit of measure, I converted it – this gave me 441.3 watts or 0.44 kW. Further considerations will involve the carburetion mixture during the test runs, such as being 'rich' or 'lean'.

Tools and instruments required

- Suitable workshop and bench with fume extraction
- One solid piece of timber to mount the engine
- Electric starter and glow-plug driver
- Methanol fuel with silicon lines
- Newton measuring gauge

Planning the test (method)

Safety note: Due to the nature of this test my teacher should start and rev the engine throughout the testing process.

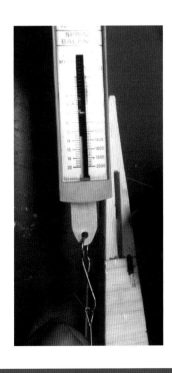

Attached Newton gauge

While the teacher is doing this I can take the readings at the measuring gauge.

1 Assemble the engine with the propeller, spinner and muffler.

2 Attach the OS engine to the test timber with screws.

3 Secure the timber to the bench and locate it under the vice.

4 Attach the measuring gauge to the block of timber and to a solid fixture on the bench.

5 Attach fuel lines and prime the carburettor.

6 Start and run engine.

7 Record data from both 'rich' and 'lean' runs.

Diagnostic testing results

Number	Description	Measurement
Test 1	Initial test run	Overload
Test 2	Mixture setting 'rich'	11–12 N
Test 3	Mixture setting 'lean'	15–16 N

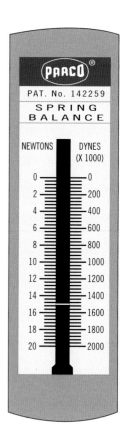

Safety note: Due to the extreme nature of this test it is paramount that my teacher should start and rev the engine throughout the testing process. While teacher is doing this I can take the readings at the measuring gauge.

The diagnostic test was very helpful in finding out how many newtons the OS Max 25 LA engine could pull while turning a 9 × 6 propeller. I found the test quite difficult, the reading on the gauge move quite a bit so it was hard to accurately record data.

Test 1

The recording I obtained from the first test wasn't very helpful because the engine overloaded as this was the first time the engine had run and the readings were irregular.

Test 2

The recording I obtained in the second test was with the mixture setting on 'rich'. The measuring gauge had a stronger reading with 11–12 N recorded, although this was still not the maximum static thrust.

Test 3

The recording I obtained in the third test was with the mixture setting on 'lean'. The Newton measuring gauge had a stronger reading again with 15–16 N recorded. I am satisfied that the result recorded here is accurate and precise.

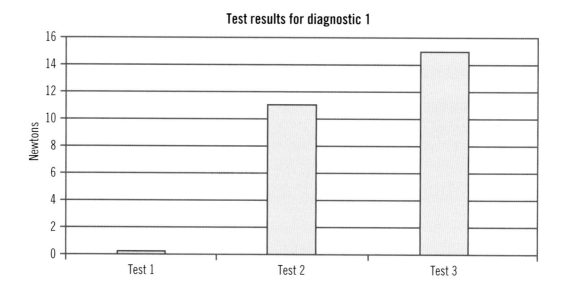

Note: Test 1 overload; no clear reading on the Newton measuring gauge.

Evaluating the design plan and production activities

This stage is concerned with the whole process of designing, planning, making and testing a complete and operational system. You need to reflect upon all the activities involved in the task and identify successes and difficulties, lessons learnt and changes made to the planned processes and product. A well-documented log or record of progress should help you to recall all of your experiences throughout the design and production phases. You should also be aware of any further improvements that can be made to the product, based upon analysis of completed tests and assessment criteria related to the product specifications.

Important points in evaluation reports

The following points should be discussed in an evaluation report. There may also be other points you can add.

1 The effectiveness of the design and production plan

2 Changes made to the plan and modifications to the product, with justifications for these

3 Suitability of the product in satisfying the needs of the brief and specifications

4 Recommendations for change and modifications to the plan and the product

A thorough and honest evaluation report is essential. It will help you and others to understand the full complexity of the completed task and the strengths and weaknesses of the design plan and the product. You should use both notes and diagrams in your report. Remember that you are producing a technical report on a technical process and system, so making diagrams is strongly advised.

View student folio samples and a usable design folio template on the website **www.cengage.com.au/syseng**.

LEARNING ACTIVITY 9.5

1 Read through the following evaluation report. Note how the student covers all four discussion points, although under three headings.

2 Assess how well the report addresses each point and make suggestions on how and where the report can be improved by additional discussion, details and diagrams, and so on.

3 Use the four discussion points to describe and evaluate a recent production task that you have completed. Include sketches and diagrams where possible.

Student sample: evaluation report

Effectiveness of the design plan

Having previously purchased laser kit components for a light and sound unit, I decided to manufacture a laser light unit based on the laser kit design. With my manufactured version laser it was necessary to make some changes. The first of the changes was the size of the printed circuit board. I cut my circuit board larger than the kit PCB. I did this to allow for more space to draw the tracks on the board. I did the artwork by hand so I could not match production line quality.

I used smaller motors on the copied board as I was unable to obtain motors of the same size and specifications as those in the kit. These motors were able to handle the same voltage but did not have as high a speed rating as the motors that came in the kit. This had no effect on the way the system operated as the motors do not operate at extremely high speed. Two types of transistors that were on the original board were unavailable. I needed to find suitable substitutes for these transistors for the copied board. To resolve this problem I substituted the 2SC3242 transistor in the copied board and three C 8050 transistors. These transistors function very similarly to the other transistors and were good substitutes.

Effectiveness of the production plan

I tried to keep to my production plan. Sometimes the stages of my production took longer than expected. All sorts of problems arose when I least expected them; this set me back even more.

One of the problems I encountered during construction of the original laser was that one of the transistors on the copied board had a dry solder joint on one of its legs. To the naked eye this dry solder joint appeared as a normal solder joint. I thought it was connecting the transistor to the PCB, but in actual fact the solder was not making a true connection between the transistor and the PCB. This problem caused one of the motors to not function. It was problems like this that caused delays in my production and required me to spend more time trying to find the faults.

I encountered a problem with the copied board as some of the copper that should have been removed in the etch tank remained and caused connections between two tracks. In order to break these connections I needed to scratch away the copper that was joining these tracks. This was only one of the minor, but important, tasks that again caused delays in production.

View detailed student sample evaluations on the website **www.cengage.com.au/syseng**.

ISBN 9780170227452

Suitability of the product

Generally both of the laser light systems function very well. Apart from a few problems experienced during construction the overall finished product is good. All of the specifications were met.

The kit and the copy both provide different speeds for each of the motors. One of the motors in each system can operate in reverse direction and one on each board can be stopped. Both displays show various patterns as required.

However, one improvement that could be made is to obtain a brighter laser light diode for each unit. The pattern produced by the current light diodes can only be seen best in a darkened room. If they were replaced with brighter light diodes, the pattern and the whole product would be a lot more effective and more impressive.

Your next task

When you complete this chapter you should read through case study 6, 'Vehicle style and design'. The case study tells how a commercial designer in the motor vehicle manufacturing industry uses a process similar to the systems engineering process to research, design, plan, manufacture, test and evaluate a concept vehicle.

Note how the designer researches the specific market sector and how ideas are developed and realised through design work, CAD applications, modelling, prototyping, making and testing. You are expected to use these skills and techniques in your project work.

It should become clear to you that what you are doing through design and production work is similar to the methods used by all professional designers and manufactures. The knowledge and skills you learn and perfect throughout the systems engineering process will be of great benefit to you if you pursue a career in any industrial or commercial sector.

Systems engineering project ideas

- Adjustable laptop stand
- Automatic door control device
- Automatic dust extractor
- Automatic feeding device
- Automatic room fan
- Automatic security door
- Blow-moulding machine
- Burglar alarm for the home
- Childproof medical container
- Computer-controlled buggy
- Computer-controlled drill
- Computer-controlled security system
- Door alarm system
- Easy-lifting devices
- Electric guitar

- Electric tool press for a workshop
- Electromechanical board games
- Electronic dice circuit
- Electronic percussion instrument
- Electronic pinball machine
- Electronic toys and games
- Engine conversion systems
- Engine-powered generator
- Fuel-level sensor
- Ground level meter
- Home intercom system
- Ignition lock for a car
- Ladder levelling device
- LED scroll name display
- Light display unit

- Light-following vehicle
- Line-following vehicle
- Materials compression tester
- Mechanical locking device for bicycles
- Metal detector
- Mini forklift
- Motorised barbecue
- Motorised hovercraft
- Motorised model boat
- Motorised trolley
- Night and day light sensor
- Noise-activated alarm
- Noise-level monitor
- Optical alarm device
- Optical communication device
- Optical display device
- Optical sensing device

- Pneumatic bench vice
- Pneumatic press
- Pneumatic saw
- Rain gauge
- Remote adjusting monitor or TV screen
- Remote controlled aircraft
- Remote controlled tripod
- Remote controlled vehicle
- Remote control security gate
- Robot arm
- Solar tracking system
- Sound and light system
- Table soccer game
- Tensile testing device
- Vacuum-forming machine
- Water-level indicator alarm
- Wind-powered generator

Weblinks

www.vcaa.vic.edu.au/
excellenceawards

www.technologystudent.
com

www.worksafe.vic.
gov.au

www.safeworkaustralia.
gov.au

www.safetyrisk.com.au

www.designcouncil.
org.uk

www.engineersedge.
com

www.matweb.com

Google Images search:
design process stages

The website **www.vcaa.vic.edu.au/excellenceawards** contains information and photographs of some excellent VCE projects produced by students in recent years.

For further ideas on designing systems, projects and design methodology, visit **www.technologystudent.com**. This site also has a design template that you can use as a guide to your own design and planning folio work.

END-OF-CHAPTER ACTIVITIES

1 Explain each of the following terms.
   a Design brief
   b Factors influencing design
   c Design parameters
   d Specification
   e Diagnostic testing
   f Evaluation

2 Write a design brief for a home alarm system.

3 Research mechanical locking devices and write an appropriate product specification for one of them.

4 A typical risk-assessment plan comprises the following three activities. State briefly what is involved at each stage.
   • Identify possible risks.
   • Assess each risk.
   • Remove or control the risk.

5 Use the example risk-assessment plans in this chapter as guides to produce a plan for a practical task requiring the use of machinery.

6 Explain and give reasons for when and why systems should be tested.

7 Write a brief description of a system that you have tested. List each stage or procedure followed during the test.

8 Use the four evaluation report discussion points below to describe a recent production task that you have completed. Include sketches and diagrams where possible.
   • The effectiveness of the design and production plan
   • Changes to the plan and modifications to the product, with justifications
   • Suitability of the product in satisfying the needs of the brief and specifications
   • Recommendations for change and modifications to the plan and the product

CASE STUDY 6

Vehicle style and design

This abridged case study by Nicolas Hogios, Manager of Product Design, Toyota Motor Corporation Australia, describes some of the challenges and tasks involved in the design, development and launch of the Sportivo coupe concept vehicle. The case study develops a number of the design concepts and procedures practised in industry and as outlined in both the design chapter and the manufacturing and technology case study in this book. Nicolas also describes an interesting approach to designing, planning and manufacturing that can be taken to produce quality engineering systems projects in schools.

The Sportivo coupe concept vehicle

Project purpose

- **Excitement**: Concept cars are created to capture the imagination of the general public, and enhance excitement. Motor show goers can be 'wowed' by a new styling concept, or a new technology, years before it actually reaches full-scale production.
- **Testing the market**: Concept cars can test market reaction to an idea or technology. Will people accept a particular idea or technology, or is it too far ahead of its time? A concept car can 'warm' people to ideas, making unusual cars acceptable for release years down the track.
- **Improving skills**: The task assists in the improvement of the skills and capabilities of a company. Concept cars tend to have a short time line and are not limited by the restriction of a production car. Because there is only a single car being made, new ideas can be explored with creative freedom, so new skills and ways of thinking are required by staff.
- **Creative freedom**: New 'styling design' ideas are a big part of concept car conception. From a styling designer's perspective, creative freedom is increased. A stylist can take more risks and explore ideas further, unlike a production car where hundreds of millions of dollars of development and tooling are at stake!

The design studio environment – equipment, skills, people

The various aspects that make up an automotive design studio are as follows:
- styling design – industrial design-trained designers responsible for exterior, interior and colour/trim design
- technical designers – studio engineers and CAD operators responsible for the technical feasibility of styling ideas
- A-class surfacing – CAD surfacing experts who create the final exterior and interior electronic surfaces that are ultimately used for tooling
- clay modelling – essentially sculptors who create the designer's vision in a 3D clay model
- fabricators – sheet metal, hard model and composites experts who create the non-clay models and prototypes
- studio administration – responsible for the day-to-day activities that keep the studio environment running smoothly.

The process – research, design, plan, produce, test, evaluate

Below is a step-by-step review of the planning, designing and fabricating process followed in developing the concept car.

Research

Customer research is more often than not required to 'kick off' the whole styling process, to get to the end result more concisely. It is less important for a concept project, as the aim of the project is to push the boundaries. However, for a production car, research is vital to 'hit the mark'.

Research for the Sportivo coupe involved the following:

- Present popular culture images to 14- to 18-year-old teenagers to understand mindset of the youth market.
- Teenagers were asked to comment using post-it notes.

Concept sketch phase

At this stage loose sketch ideas are quickly generated to explore a number of 'loose' ideas. Little thought is given to final build requirements as this stage is really an idea generation process.

Initial idea consultation for the Sportivo coupe was the following:

- Eight exterior and six interior sketch concepts were created.
- A second research event: the same teenagers were asked to comment on actual designs, again using post-it notes and discussion.
- The final design theme was chosen.

Feedback from the teenagers

- A stylish coupe body was the preferred image.
- Four seats were required to carry friends and socialise.
- Personal, integrated technologies were expected.
- Ability to communicate between cars was important.

Key design direction: personal and integrated technologies

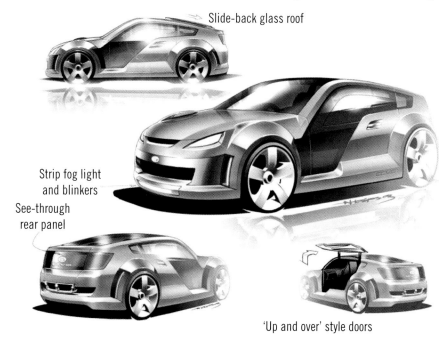

Slide-back glass roof

Strip fog light and blinkers

See-through rear panel

'Up and over' style doors

All-glass tailgate

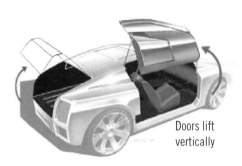

Doors lift
vertically

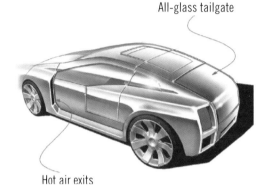

Hot air exits

Electronic design

Here the 'idea' begins its transition into a tangible, 3D proposal. This is done either as clay or as a computer-generated model. It is vital that the idea is not lost in the transition from the 2D sketch to the 3D model. This is one of the designer's biggest challenges.

Modelling for the Sportivo coupe

- A CAD model of final design was created.
- A 30% scale model was machined in foam and reviewed.
- A second 30% scale model was machined in foam and reviewed.
- The model was refined.
- A full-sized model was machined in foam.
- An interior package was created.
- A 21-inch wheel model was created.
- A space frame was simultaneously created on CAD (CATIA) to bond the body to the chassis. CATIA is a top-end engineering software package used by car companies and large-scale aviation companies.
- The gull-wing door system was designed on CATIA.

ISBN 9780170227452

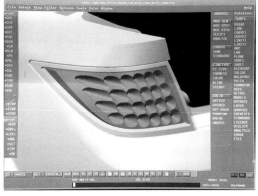
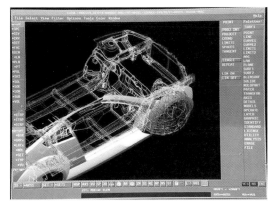
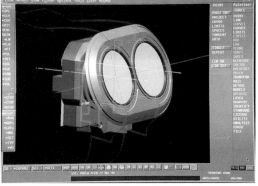

Nicolas Hogios, Manager of Product Design, Toyota Motor Corporation Australia

Model fabrication

This process takes the final design surfaces and translates them into a working hard model. Sometimes it is simply a rolling chassis, a frame to attach the exterior panels and house the interior. However, in the case of the Sportivo coupe it was a fully functional running prototype.

Fabrication for the Sportivo coupe

Mechanical

- The basic car chassis was modified and the space frame fitted.
- A standard 2.4-L engine was turbocharged and intercooled.
- A gearbox was modified and fitted.
- An all-wheel-drive system fitted.
- Massive racing brakes and cross-drilled rotors were fitted.
- 21-inch wheels were cast.
- Gull-wing door system frames were built.

Nicolas Hogios, Manager of Product Design, Toyota Motor Corporation Australia

Body

- A negative of the body data was machined out of solid blocks and assembled to make tooling.
- A one-piece (other than doors, bonnet and boot lid) carbon fibre body was created from this tooling.
- The carbon fibre body was attached to the chassis and space frame.
- Gull-wing door panels, bonnet and boot lid were attached to the body.

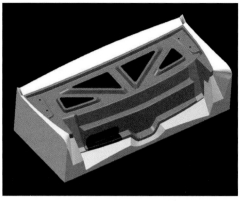

Nicolas Hogios, Manager of Product Design, Toyota Motor Corporation Australia

Interior

- Foam prototype panels were made from data and adjusted by hand.
- Panels were scanned and remodelled.
- Final hard panels were made.
- Seats were fabricated by hand using fibreglass and soft trim.
- Steering wheel, gearshift, grab handles and so on were all machined.

Final build: production

With such a complex product as a fully functional automobile, there are literally hundreds of mating parts to manage. In the case of the Sportivo coupe, a short development time meant that there were going to be some part mismatches. At this point it is effectively the skill of the fabricators that solves these issues. This is a very chaotic time and usually occurs very close to a motor show launch date. This involves a huge number of hours and very late nights!

Nicolas Hogios, Manager of Product Design, Toyota Motor Corporation Australia

Launch: evaluation

The launch of the Sportivo coupe at the Melbourne Motor Show was a spectacular success, to say the least. The media were stunned and stayed around the vehicle long after the 'reveal' had finished. The public response was just as overwhelming, with crowds flocking to see the 'star of the show'.

We invited the original 14- to 18-year-olds back to check on our interpretation of their ideas. During the 'big unveil' they were there, next to the 'car of their dreams' that they had had a hand in creating.

The car was featured heavily in the media. This 'free advertising' more than paid for the cost of the project. Years after the car was first revealed, its use as a publicity vehicle is still in full swing, and it is featured on television shows, advertisements and billboard advertising.

Nicolas Hogios, Manager of Product Design, Toyota Motor Corporation Australia

Concept versus production vehicles

What are the procedural differences between a 'one-off' futuristic concept car and a 'production line' daily driven vehicle? Well, the differences are quite immense!

A production program runs for a lot longer than a concept car program. Numerous manufacturing constraints must be addressed before a design is considered 'feasible'.

Close collaboration with engineering, marketing and purchasing departments is essential every step of the way to ensure not only that the image of the car is correct, but also that the car can be built to a high level of quality for the right price.

The design studio normally works with clay models. This allows the designer to refine a design to perfection and make surface changes for engineering or styling modifications. During a production process the model goes through countless iterations before being signed off for production.

Clay modelling is often used on concept car projects, but in the case of the Sportivo coupe there was insufficient time, so an electronic process was employed, as outlined earlier.

The process of producing a one-off concept vehicle is similar in many respects to the process followed by students studying systems engineering. Both situations require a lot of planning, modelling, prototyping, and testing as you go along. This is needed to ensure that the one and only final product has a greater chance of being a success. You generally only get one go! The evaluation stage enables feedback and a true assessment of the whole project. This, however, is where it ends, unlike normal production vehicles where the process can be repeated so that vehicles are continually redesigned, modified and updated.

ISBN 9780170227452

10

PRODUCTION: EQUIPMENT, SAFETY AND MATERIALS

In this chapter you will learn about the correct and safe use of some common engineering tools and equipment used in production work. In doing so you will examine a range of materials and related processes that could be used for production tasks. The chapter also addresses the need to consider relevant Australian standards, occupational health and safety issues, and risk-managing production activities that are potentially hazardous.

Workshop equipment

When we work with systems we need to use a wide range of tools, equipment and components, some of which are highly specialised. We use tools and equipment for preparing, marking out, processing, assembling and testing components and technical systems. It is essential that precautions are followed for correct use and to avoid injury. Some important precautions are:

- Make sure the work area is kept clear, clean and has adequate lighting.

- Wear eye and ear protection when cutting, sawing, drilling and grinding.

- Do not wear loose clothing when operating machines.

- Inspect the condition of all tools and equipment before use.

- Never leave machines or power tools running unattended.

- Check that the equipment being used and the components being assembled meet the relevant Australian Standards.

When you assemble or repair a system you should choose the right tools. Using the wrong tool can result in damage to some part of the system; it can create problems that will be expensive to fix; and in some cases it can cause the system to cease operating.

There are many tools to choose from. Some are specialised and would be used in industry; many can be found at home and in school systems areas and workshops.

Soldering tools

Soldering irons are an important tool when assembling an electronic circuit. Most irons run from 240 V mains; however, most common low voltage types usually come as part of a soldering station. The soldering station, which is more expensive, transforms or reduces voltage and includes some means of controlling the temperature. Soldering irons vary in size and some have interchangeable tips of different shapes.

Heat-sink clips are used to protect electronic components from overheating during the soldering process and are usually made of a material with very high thermal conductivity that will conduct the heat away from the part to be protected. Heat sinks work on the principle that heat will always flow from a hot object to a colder one.

Soldering iron and transformer

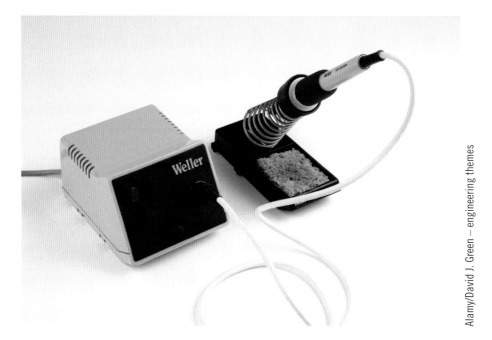

Selecting soldering irons

Where possible select soldering irons that have temperature control.

Using a soldering iron

Ensure that the soldering iron and its components are clean. Solder will not 'stick' to dirty surfaces.

The amount of solder used is important – too little and the joint will be weak; too much may cause short circuits with adjacent joints.

The soldering process is examined more thoroughly in Chapter 5, 'Electrotechnology'.

Pliers

After the screwdriver, pliers would be the next most versatile group of tools. They are used to grip, turn and cut. There are many different types of pliers:

- Combination pliers usually have two sets of serrated jaws, one straight and the other curved. One type, known as fencing plier, has cutting blades on the outside of the body.

- Diagonal cutting pliers have two cutting blades and are used to cut wire and small sections. Cutting pliers used in electronics must be able to cut close to the end of a soldered connection.

ISBN 9780170227452

- Long-nose or needle-nose pliers have long thin jaws for gripping objects that are in hard-to-reach places. Some types also have cutting blades.

- Bent-nose pliers are similar to long-nose pliers, but the nose is bent at an angle to assist the user to reach components that are behind other parts.

- Circlip pliers have round tapered jaws that are used to assemble circlips. There are types for external and internal circlips and often the ends of the jaws are bent at an angle.

- Multigrip pliers are sometimes called slip-joint pliers. The fulcrum or pin can be locked in one of a number of holes to enable the width of the jaw opening to be altered.

- Vice-grip pliers are adjustable and can be locked onto a part so that you have both hands free. The pliers are easy to release and they can be used as a pipe wrench, adjustable wrench or a clamp. They come in a variety of sizes and shapes.

- Wire strippers are used to cut and remove the insulation on electrical wires, leaving the wire exposed and undamaged.

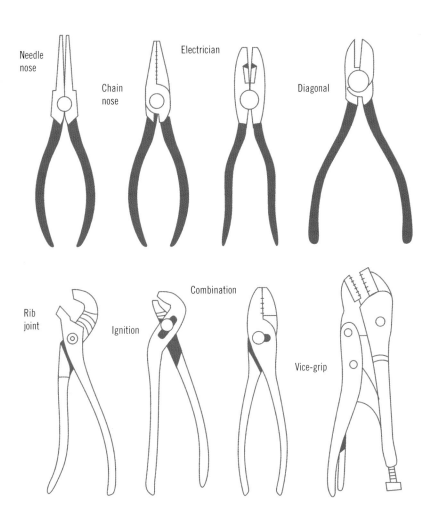

Selecting the right pliers

Size is important. More pressure can be applied to the object being gripped if the handgrips are longer.

Pliers designed for use with electrical or electronic systems should have insulated handgrips.

Using pliers

1 Keep the pliers clean and dry.

2 Check to make sure the serrations on the jaws are not worn.

3 Do not use pliers to tighten or loosen screws and nuts. The corners of the screw head or nut will be 'rounded' and this will damage the fastener.

4 The pin or fulcrum can be lubricated with substances such as WD40. Wipe clean before using the pliers.

5 Take care when gripping fragile objects.

6 Use insulated pliers when working on electrical equipment.

LEARNING ACTIVITY 10.1

1 With your teacher, carry out a condition and safety check on the tools and equipment used in your workshop.

2 Use the information given on tools and equipment to examine the equipment to see it is in good working order.

Electrical power tools

Nowadays, an increasing range of tools are powered by electricity. Examples of these include drills, grinders, sanders, polishers and saws. Safety is very important when using these power tools. Here are some safety precautions required when using power tools:

1 Before you use a power tool make sure you know how to use it. Read the user manual if in doubt and follow instructions.

2 Check if the equipment complies with relevant Australian Standards.

3 Every time you use a power tool, check for damage first. Inspect cords for cracking, fraying or other signs that the insulation has been damaged. Check switches and trigger locks and make sure plugs have no loose, missing or damaged pins.

4 Ensure that the power cord is clear of the work location.

5 Ensure all guards or shields are in place.

6 Switch off tools before you connect them to the power and when they are not in use.

7 Do not disconnect the power supply by pulling or jerking the cord to remove the plug.

8 Do not pick up or carry tools by the cord.

9 All handheld power tools should automatically cut off when the tool is released by the operator.

10 Wear appropriate safety gear, such as ear protection and goggles.

Production equipment

Depending upon the type of work area, facility and specialisation you work in, you should encounter and develop skills in using a range of engineering equipment, machines and hand or power tools during your production activities. Some common production equipment is listed below.

- Vacuum formers
- Line benders
- Strip heaters
- Ovens
- Engineers lathes
- Drilling machines
- Milling machines
- Welders

- Electromechanical control devices
- Computers
- Engine hoists
- Compression testers
- Multimeters
- Routers
- PCB etch tanks
- CNC lathes

Before using any of the above or similar equipment it is important to be trained correctly. This ensures the safety of the person operating the equipment and prevents unnecessary damage to both the production equipment and the system being produced or tested. There are obvious advantages in this as the finished product will have a higher degree of reliability and the final product user is less likely to suffer injury.

All of these considerations must be factored into the design and planning for production and the operation of systems projects. Doing this helps to reduce or eliminate the risk of potential failure and the consequences of this. A formal and sequential approach can be taken by applying a risk assessment plan.

Risk assessment

Risk assessment is basically a process of analysing all the possible risks related to the design and configuration of a system, and in producing, testing, operating and maintaining a system throughout its life.

Designers and manufacturers assess designed products at the planning and preproduction stages to assess their degree of safety and reliability. They need to select appropriate components and materials that comply with Australian Standards. The final product should meet 'standards' requirements and guarantee safety and reliability to the marketplace.

The most appropriate production equipment and processes should be employed. This often means careful consideration of factors such as production cost, ease of manufacture, quality and reliability. No matter what the outcome of the production options and production methods employed, manufacturers are obliged to satisfy Australian Standards requirements related to product design, operation and use. They also need to ensure that working conditions satisfy relevant requirements of the *Occupational Health and Safety at Work Act*. Employers therefore need to provide adequate training for employees and ensure that they work in a safe, hazard-free environment.

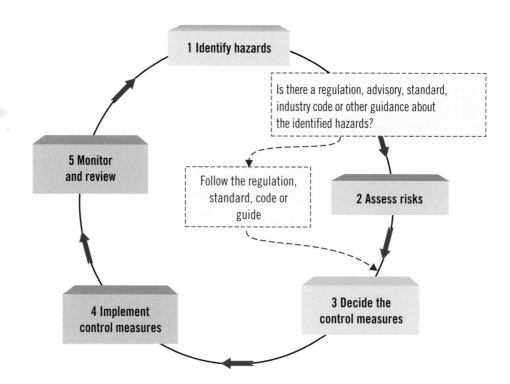

Risk management cycle – a constant process

1 Identify hazards

Is there a regulation, advisory, standard, industry code or other guidance about the identified hazards?

Follow the regulation, standard, code or guide

2 Assess risks

3 Decide the control measures

4 Implement control measures

5 Monitor and review

As a designer and producer, you need to follow similar procedures to those previously outlined. In doing so, you should establish you have addressed the following four points.

1   You are qualified and have the skills to perform any planned tasks.

2   The equipment and planned production methods are hazard-free.

3   Planned testing and maintenance procedures are risk-free.

4   The system or product is designed for safety and ease of use.

With the above points in mind when you are designing and planning, you should attempt risk-assessment tasks for the proposed design, as well as for production tasks, testing and operating the completed system. Depending on the time available, you may decide to attempt risk assessments for the major production and testing tasks, and for obvious risk situations only.

A sample plan for risk assessing 'PCB etching' has been completed below. You may choose to use this as a guide in planning your production work. Chapter 9, 'The systems engineering process', also examines risk-assessment procedures and uses completed student samples.

A risk assessment plan comprises the following three activities.

1   Identify possible risks.

2   Assess each risk.

3   Remove or control the risk.

Risk-assessment plan

PCB artwork etching process: use of tools, equipment, processes (including chemicals) with a degree of danger

Identify risks, hazards, safety issues	Assessment	Eliminate/control risk
Chemical usage hazard: ammonium persulfate – inhalation, skin contact and absorption possible.	Chemical hazard if contact with skin, eyes, etc. Can cause injury – from minor to serious irritation and damage to skin and eyes. Highly likely that contact will occur unless correct safety and handling procedures are followed.	Follow the manufacturer's materials data sheet advice. Teacher or technician only to use this equipment. Etch tank should be located in a suitable chemical or fume extraction unit. Wear suitable hand and eye safety protection.
Fume/vapour inhalation possible.	Chemical fume emission is possible when heater is in use.	PCB should be placed in tank basket or tray and slowly immersed into tank. Cover tank, close unit door. Switch on heater, pump and extractor. Check condition of boards during process.
PCB artwork must be complete and accurate for operational use.	Possibility of over/under-etching tracks or boards.	Switch off heater, pump and extractor when process is completed. Remove basket/tray and flush etched boards. Quality control check or test.

LEARNING ACTIVITY 10.2

1   What are the advantages of being trained to use equipment correctly?

2   List and describe the stages involved in risk assessment.

3   Attempt risk assessments for two of the following tasks.

- Changing or testing a car battery
- Drilling a PCB
- Using a hand or scroll saw to cut plastic
- Setting up and using an oscilloscope to test a circuit
- Using a vacuum former to form plastic
- Connecting a speaker

4   Search the following sites for information on occupational health and safety, risk management and planning.

- **www.worksafe.vic.gov.au**
- **www.safeworkaustralia.gov.au**
- **www.safetyrisk.com.au**

Materials for production

When we design systems we want them to produce the desired output and to be reliable and safe to use. To achieve this outcome, the individual parts of the system must be made from the most suitable material. If there is a wide variety of a material to choose from, how do we go about selecting a material? There are many things we have to think about, such as price and availability, but the most important consideration is the properties of the materials. Even simple systems like a hair dryer demonstrate the use of a wide range of materials.

Steel shaft, copper wire, carbon brushes and ferromagnetic metal are used in the motor

Nickel chromium wire heating element

Rigid plastic body

Plastic moulded plug with brass pin

Hair dryer

Plastic-covered copper wire

Shutterstock.com/EuToch

Common materials and their properties

In technology we are increasingly using materials including plastics such as high-impact polystyrene for vacuum-forming moulds, boxes, circuit housings and so on, and acrylic (Perspex) for forming and fabricating. Nylon is another common material that is used for light mechanical assembly work and for components such as washers, pins, and project kit parts. Stainless steel components are used where strength is important. The ability of stainless steel to resist corrosion together with its stainless surface finish are also important characteristics. Fibreglass as a moulding compound is used much less due to health and safety concerns associated specifically with handling the raw material in its basic form.

So-called 'new materials' composites and fibres such as Kevlar and Technora have been around for a number of years (Kevlar in various forms since the 1960s) and are now being used more frequently by many of us, often without realising it. Kevlar, for instance, is super-strong (in fact, up to five times stronger than steel), tough and stiff. It also has a high

ISBN 9780170227452

resistance to friction, heat, flames, chemicals and electrical conductivity. Applications include electronic component bodies, circuit boards, clothing, fibre moulding and forming, body armour, motorcycle helmets, kayak oar blades, belts, hoses, tyres, cables, fishing gear, golf balls, fibre-optic cables ... the list is endless!

Material properties

One meaning of the word 'property' is the quality or characteristic of a thing. There are a large number of properties of materials and they can be divided into groups. A simplified classification of the properties of materials used in engineering is shown below.

- Electrical and magnetic

- Chemical

- Thermal

- Physical

- Mechanical

- Optical

- Acoustic

Electrical and magnetic properties

Electrical conductivity

Electrical conductivity is the ability of the material to allow an electric current to pass through it. A material with good electrical conductivity is known as a conductor. Metals such as silver, aluminium and copper are good conductors of electricity. Brass is often used in components such as switches and connectors. Copper is the most commonly used electrical conductor.

Shutterstock.com/Brian K.

Electrical resistivity

The ability of a material to resist the flow of electricity is referred to as the property of electrical resistivity. A material with good electrical resistivity is known as an insulator. Glass, ceramics and rubber are good insulators. Plastic is one of the most used materials in situations where insulating properties are required. Ceramics are used in situations where the operating conditions are severe, such as for insulators on electricity supply lines and the bodies of spark plugs.

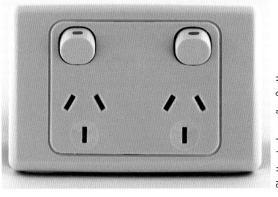
Power point

Shutterstock.com/Ian Scott

There is another group of materials known as semiconductors that fit somewhere between conductors and insulators. At low temperatures the pure semiconductors act like insulators but if the temperature increases, impurities are added, or in the presence of light, the conductivity of semiconductors is increased significantly. The common semiconductors include elements such as silicon, germanium and selenium, and compounds such as gallium arsenide, zinc selenide and lead telluride. Semiconductors are used in the manufacture of electronic components such as integrated circuits, transistors and diodes.

Integrated circuit

Shutterstock.com/Ragnarock

Magnetic properties

The magnetic property of a material is its ability to act as a permanent or non-permanent magnet. It is associated with metals containing iron and they are often called ferromagnetic metals. Alloy steels are used to make permanent magnets.

An iron–nickel alloy acts as a magnet when in the presence of an electric current. This type of non-permanent magnet, known as an electromagnet, is used in electronic devices such as relays (switches) and electric bells. Electromagnets are also used in machines that lift and move steel and iron objects.

Magnet

Shutterstock.com/James Steidl

ISBN 9780170227452

Electrochemical properties

When two dissimilar metals are in contact in wet situations, one of the metals may corrode. An electric current is created when one metal acts as an anode (positive terminal) and the other a cathode (negative terminal). Ions (atoms with a negative charge) move from the cathode to the anode. Where two dissimilar metals are in contact, the metal lower on the galvanic series list (shown opposite) will be the one to corrode. The further apart the materials are on this list the greater the chance of corrosion.

Magnesium is used in hot water units as a 'sacrificial anode'. Because magnesium is lower on the galvanic list it will corrode and protect the other metal parts of the unit. Zinc anodes are also used in boats to protect other metal components.

> **Electronegative**
> Gold
> Silver
> Nickel
> Brass and bronze
> Lead
> Tin
> Iron
> Steel
> Aluminium
> Zinc
> Magnesium
> **Electropositive**

An electromagnet in use

Getty Images/Science Photo Library

LEARNING ACTIVITY 10.3

1 Explain why in designing systems we must know about the properties of materials.

2 Describe three situations in which the electrical conducting and insulating properties of materials are important for use in a home.

Chemical properties

Corrosion resistance

Corrosion resistance is the ability of a material to resist corrosion when left unprotected. 'Rusting' is the word often used to describe the corrosion process in steel and iron. Metals with no iron content, such as aluminium, brass and bronze, will not rust. Bronze is used to make boat propellers because it also resists the corrosive effect of sea water.

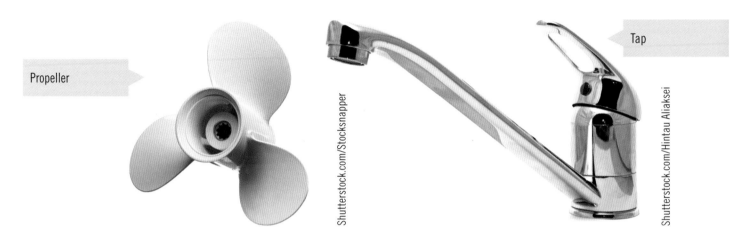

Propeller

Tap

Shutterstock.com/Stocksnapper

Shutterstock.com/Hintau Aliaksei

Copper and brass are used in the manufacture of plumbing and water-system fittings. The surfaces of metal parts are often coated with a thin layer of corrosion-resistant metals such as nickel and chromium.

Steel and cast iron, with a high iron content, will corrode (rust) after contact with water. Stainless steel is the exception because it contains significant amounts of nickel and chromium. Plastics and ceramics are examples of materials that do not rust.

Resistance to attack by chemicals

A material may need to resist reaction with chemicals. Glass has excellent resistance to attack by chemicals and it is used in science laboratories and in industries where chemicals are processed. Plastics, such as high density polyethylene (HDPE), are used to make containers for chemicals.

Resistance to ageing

This is the ability of a material to resist any adverse effect on its characteristics over a long period of time. Some paper will become discoloured, and wood, glass and some plastics become brittle.

Resistance to ultraviolet light

This is the ability of a material to retain its properties after exposure to ultraviolet light (sunlight). Some plastics and fabrics will change after long exposure to ultraviolet light. The plastics will become brittle, and fabrics fade after long exposure to sunlight. Metal, glass and some plastics such as polypropylene, to some extent, are materials that can be exposed to sunlight without adverse effects.

ISBN 9780170227452

Thermal properties

Specific heat

The specific heat of a material is the amount of heat energy required to raise the temperature of 1 kg of the material by 1°C. Generally metals have a lower specific heat than materials such as concrete and water. Specific heat is important in systems where the operating temperatures are high.

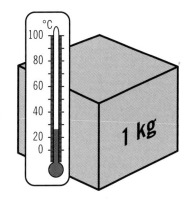

Thermal conductivity

Thermal conductivity is the ability of the material to transmit heat energy. Materials that transmit heat are described as heat conductors and materials that resist the transmission of heat are known as heat insulators. Metals are good conductors and plastics are insulators. A soldering iron is an example of the use of thermal conductivity.

Soldering iron

Shutterstock.com/Ruslan Rizvanov

The following table shows the thermal conductivity rating of some common materials. Silver is the best conductor and it is given a rating of 100.

Material	Rating	Conductivity
Silver	100	Good conductors
Copper	90	
Aluminium	48	
Brass	27	
Glass	0.15	Good insulators
Asbestos	0.06	
Wood (kiln dried)	0.05	
Cork	0.01	
Felt	0.01	

Thermal expansion or contraction

Most materials expand when they are heated and contract when cooled. Thermal expansion (or contraction) is the increase (or decrease) in length for each 1 m of length of the material when the temperature is increased (or reduced) by 1°C.

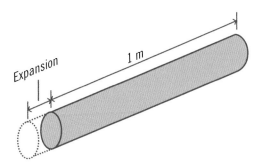

The rate of expansion is very important when selecting the material for moving parts in a machine. Aluminium expands (or contracts) at twice the rate of that steel does. The expansion rate is also considered when designing bimetal thermostats. The expansion of some common materials is shown below.

Material	Expansion (mm)
Rubber	0.670
PVC	0.150
Aluminium	0.023
Silver	0.019
Brass	0.018
Copper	0.017
Steel	0.011
Glass	0.003

Melting point

The melting point is the temperature at which a material changes from solid to liquid. Melting point is an important property when materials have to be cast or welded. Metals, glass and thermoplastics are examples of materials that change from a solid to a liquid state when heated to the melting temperature. The material in heating elements and electric light filaments is made of a nickel–chromium alloy that has a very high melting point. The melting point of some common materials is shown in the table below.

Material	Melting or softening point (°C)
Tungsten	3380
Porcelain	2400
Steel	1370
Glass	1100
Copper	1083
Aluminium	660
Lead	327
Rubber	125

ISBN 9780170227452

Reaction to heat

How the material behaves when heated is described as its reaction to heat. Materials such as paper and cotton will burn, while glass and metals will melt and become liquid. Thermoplastics soften and can be reworked when heated. Reheating cannot soften thermosetting plastics after the initial curing has been completed. A material's reaction to heat will determine where and when the material will be used in components.

Thermoforming properties

Thermoforming properties relate to the temperature at which a material can be formed and the ease with which it can be formed. Materials such as metal, glass and thermoplastics become soft when heated and can be formed into new shapes. High-impact polystyrene and acrylic are common examples of this. When steel is heated and glows red it becomes soft and can be easily bent or twisted. Thermoplastics are materials for which thermoforming properties are important.

LEARNING ACTIVITY 10.4

1 Describe three situations in which corrosion-resistant metals are used in the home.

2 Water is used to cool the metal parts in a car engine. What would happen if the cooling system failed?

Physical properties

Density

When people describe a material as being light or heavy they are really referring to its density. The definition of density is the mass per unit volume (kilograms per cubic metre). Aluminium is known as a light material, lead as a heavy one. This is because aluminium is less dense than lead.

Mass is the amount of matter in a body. 'Matter' is a word used in science to describe anything that is made up of atoms, occupies space and has weight. Other words for matter are 'materials' and 'substances'. Matter is usually divided into three groups – solids, liquids and gases. The density of some common materials is shown in the table below. All the materials above water in the table will sink in water and those below it will float.

Material	Density in kilograms per cubic metre
Gold	19 300
Lead	11 300
Steel	7 850
Aluminium	2 800
Glass	2 700
Plastic – PVC	1 300
Rubber	1 100
Water	1 000
Plastic – low-density polyethylene	910
Paper	780
Wood – pine	450

Aluminium alloys are used in the manufacture of aeroplane parts because of their low density. An increasing number of car parts are made of plastic to reduce the weight of the vehicle.

Porosity

Porosity is the ability of a material to allow or prevent the flow of liquids or gases through it. Materials are often described as porous or non-porous. Plastic and metal are non-porous materials that are used in the manufacture of pipes and tubes.

Paper and cotton are examples of porous materials, and specially manufactured porous materials are used in filters for gases and liquids. Non-porous materials, such as metal, plastic and glass, are used to make pipes, tubes and containers for gases and liquids.

Mechanical properties

Strength

Strength is the ability of a material to withstand stress without failure. This is one of the most important properties of a material, and to understand the description it is necessary to look at the idea of stress. The technical definition of stress is the force per unit area tending to change the dimensions (shape) of the material. It is calculated by using the formula below. In the metric system, force is measured in newtons and the area in square metres. Stress measured in newtons per square metre (N/m^2).

This is a useful method of calculating the ultimate limit of strength for different-sized pieces of material. If the ultimate stress for a particular material is $10\,N/m^2$ then the ultimate total load (force) can be determined as follows:

Safe load = safe stress × area

There are four types of stress: tensile, compression, torsional and shear.

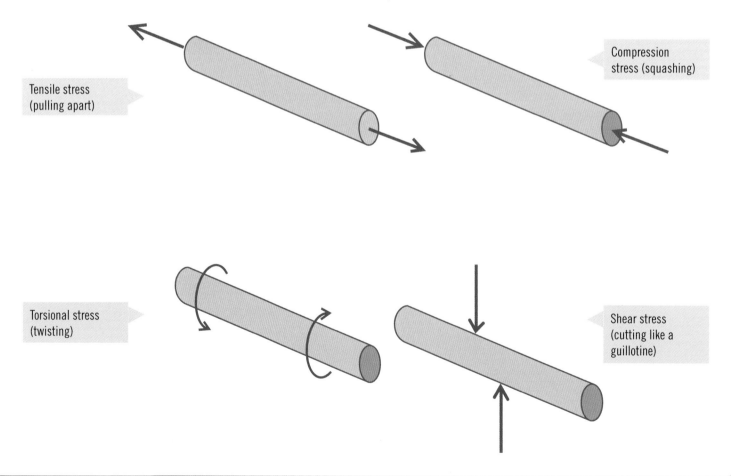

Tensile stress (pulling apart)

Compression stress (squashing)

Torsional stress (twisting)

Shear stress (cutting like a guillotine)

ISBN 9780170227452

Tensile strength

This is the ability of a material to resist failure under tensile stress (pulling apart). Steel is a material with excellent tensile strength. One type of steel known as high-tensile steel is used in situations where tensile strength is very important, such as for crane cables and in building construction.

Compression strength

This is the ability of a material to resist failure under compression stress (squashing). Cast iron and steel are materials with very high compression strength. The base of large and heavy machines is usually made of cast iron. Steel rails are used in train and tram systems.

Torsional strength

This is the ability of a material to resist failure under torsional stress (twisting). Kevlar and steel with a high carbon content are materials used where torsional strength is important. Examples include screws, screwdriver blades, rotating shafts and the driving **axles** on cars.

Shear strength

This is the ability of a material to resist failure under shear stress. Metals such as cast iron and steel have good shear strength. A tow-bar ball is an example of a situation where shear strength is important. Materials with high shear strength are harder to cut with tools such as scissors, tinsnips and guillotines.

Elasticity

Elasticity is the ability of a material to return to its original shape after having undergone some shape change (e.g. springs back after bending, twisting or stretching). Rubber and plastics known as elastomers are very elastic materials. Even hard materials such as Kevlar and steel have elastic properties. They can be stretched or squashed a very small amount and still return to the original shape when the stress is removed.

There is a limit to the elasticity of each material. This is the point at which the material will not return to its original shape. This is known as the elastic limit of the material.

Plasticity

Plasticity is the ability to undergo a permanent change in shape without failure. Soft metals, such as copper and lead, when bent or squashed will retain the new shape without breaking. Putty and sealing compounds are examples of very plastic materials.

Stiffness

Stiffness is the ability of a material to resist any change in shape when a load is applied. The shape may change in three ways:

1 elongation (increase in length)

2 contraction (reduction in length)

3 deflection (bending).

Sometimes the property of stiffness is called springiness. A stiff material is one that resists any change in shape. If all materials are elastic, it is the ones that resist being stretched squashed or twisted that we describe as stiff. Steel, Kevlar, concrete and bricks are stiff materials, but they can be stretched, squashed or bent, even if only to a very small extent that is not visible to the human eye.

Some common materials are listed on the right in order of stiffness. Examples in which stiffness in systems components is required are fibreglass bases for printed circuit boards, thick sheet metal, cast iron and cast steel for machine bodies, shafts, axles and brake pedals in cars.

Hardness

Hardness is the ability of a material to resist scratching, abrasion, indentation or penetration. Hard materials also resist wear. Diamonds and tungsten carbide are examples of very hard materials. They are used to make cutting tools. Melamine formaldehyde, usually called melamine, is a hard plastic that resists wear and scratching and is used on bench- and tabletops.

Heating to high temperatures (red heat) and quenching quickly in oil is a process that is used to harden special high-carbon steels. High-speed steel (HSS) is used to make metal-cutting tools.

High
Diamond
Steel
Copper
Aluminium
Glass
Bone
Concrete
Wood
Some plastics
Rubber
Low

Circuit board

iStockphoto

Toughness/brittleness

Toughness is the ability of a material to withstand repeated applications of stress without breaking (such as hammering, or bending backwards and forwards). Materials like steel and Kevlar are tough materials; others such as glass, which break easily, are described as brittle.

ISBN 9780170227452

Acrylonitrile butadiene styrene (ABS) is a plastic that will resist breaking when hit by sudden shock. It is often used as a substitute for metal. ABS is used to make the bodies of appliances such as vacuum cleaners and sewing machines.

Workability

This is the ability of a material to undergo a change in shape without failure is known as workability. It covers the properties of ductility and malleability.

Ductility

This is the ability to be changed in shape by mainly tensile stresses (wire-drawing processes).

Malleability

This is the ability to be changed in shape by mainly compressive stresses (rolling or forging processes).

Machinability

This is a measure of how easily a material can be machined. 'Machining' is the term used to describe cutting processes. Extremely soft and very hard materials are difficult to machine.

LEARNING ACTIVITY 10.5

1 Name a system where the density of the material is important to performance.

2 What mechanical properties would be desirable for bicycle frames?

3 What properties are essential features in compression springs?

Optical properties

Colour

Some materials have a distinctive natural colour and others can be produced in a range of colours. Metals can often be recognised by their colour. Individual metals have their own distinguishing colours; brass is gold, aluminium is silver and cast iron is grey. Plastics and glass are examples of materials that can be produced in different colours.

Light transmission

The ability of a material to transmit light can be important when designing projects. Materials, such as clear glass and plastic, we describe as transparent (clear) because they allow light to pass through. Other materials, like ceramics and metal, do not allow light to pass through and they are described as opaque. Camera and microscope lenses, instrument panels, light globes and optical-fibre cables are examples of using light-transmitting materials.

Light reflection

When light strikes an opaque surface, some of it is reflected and some is absorbed. An opaque surface is one that light cannot penetrate. Metals with a polished surface are good reflectors. Silver and aluminium are often used in situations where light has to be reflected, such as for mirrors and compact disks. Many other materials, especially those with dull surfaces or dark colours, are poor reflectors of light. In a torch, for example, the lens must be transparent and the reflector is made of a highly polished metal.

Shutterstock.com/Sergey Melnikov

Shutterstock.com/Ivaschenko Roman

Acoustic properties

The **acoustic properties** of a material affect its ability of a material to reflect and transmit sound.

Sound reflection

Sound reflection is the ability of a material to reflect sound waves. Sound waves striking a surface may be absorbed or reflected. Porous materials, such as fabrics and 'foamed plastics', tend to absorb sound. Hard materials, such as concrete and metals, reflect sound. Concrete barriers are used to reflect sound along freeways and protect people living nearby from the sound of traffic.

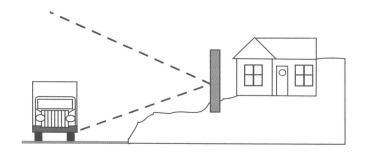

Sound transmission

The ability of a material to transmit sound waves is referred to as sound transmission. Sound waves need a material (solid, liquid or gas) to be transmitted from one place to another. Sound generally travels faster in solids than in liquids, and faster in liquids than in gases.

The speed of sound transmission in some common materials

Material	Speed (metres per second)
Air (18°C)	342
Cork	500
Water	1440
Steel	5000
Wood	3000–5000
Glass	5000

ISBN 9780170227452

END-OF-CHAPTER ACTIVITIES

1 List and describe the stages involved in risk assessment.
2 Attempt risk assessments for two of the following tasks.
    a   Etching and drilling a PCB
    b   Using a milling or drilling machine
    c   Producing and testing your current production task
    d   Testing a remote vehicle or aircraft
3 Use the system you are studying or working on to complete this activity. Suggest alternative materials that could have been used for your project and provide possible reasons why they were rejected.
4 Describe three situations where corrosion-resistant materials are used in the home.
5 Describe three situations where heat-resistant materials are used in the home.
6 What is meant by the terms 'characteristics' and 'properties' of materials?
7 Describe three situations where good electricity-conducting properties are useful.
8 Describe three situations where good heat-conducting properties are useful.
9 Describe three situations where good heat-resistant properties are useful.

REVISION TASKS

Use this section to help test your understanding of selected technologies and the principles and concepts covered in this book. Attempt to answer the questions in full, as the terminology and topics are similar to questions set in school tests and external examinations.

Chapter 1

1. Name an integrated system that you have worked with and list two of its subsystems. Categorise each subsystem by type (mechanical, electronic, electrical, mechatronic, electrotech and so on).

2. Describe the input, process and output of each of the above subsystems.

3. State the specific values for the inputs and outputs of each of the subsystems identified above. For example, 'the output of the 9V DC motor is 5000rpm'.

4. Is the above system an open or closed loop? State why you think this is so.

5. Describe what control devices, if any, are used in the above integrated system.

6. Draw a block diagram that represents an open loop system that you have studied.

7. Draw a block diagram that represents a closed loop system that you have studied.

8. What feature of a closed loop diagram identifies that it is an actual closed loop system?

9. In closed loop systems the output is always monitored. Explain why.

10. In closed loop systems 'feedback' is an important concept. For a system that you have studied describe what is meant by feedback.

11. Give three reasons why controlled closed loop systems are thought to be more effective than open loop systems.

Chapter 2

12. Select a system (such as a fuel cell, a mobile phone, electric vehicle or LCDs) and investigate the development of the product. Find out what the system replaced, some of the changes in designs for the product over time, and how it operates. Discuss the advantages and disadvantages of the product as it is now to its users.

13. What are the main features of lean manufacture as described in Chapter 2 and the 'Manufacturing and technology' case study?

14. Compare a microwave oven to a conventional oven. List the similarities and differences in terms of the following:
    - how each one heats food
    - the time each takes to heat

- the advantages and disadvantages of using each
- situations where it would be most appropriate to use each type of oven.

15 Identify three recent technological developments (such as solar-powered ventilation) that are designed to reduce the negative impact of systems on the environment and people. Explain what the developments are and how they reduce the impact.

16 Describe a recent technological development (system, material or component) that has greatly improved the technical and functional characteristics of a product. Describe how the product is improved.

17 Jet skis are popular recreational devices. They are frequently used around the shore and in popular beach areas. In the past this has been a problem because of noise pollution and the danger to swimmers in the area.

   a What advantages do jet skis offer to users?
   b What disadvantages are there?
   c What can be done to make the situation more satisfactory to jet ski users, beach users and swimmers?

Chapter 3

18 Name the control devices used in each of the following situations.

Situation	Control device
Controls oven temperature	
Controls water level	
Controls a car engine temperature	
Uses a small amount of energy to control a larger one	
Controls opening and closing of car engine valves	

19 Identify the listed energy conversions that take place in a motor car.

Source	Energy conversion		
Battery	From chemical	to	
Burning fuel	From	to	
Starter motor	From	to	
Headlights	From	to	light and heat
Alternator	From	to	

20 Complete the following table, giving the name of the energy conversion system in each case.

Energy forms	Energy conversion system
Chemical to electrical energy	
Wind power to electrical	
Electrical to mechanical	
Hydro to electrical	
Solar to chemical	

21 Describe the following technologies and their applications.

   a Solar panel

   b Solar tower

   c Wind turbine

   d Supercapacitor

22 Name the types of energy that may be stored in each of the following components.

   a Capacitor

   b Elastic band

   c Battery

   d Compression spring

23 What are the undesired energy outputs of each of the following?

   a DVD player

   b Solar tower

   c Lawn mowers – petrol and electric

   d Boiling kettle

   e Wind turbine

24 Motor vehicles are important to many of us; however, they release undesirable chemical emissions that contribute to air pollution and result in environmental and health problems.

   a What chemicals are released by motor vehicles as pollutants?

   b How do car manufacturers attempt to improve vehicle systems design to reduce this problem?

   c How does legislation deal with this problem?

25 Complete the following table by identifying the missing inputs and outputs.

Input energy	System	Output energy
Electrical	Mobile phone	
	Food processor	
	Gas/fan heater	Heat, mechanical and sound
	Bicycle	Mechanical, heat, sound
Wind/kinetic	Wind turbine	
	Solar panel	

26 A four-stroke petrol engine has an efficiency of 25%. If the price of petrol is $1.40 per litre, how much of the cost is wasted by the engine?

Chapter 4

27 Name and describe the four types of motion.

28 List two practical applications for each kind of motion.

29 Using diagrams, give one example of each type of force: tension, compression, torsion and shear.

30 Levers can be described as first, second or third order. Draw a diagram to show each type of lever and describe one example of each.

31 Define the term 'moment' and calculate the moment if a force of 50 N is applied to a lever measuring 1.3 m.

32 Describe in detail a situation where counterbalances are used.

33 What is 'mechanical advantage'? Describe a practical example of this.

34 Using the formula VR = distance moved by effort ÷ distance moved by load, calculate the velocity ratio if the effort distance is 660 mm and the load is lifted 85 mm.

35 What is the gear ratio of two gear wheels, one with 40 teeth and the other with 75 teeth?

36 Sketch and give an application for each of the following mechanisms.

   a Rack and pinion

   b Worm gears

   c Ratchet and pawl

   d Compression and tension springs

   e Bevel gears

   f Pulleys

   g Chain and sprocket

   h Cam and follower

37 A pinion wheel has 32 teeth with a 15 mm pitch. How far does the rack move if the pinion rotates through 180°?

38 What is the technical difference between single- and double-acting cylinders?

39 Explain the difference between pneumatic and hydraulic systems.

40 List and briefly describe two pneumatic systems.

41 List and briefly describe two hydraulic systems.

42 Describe how a hydraulic car jack works. Use diagrams to explain your answer.

43 Friction is a force that is applied by surfaces rubbing against each other. Explain how this can be reduced.

44 Identify two mechanical devices that rely on friction for their operation.

45 Name five subsystems in a motor vehicle.

46 Give two reasons why motor vehicle engines are inefficient.

47 Explain how motor vehicles can become more energy efficient.

Chapter 5

48 Ohm's law defines the relationship between voltage, current and resistance.

   For instance, the formula to find voltage is $V = I \times R$.

   Rearrange this to find R, if $V = 15\,V$ and $I = 20\,mA$.

49 Draw a 150R and a 500R resistor in series, then in parallel. Calculate both sets of resistance values.

50 What is the value of the resistors with bands of the following colours?

    a Brown, black, orange, gold

    b Brown, red, blue, silver

    c Yellow, violet, orange, gold

    d Blue, green, yellow, silver

    e Red, grey, brown, silver

    f Orange, white, red, gold

51 State the purpose of the following components and sketch the correct symbol for each one.

    a Fixed resistor

    b PNP transistor

    c NPN transistor

    d LED

    e Light-dependent resistor

    f Motor

    g Diode

    h Zener diode

    i Electrolytic capacitor

    j Microswitch

    k Stepper motor

    l Thermistor

    m Integrated circuit

52 Resistance is measured in ohms (Ω). When we check resistor values we often find that they are written differently, for instance 10R, 4K2, 100KV, 1K2, 100V, 4M2. What are these individual values? What is the total value of the six resistors?

53 Capacitors store energy in electronic circuits. What is the unit of capacitance?

54 What is the value of each capacitor, in farads: 10 µF, 100 nF, 100 F, 50 pF?

55 Explain, using sketches, the difference between PNP and NPN transistors.

56 Explain what is meant by AC and DC.

57 Explain and do a PMI assessment to compare analogue and digital multimeters.

Chapter 6

58 List the advantages of using CNC processes.

59 What advantages do CNC and digital manufacturing have over manual production techniques?

60 What are the advantages in using CAD as opposed to conventional manual drawing design work?

61 What is 3D printing?

62 What is a schematic drawing?

ISBN 9780170227452

Chapter 7

63 List as many applications as you can for control systems in industry.

64 Explain what you know of PIC applications and advantages.

65 What are the advantages of using flow charts in PIC programming?

66 Identify applications and the advantages of radio control systems.

Chapter 8

67 Name one fault that could occur in a system that you have worked with and describe what could cause this.

68 Name and describe one type of test equipment that could be used to locate the fault.

69 Explain the technological principle on which this test equipment is based.

70 Explain in detail how to test for the identified fault.

71 Explain how the identified fault could be corrected or repaired.

Chapter 9

72 List the stages in the systems engineering process and briefly describe what is involved at each stage.

73 Why do you think the process is vital to the task of project management?

74 In point form, explain how you project-managed your production tasks.

75 Why are product specifications important? Explain how specifications relate to the design brief, project evaluation and final assessment criteria.

76 Suggest how you would get ideas for a project you are considering. What type of reference material and information sources would you use to get some initial ideas and possible project designs?

Chapter 10

77 What is involved in performing a risk-assessment plan?

78 Why is risk assessment important?

79 Describe a workshop task that involves an element of danger. Explain what precautions you would plan to reduce the risk.

80 Why is it important to know the properties and characteristics of materials before selecting them for project work?

81 List the different mechanical properties and briefly describe each.

82 Describe two situations in which good electrical-conducting properties are useful.

83 Describe two situations in which good electrical-insulating properties are useful.

84 Describe two situations in which the electrical conducting and insulating properties of materials are important for use in the home.

85 Describe two situations in which good heat-conducting properties are useful.

86 Describe two situations in which good heat-resistant properties are useful.

87 Describe three situations in which good acoustic properties are useful.

Visit www.vcaa.vic.
edu.au/vce/exams/
index.html for advice
on assessment and
examination criteria,
past papers and reports
on outcome assessment
and examinations.

88 If you were to make a small mechanical or controlled vehicle, what materials would you use for its chassis and body? Explain your choice of materials.

89 Select and explain what materials you would use for a power supply or electrical transformer body.

90 Describe how you selected materials and components for your production tasks. Did you choose any of these specifically for their properties or characteristics? Explain why this should be so.

ISBN 9780170227452

A–Z: Systems terminology

Acceleration   the rate of change in velocity.

AC electricity   alternating current flow, or change in direction and strength of electrical current, as in mains electrical supply.

Acoustic properties   the properties of a material that affect its ability to reflect and transmit sound.

Alternating current (AC)   a form of electricity that keeps changing its direction of flow. AC current varies over time, creating a sine-wave waveform.

Ampere/amp (A)   the unit of electrical current measurement. Amount of electric charge flowing through a conductor. Can be likened to the litres per minute (LPM) of water flowing through a pipe.

Amplify   to increase a signal, such as sound.

Amplifier   a device that boosts an electrical signal.

Anode   the positive terminal of a component such as an LED.

Automatic circuit   a circuit that operates continually without human intervention.

Axle   a shaft for a fixed wheel.

Base   the terminal that controls current through a transistor.

Bearing   usually used where a rotating surface is supported by a non-moving surface.

Belt   used to link pulleys for rotation. The belts are in tension and use friction as a means of gripping the wheels to transmit motion.

Bending   a combination of tension and compression forces.

Bevel gears   gears that transfer rotary motion through an angle, usually of 90 degrees.

Brake   a mechanism that uses friction to stop or slow a moving object such as a motor vehicle.

Bush   a simple form of bearing used to absorb movement, reduce friction and wear of metal components.

Cam   a mechanism that converts motion, usually rotary to linear, reciprocating or oscillating motion. The resulting motion depends on the shape of the cam and the follower design.

Cam follower   device that is in contact with a cam as it rotates.

Capacitance (C)   the amount of electrical charge that can be stored.

Capacitor   an electronic device that stores small amounts of electrical charge.

Cathode   the negative terminal of a component.

Chain   used to link sprockets together to transfer rotary motion.

Chemical energy   that part of the energy in a substance (such as oil, gas, coal, nuclear) that is released by a chemical reaction.

Circuit (electronic)   a circuit made up from electronic components and works by connecting to the positive and negative terminals of a power supply.

Circuit (pneumatic)   an arrangement of components that uses compressed air to produce controlled movement.

Closed loop cycle   the continuous flow and controlled feedback cycle within a system.

Closed loop system   a system that feeds back information to its monitor or controller to modify the input or process so the desired output is constantly maintained. This is a controlled system.

Clutch   the mechanism through which the power of an engine or motor is transferred to the driving shaft. The clutch disengages the power unit from the drive shaft to allow gear changes.

Collector   one of the high current terminals of a transistor, the input terminal.

Compression   a pressing or squeezing force.

Compressor   a machine used to produce compressed air for use in pneumatic systems.

Computer-aided design (CAD)   the use of computers to aid the design process.

Conduction   heat transfer within a solid due to energy transfer between molecules and atoms.

Control   to monitor and determine the function of a system.

Corrosion resistance   the ability of a material to resist corrosion when left unprotected.

Crank and slider   a mechanism for converting linear motion to circular motion. A common example is a piston and cylinder.

Current (I)   electrical current is a flow of electrons in a conductor and is measured in amps (A).

Cylinder   a cylindrical space in which a piston moves up and down. When compressed air is introduced, the piston inside the cylinder will move. There are two types   single acting and double acting.

Density   the mass per unit volume (kilograms per cubic metre; kg/m^2) of a material.

Design brief   a brief statement that indicates what is required to satisfy a given situation or problem. The statement contains an outline of a context, problem, need or opportunity, and specifications that apply to the problem.

Design process   a process of thought and creativity that is used to generate ideas and develop best solutions to needs and problems.

Diagnostic test   a test of a system to evaluate its performance or to find actual faults.

Diode   an electronic device that allows electricity to flow in one direction.

Direct current (DC)   a form of electricity in which all electrons move in the same direction, conventionally from positive to negative. DC current does not vary with time, creating a flat waveform.

Driven shaft   the shaft or spindle on which the driven or output wheel is mounted.

Driver shaft   the shaft or spindle on which the input gear or pulley wheel is mounted.

Efficiency   a measure of how well energy is used, as determined by energy out divided by energy in. When one form of energy is converted to another, the fraction of energy converted and not lost gives the efficiency of the conversion.

Effort   the input force to a machine.

Elasticity   the ability of a material to return to original shape after it has undergone a change to that shape.

Electric motor   a motor that converts input electricity to output rotary motion.

Electricity   the flow of electrons.

Electrical conductivity   the ability of the material to allow an electric current to pass through it.

Electrical resistivity   the ability of a material to resist the flow of electricity.

Electrochemical properties   properties governing the relationship between chemical and electrical change and their effects. For example, a chemical reaction from a battery is used to provide electrical power. Conversely, electrical charge is used in materials processing such as the electroplating of metals.

Electromotive force (EMF)   the force that pushes electrons around an electric circuit to give an electric current.

Electron   in an atom, a very small particle which carries a negative charge.

Emitter   one of the high current terminals on a transistor, the output terminal.

Energy   capacity for performing work.

Equilibrium   the condition in which all acting influences or forces are in a stable, balanced state.

Etching   the process of using acid to remove metal from a surface area to create artwork, such as printed circuit board tracks.

Evaluate   assess or analyse the effectiveness of a situation, activity or device.

Farad (F)   the unit of capacitance.

Factor of safety   how much stronger a material is than the load.

Feedback   information obtained about a system, usually from sensors, that is fed back to the controller. See **closed loop system**.

Fission   the splitting of the nucleus of an atom with accompanying release of energy.

Force (*F*)   a push or a pull. When a force is applied to an object its direction of travel or its speed will change: force = mass × acceleration.

Frequency (*f*)   used to describe waveforms; the number of vibrations or oscillations every second. Measured in hertz (Hz) or cycles per second.

Friction   the force which resists motion when two surfaces are rubbing together.

Fulcrum   the 'pivot' point of a lever around which the load and effort move.

Fusion   the joining together of two or more entities, such as an atomic reaction when a number of atoms are combined to form a larger single atom.

Gears   circular discs or rods with teeth. There are many different types, such as worm, pinion, spur and bevel.

Gear ratio   a mathematical representation of the gear teeth in gear trains (e.g. if a 60-teeth gear drives 30-teeth gear, the gear ratio is 60:30 or 2:1). Used to calculate turning speeds.

Hardness   the ability of a material to resist scratching, abrasion, indentation or penetration.

Heat sink   a metal device attached to electronic components to keep them from overheating; it absorbs heat.

Hydraulic system   a system using of fluid, usually oil, to produce force and movement, as in hoists and brakes.

Integrated circuit (IC)   a single electronic component that contains within it circuitry to perform a set of functions, enclosed in a small plastic case.

Integrated system   a system that contains mechanical, pneumatic or hydraulic functions together with electrical or electronic (electrotechnology) functions.

ISBN 9780170227452

Input what goes into a system, the starting point, where the raw elements (e.g. information, energy and materials) are applied.

Insulator something that prevents the flow of electrons.

Kinetic energy the energy of moving objects; measured in joules.

Lean manufacturing manufacturing practice where consideration is given to efficiency in production processes, cost, waste reduction, energy efficiency and lean product design features, etc. See the 'Manufacturing and technology' case study and Chapter 2.

Lever a simple machine or device that provides mechanical advantage. It has three main parts: effort, load and fulcrum.

Linear motion straight line motion, on one axis, in one direction.

Linkages a collection and connection of parts linked together to manage force and movement.

Live centre a tool that is placed into the tailstock and used to support the work piece during the machining process.

Load (N, newton) (mechanical) a force or burden (load = mass × acceleration) ($N = m \times a$).

Load (Ω ohms, or R electrical) a resistive device at the output where the electrical power is dissipated.

Logic gate a configuration of transistors that performs a defined switching sequence or logic function; an electronic decision-making circuit. AND, OR, NOT, NAND and NOR gates are examples.

Lubricant a fluid used to reduce friction between surfaces.

Machinability a measure of how easily a material can be machined.

Magnetic properties the ability of a material to act as a permanent or non-permanent magnet.

Mass the amount of matter in an object.

Mechanical advantage (MA) the ratio of the force performing the work done by a mechanism to the input force, such as provided by a lever; the ratio of load and effort applied to a machine.

Mechanism a mechanical system constructed from simple machines that can include levers, wheels, axles, pulleys and gears; a device that produces useful forces and motion. A combination of these is what we know as a mechanical system, or a machine.

Melting point the temperature at which a material changes from solid to liquid.

Moment the turning force calculated by multiplying force by the distance of the force from the fulcrum.

Monitor to check or observe an operational system, usually with sensors.

Newton the unit of force and weight.

Ohm (Ω) the unit of electrical resistance measurement.

Open loop system a system that has no monitoring or self-adjustment, which results in an output that is unaffected by the inputs, and its function can be altered only by human intervention; a system that is operated manually and where control is attempted by human intervention.

Optical properties a material's colour and ability to reflect and transmit light.

Oscillating motion back and forward motion on an arc about a fixed point.

Output the outcome of processes that occur within a system.

Photovoltaic cells cells used in solar energy systems and solar panels to convert light to electrical energy.

Plasticity the ability of a material to undergo a permanent change in shape without failure.

Pneumatic system –the use of compressed air to operate mechanisms by transferring force or motion.

Pneumatic valve a valve that allows compressed air to enter and leave a pneumatic device.

Porosity the ability of a material to allow or prevent the flow of liquids or gases through it.

Post-processing interpretation of data from the CAM software and writing of the numerical code that will be outputted to the machine.

Potential difference the voltage (or electrical force) across two points in an electrical circuit. Measured in volts (V).

Potential energy energy stored in an object with the ability to do work.

Power the rate at which work is done or energy used; electrical term (power = voltage × current), ($P = V \times I$), and 1 horsepower (hp) = 746 watts of power.

Printed circuit board (PCB) a circuit board usually made of fibreglass, on which copper tracks are 'printed' to make an orderly connection of components.

Process an activity in a system where the task of converting the input to the output occurs.

Programmable integrated circuit an electronic component that can be externally programmed to perform a series of functions.

Pulley a wheel over which a belt will run, enabling it to transfer motion.

Rack and pinion a rotary and linear mechanism for changing rotary motion to linear motion.

Reciprocating motion motion that is backwards and forwards on an axis.

Rectification the process of changing alternating current (AC) to direct current (DC).

Relay electromagnetic device or switch that allows one circuit to switch another, usually at a different voltage or current flow.

Reservoir in pneumatics, something that stores air for a short time, putting a time delay into pneumatic circuits.

Residual current device a device that disconnects a circuit whenever it detects that the current is not balanced between the energised conductor and the neutral conductor.

Resistance (R) electrical resistance of current (electron flow) in a conductor. Measured in ohms (Ω).

Resistor a device that provides a specified amount of opposition to the flow of current.

Risk assessment the process used to determine and identify hazards or dangers involved in activities or tasks; assessing the risk, then planning or managing appropriate action.

Rotary motion continuous movement about a circle.

Sensor a device that is used to observe and measure the performance of a system.

Shear a cutting or slicing force.

SI unit *Système International d'Unités* (International System of Units). Modern term for the metric system.

Solar cell an electrical device that converts light energy directly into electricity. See **photovoltaic cell**.

Solenoid a closely wound coil of wire. When current flows through the coil it acts like a magnet and creates movement.

Specific heat the specific heat of a material is the amount of heat energy required to raise the temperature of 1 kg by 1 degree Celsius.

Specification an extension of the design brief. This details more precise requirements of what a product or system should do; for instance, output speed in rpm, input voltage DC. The specification can be used as a set of criteria for assessing an operational system.

Sprocket a mechanism that transfers rotary motion from one shaft to another. A bicycle uses this arrangement.

Stiffness the ability of a material to resist any change in shape when a load is applied. The shape may change in three ways: elongation (increase in length), contraction (reduction in length) and deflection (bending).

Strength the ability of a material to withstand stress without failure. There are four main types of strength: tensile (pulling apart), compressive (squashing), torsional (twisting) and shear.

Subsystem a system within a more complex system – for instance, an engine in a motor vehicle.

Subtractive process a machining process that uses a removal method to remove the excess material from the workpiece.

Supercapacitors capacitors that use a carbon surface to store electric charge. The surface area and energy density available is thousands of times greater than in traditional capacitors that use metal surfaces.

System a configuration of essential subsystems and components that performs a useful function. A system has inputs, processes and outputs. If any of the parts of a system were to fail, the system would malfunction or fail as a result (see **open and closed loop systems**).

Systems engineering process the process followed in this book to research, design, model, make, test and evaluate engineering systems. See Chapter 9 and the 'Vehicle style and design' case study.

Tailstock a device on a centre lathe that is used to support the work piece or other tools while machining.

Tension a pulling force.

Thermal conductivity the ability of a material to transmit heat energy through it.

Thermal expansion or contraction most materials expand when they are heated and contract when cooled.

Thermoforming properties properties that relate to the temperature at which a material can be formed and the ease with which it can be formed.

Threading die a tool that is supported by a die handle and is used to cut an external thread on a shaft.

ISBN 9780170227452

Torsion a twisting force.

Tolerance used to give the accuracy to which something is made.

Toughness/brittleness the ability of a material to withstand repeated applications of stress without breaking (e.g. hammering, or bending backwards and forwards).

Torque a turning force usually of an axle or rotating arm. Measured in newton metres.

Transducer a device that changes one form of energy to another form of energy; usually described as either an input or an output transducer.

Transformer a device that changes an input voltage to a varied output voltage.

Transistor a semiconductor with three terminals: collector, base and emitter. Transistors amplify the input signal.

Universal joints joints used on connections between rotating shafts when the shafts are not in line or at angles to each other.

Variable resistor an electronic component that varies the amount of resistance in a circuit.

Velocity ratio (VR) the distance moved by the effort divided by the distance moved by the load. Also called the gear ratio when using gears.

Viscosity the thickness of a fluid.

Voltage (V) the electromagnetic force by which electrons move. Measured in volts (V).

Watt (W) the unit of power.

Weight the force with which gravity pulls on a mass. Measured in newtons (N); a mass of 1 kg has a weight of about 10 N.

Work done whenever a force moves an object; given by the size of the force multiplied by the distance the object moves. Work = force × distance (Nm).

Workability the ability of a material to undergo a change in shape without failure.

Worm gear a spiral or helix-type gear (with one tooth) that enables high gear ratios. As the worm rotates through one revolution it moves the meshed worm wheel by one tooth.

Index

ISBN 9780170227452

ISBN 9780170227452